Praise for *By Ha...*

"[Shows] the 'chronic, unpredictable violence . . . historical retrieval is only part of [Margaret] Burnham's . . . makes a case for reparations, to pick up 'where law has failed.'"
—Jennifer Szalai, *New York Times Book Review*

"Margaret Burnham's rich historical analysis documents the longstanding failure of federal laws and institutions. . . . [and] shines a light on the resourcefulness of African Americans who organized to help one another and fight for justice."   —Debbie Elliott, NPR

"Burnham illuminates a continuum of white supremacy. . . . She also examines Black Americans' long-standing 'practices of dissent and resistance' and describes reparations as an ethical imperative."   —*The New Yorker*

"A stunning work of scholarship. . . . This is a truly important work, arriving at a pivotal moment in our own time."   —Nikki Leahy, *Southern Review of Books*

"Indispensable. . . . Burnham launches a vital and restorative reckoning with the reprehensible devastation of lives, communities, justice, and memory."
—Martha Minow, author of *When Should Law Forgive?*

"[A] necessary and important book. . . . It is timely and essential reading."
—Saidiya Hartman, author of *Wayward Lives, Beautiful Experiments*

"Rigorously delineated, passionately argued. . . . [Burnham asks] us to finally acknowledge the history of ever-present resistance, even under the most insurmountable conditions, and to consider what justice might mean today."
Angela Y. Davis, Distinguished Professor Emerita, History of Consciousness and Feminist Studies, University of California, Santa Cruz

"A vitally important history, . . . [S]earing, unforgettable, and profoundly moving."
—Patricia J. Williams, author of *The Alchemy of Race and Rights* and *Giving a Damn*

"[A] powerful, moving, and groundbreaking account of the interconnections between race, law, and citizenship in US history."
—Keisha N. Blain, coeditor of *Four Hundred Souls* and author of *Until I Am Free*

"[A] narratively lively yet stunningly exhaustive interrogation. . . . [This book] ought to become indispensable to all legal and civil rights considerations, and the *cause célèbre* of our time—reparations."
—David Levering Lewis, Pulitzer Prize–winning author of *W.E.B. Du Bois*

BY HANDS
NOW KNOWN

JIM CROW'S LEGAL EXECUTIONERS

MARGARET A. BURNHAM

W. W. NORTON & COMPANY
Celebrating a Century of Independent Publishing

Frontispiece: Elizabeth Catlett, *I have special reservations*

For information about permission to reproduce selections from this book, write to Permissions, W. W. Norton & Company, Inc., 500 Fifth Avenue, New York, NY 10110

For information about special discounts for bulk purchases, please contact W. W. Norton Special Sales at specialsales@wwnorton.com or 800-233-4830

Manufacturing by Lakeside Book Company
Book design by Chris Welch
Production manager: Lauren Abbate

Library of Congress Cataloging-in-Publication Data

Names: Burnham, Margaret, 1944–author.
Title: By hands now known : Jim Crow's legal executioners / Margaret A. Burnham.
Description: First edition. | New York, NY : W. W. Norton & Company, Inc., [2022] | Includes bibliographical references and index.
Identifiers: LCCN 2022036502 | ISBN 9780393867855 (hardcover) | ISBN 9780393867862 (epub)
Subjects: LCSH: African Americans—Civil rights—History—20th century. | African Americans—Crimes against—History—20th century. | Discrimination in criminal justice administration—United States.—History—20th century. | African Americans—Social conditions—To 1964.
Classification: LCC KF4757 .B87 2022 | DDC 342.7308/73—dc23/eng/20220924
LC record available at https://lccn.loc.gov/2022036502

ISBN 978-1-324-06605-7 pbk.

W. W. Norton & Company, Inc.
500 Fifth Avenue, New York, N.Y. 10110
www.wwnorton.com

W. W. Norton & Company Ltd.
15 Carlisle Street, London W1D 3BS

1 2 3 4 5 6 7 8 9 0

In honor of my parents,
Louis Everett Burnham
and Dorothy Challenor Burnham,
whose gift to me was this cause

CONTENTS

PART III
PATEROLLERS AND PROSECUTORS

PART IV
THE *SCREWS* EFFECT
RACIAL VIOLENCE IN THE SUPREME COURT

PART V
BLACK PROTEST MATTERS

PART VI
"HE THAT STEALETH A MAN"

PART VII
"A MINT OF BLOOD AND SORROW"

INTRODUCTION

"The Black Man Is a Person Who Must Ride 'Jim Crow' in Georgia"

—W. E. B. DuBois

In June 1944, a person named Sam Rayburn sent a letter to the New York office of the National Association for the Advancement of Colored People about a death in Donalsonville, Georgia. An "elderly Negro woman" had been examining a can of oil at a general store. The white man in charge told her to put the can down. She did so, then turned, perhaps on her heels, and left. The man, whose age Rayburn put at about twenty, followed her from the store onto the street and beat her with an ax handle, causing her death. Rayburn, the letter writer, did not name the victim or the perpetrator, but did say it was rumored that the white man had been arrested and promptly released. "Donalsonville," the letter continued, "is a small town completely icolated . . . Please interceed if there is any possible chance." A lawyer for the NAACP, likely overworked, advised Rayburn to look to local authorities or Georgia's governor, Eugene Talmadge, for an investigation.

Rayburn's letter was all that kept this incident from disappearing into thin air. It never made it into any newspaper or historical account.

Remaining a mystery is the name of the killer, although the extant legal records allow us to say with some confidence that he was never prosecuted. We know nothing—not the race nor the gender—of Sam Rayburn. In 2020, researchers learned that the victim was one Ollie Hunter, that she was in her midsixties, and that she was likely single when she was killed. If there was any legal process in Donalsonville, it appears not to have been preserved. The case never reached federal authorities.

Scanty though the facts are, they suggest how lethal, for women and for men, the most commonplace encounters under Jim Crow could be. And they tell us something about the role of law, for they suggest that the dispute mechanisms that are at the heart of the country's sense of exceptionalism—reliance on neutral laws and evidence-based determinations—yielded to a strikingly different system under Jim Crow. What cultural norm did Ollie Hunter violate? Did she curse the store manager? Throw the can onto the counter? Exit the store too quickly? Was there bad blood between the two? Who was the killer? Did he raise his family in Donalsonville after the murder? Did his descendants remain there? Who were the local journalists who deemed the case too trivial to report? The prosecutor who, so far as we can tell, let the case die? We are left to speculate on details and motives, but what we do know about the slaying tells us a great deal about the role of direct, physical violence in sustaining Jim Crow. Based on these facts, at that time and place, the transgressor was the Black "elderly" woman, not the young white grocer, and her sentence was death.

Although much has been written about the South in general and southern Jim Crow in particular, the system of white supremacy that prevailed between the late nineteenth and mid-twentieth century is ancient history for the current generation. They may recognize the names Rosa Parks and Fred Shuttlesworth, and know something about lynching, but they likely have little sense of the quotidian violence that shaped routine experiences like grocery shopping and tied the nation's legal institutions to its racial culture. Much of that history was never preserved. The chronic, unpredictable violence that loomed over everyday Black life, dictating the movements and postures of white storeowners and Black customers, is what sustained Jim Crow for over half a century. Conflating private and public authority, and immunizing whites who served as its unofficial policemen—like the grocer—Jim Crow blurred the lines between formal law and informal enforcement. C. Vann Woodward captured this in his 1955 classic, *The Strange Career of Jim Crow*: "the Jim Crow laws put the authority of the state or city in the voice of the street car conductor, the railway brakeman, the bus driver . . . the hoodlum of the public parks and playgrounds."

Although closely correlated with life in the postbellum South, Jim Crow took different forms across the country, embedded in culture, articulated in law, and entrenched in politics. Often portrayed as defining a strictly dualistic system with segregation on the one hand and integration on the other, Jim Crow was as pervasive in northern spaces where no signs demarcated racial positioning as it was in southern spaces where the races rubbed elbows but occupied different worlds. It was not so much tied to a geographical place as it was a national project, supported not just by the violence of "the locals" but by a national legal system that endorsed and sustained a missionary commitment to a future of perpetual white rule.

While researchers have examined the history of the Jim Crow regime and its contemporary footprint, particularly in the realm of criminal justice, the erasure of important parts of this narrative—Ollie Hunter's case and those like it—leaves us with crucial gaps in our understanding of the period. Using newspaper accounts, courtroom testimony, legislation, and judicial rulings, *By Hands Now Known* addresses those gaps. It seeks to illuminate how direct physical violence, a defining feature of Jim Crow, shaped the legal terrain in the South during the first half of the twentieth century—transforming, in fundamental ways, concepts of federalism, citizenship, and democratic rights and privileges. Neither sporadic nor irrational, but rather inescapable and uncontrolled, the violence was a marker of legal personhood and freedom. Its ideologies and constructions—of racialized masculinity, of Black pain, suffering,

and silence, of color-coded public spaces, of southern redemption—
have endured into the present. As a uniquely American phenomenon,
the mob violence that riddled the southern landscape from Appomattox until World War II indubitably epitomized racial vulnerability.
But the national obsession with lynching has also obscured the mun-
dane, largely hidden violence that, while it lay at a different point on
the spectrum, was equally essential to Jim Crow. Twice erased is the
murder of Ollie Hunter: submerged, seamlessly, into the landscape of
southern life at the moment of her death, and then omitted, brutally,
from historical accounts of the period.

THE EARLY TO MID-TWENTIETH CENTURY was a critical period in
solidifying white supremacy and incorporating its premises into legal
codes and practices. This study of the Jim Crow legal system examines the experiences ordinary citizens had with police, prosecutors,
and courts. It draws on cases, some well known and many, like that of
Ollie Hunter, newly discovered, that have been collected by researchers at Northeastern University and the Massachusetts Institute of Tech-
nology under my direction and that of MIT political scientist Melissa
Nobles, my research partner. In 2007, Nobles and I set out on a journey
to unearth this forgotten history of racially motivated homicides, for
the families, of course, but we also wore our scholars' hats as we did the
work. Without these accounts, we thought, we could not fully map the
Jim Crow system in the United States, or grasp how it seeped deep into
the interstices of the US legal system, or the precise content of its residue today. Without them we could not measure the scope and nature
of authoritarianism in the southern states, or the patterns and dynamics
of Black resistance.

We knew that these histories had been largely ignored in official
accounts of the period. But as we traveled across the country and visited with families, we met with hundreds of people who insisted on
keeping these memories alive for their own posterity. Preserving pho-

tographs and old newspaper clippings, they cultivated a kind of vernacular history that they were eager to share with us. Despite these individual efforts, however, a careful account of lethal state violence remained unavailable to a wider public. It was our sense that as long as these events translated as idiosyncratic, one-off, private experiences of grief, multifaceted systems of racial injustice would remain hidden, and, concomitantly, the need for structural remedies would seem unwarranted. We brought together our professional expertise and the critical work that community historians were doing to compose a more comprehensive and accurate picture.

To track these cases we created a database of racial violence incidents—namely, homicides—in the US South during the Jim Crow era. We narrowed our scope to the South—fully mindful of the myth of southern exceptionalism—simply because so much of the violence occurred there. We chose the mid-twentieth century because we wanted to capture the memories of elderly family members, and because we had access to federal records from that period. A good deal had already been written about the racial violence of the traditional civil rights era. Jim Crow–era violence, on the other hand, had not been fully treated when we began our research. When we called survivors from the period, often they responded, "I thought I'd never get this call." The fruit of this project is the CRRJ Burnham-Nobles Digital Archive, a collection of public documents and interviews that capture, through over a thousand homicides, the grim history of anti-Black violence in the Jim Crow South.

Drawing, in part, on these archival materials, *By Hands Now Known* tackles the three interrelated themes of federalism, racial violence, and resistance.

The federal government, including the Justice Department, had the legal tools to protect citizens from the most egregious forms of Jim Crow violence and a political duty to do so, but distance and denial severely undermined its response. In the mid-twentieth century, federal courts, oblivious to the long-term stakes, rendered nearly toothless the Reconstruction-era statutes that specifically targeted racist terror.

The government failed to grasp that what they were dealing with was not just a criminal law problem but a civil and human rights problem. Its failure to take the necessary steps to punish the violence constituted a breach of law and duty, even where the crimes were committed by private individuals. What tools were available to Washington and why were they ineffective? What permanent scars to the legal system are attributable to these failures? And how did the Black freedom movement challenge this federal abandonment?

Second, *By Hands Now Known* probes the dynamic relationship between violence (physical violence in contrast to symbolic or structural violence), political power, and citizenship during the Jim Crow era. These assaults both signified and solidified white male domination, repressed Black political participation and economic competition, and unified whites across class lines. Violence mediated the transformation from slave property to citizenship in a free labor regime. White control, including violent suppression, was inherent in slavery, but after the Civil War, the country's ruling elites, in both the North and the South, were operating under a purportedly liberal democratic regime, and therefore had to adopt different methods to control and exploit free labor. Violence that was previously lawful became putatively illegal. Nevertheless, from Reconstruction until the end of Jim Crow, Black citizenship was profoundly shaped by the white terror that served to control Black labor and mollify the white working class. The right to live free of violence—to have the legal wherewithal to protect one's property and person—was at the heart of the liberal, law-bound, democratic project. Stripping Black people of that right knocked them back to noncitizens. *By Hands Now Known* investigates these Jim Crow years of dashed hopes to illuminate how, after slavery was over, a self-described democratic republic used terror to revive a form of subcitizenship that would prevail for just short of a century. It illustrates how authoritarian southern political systems thrived within an ostensibly democratic national polity.

Third, *By Hands Now Known* excavates the history of collective resistance to racial terror in the Jim Crow era. Historians have written much about the civil rights movement of the thirties and forties, and the continuities in antiracist social movements across the twentieth century. Nevertheless, the popular view persists that Black protest, particularly in the South, was not especially robust or consequential until the late 1950s. The case studies here suggest otherwise. In September 1933, four thousand people, aroused to a "fever pitch," attended a "protest funeral" in Atlanta in the wake of the police shooting of forty-year-old Glover Davis, a blind man. With ninety police officers, some mounted, armed with machine guns and tear gas, encircling the church, the pastor forbade protest eulogies. In defiance, one minister intoned, "Lord, give us men who are not afraid to . . . denounce police brutality, and their slaying of Negroes, shooting them in the back while they flee arrest . . . give us an aroused church, both white and black . . . who despite mob violence . . . and even though the police force surround our churches . . . will stand upon the house tops and cry aloud." In 1942, thirteen years before the Montgomery boycott, Black bus passengers in Mobile, Alabama, threatened a "Walk to Work, Walk to Church, Walk to Shop" campaign, forcing the town's bus company to disarm their drivers after an operator shot and killed a soldier on his bus. And in 1948, more than 2,000 mine workers, Black and white, staged a wildcat strike in Edgewater, Alabama, to protest the police killing of a popular fifty-four-year-old Black union man.

Demonstrations such as these were but one form of Black protest. Civil lawsuits filed by survivors of racial homicides offer detailed accounts of the events, as do petitions to public officials and letter writing campaigns. These materials, the source of many of the cases examined in this book, evince sophisticated conceptions of the relationship between structural harms and police brutality, while also revealing significant divisions over politics and strategies. Though some civic and church leaders looked for consensus and favored top-down, deliberative approaches, militants—including many in the faith community—pushed back. Rejecting the prevailing script of respectability and polite subordination, they worked from the ground up, centered the perspectives of those at the bottom, perceived it as absurd to lobby for legal change in lawless spaces, and argued that only bold contestation—which could include counterviolence and sabotage—would bring about change. Also key was the Black press, without which many of these stories would have remained hidden. These big city newspapers—including the *Chicago Defender*, the *Pittsburgh Courier*, and the *Baltimore Afro-American*—transformed individual tragedies into collective experiences, nationalized Black politics, and ignited the Black imagination. In sum, these practices of protest altered legal meanings, challenged the state's pretensions to equal justice, fostered collective agency and solidarity, and dislodged official truths in favor of indigenous knowledge. These anti–Jim Crow activists lost as often as they won, but their travails, which tell us much about life under Jim Crow, comprise an essential umbilical link to the movements of the 1950s, '60s, and '70s.

A NINETEENTH-CENTURY federal case, *United States v. Cruikshank*, foreshadowed what was at stake in the twentieth-century struggle over federalism and citizenship. The case concerned a massacre that took place in Colfax, Louisiana, on Easter Sunday 1873. When the guns fell silent in a confrontation over the results of an election pitting Republicans, Black and white, against white Democrats, many of whom were former Confederate soldiers and members of groups like the Ku Klux Klan, 3 white men and somewhere between 60 to 150 Black men were left dead, and the parish courthouse, the site of the siege, was virtually in ashes. Historian Eric Foner described this event in majority-Black Grant Parish as the "bloodiest single instance of racial carnage in the Reconstruction era." It "taught many lessons," he wrote, "including the lengths to which some opponents of Reconstruction would go to retain their accustomed authority." Although 97 members of the white mob were indicted under federal law, only 9 were charged. Congress investigated the massacre and released a report describing it as a "deliberate, barbarous, cold-blooded murder" that was a "foul blot on the page of history," but the appellate courts overturned all the ensuing convictions.

The most harmful opinion came not from the US Supreme Court, but from one of its justices, Joseph P. Bradley, who was sitting on the federal appeals court along with two other judges. Bradley construed the laws that the Reconstruction Congress adopted to curtail racist terror in a manner that made it clear the federal courts would view with hostility any congressional efforts to confer all the elements of citizenship on the formerly enslaved. He read narrowly the constitutional grant of power to Congress to pass such laws. He reduced congressional power to hold individuals liable for civil rights violations. He heightened the prosecutor's burden in these cases by demanding proof of intentional discrimination. And, in effect, he reinforced the widely held belief that Black people should not be permitted to bear arms, notwithstanding the Second Amendment. The long shadow cast over federal civil rights enforcement by Bradley's opinion, which was endorsed by the Supreme Court, has crippled civil rights enforcement to this day.

In Louisiana, the reaction to Bradley's opinion was swift and brutal. Night riders in Colfax slit the throat of a Black man named Frank Foster who was, disastrously, in the wrong place at the wrong time. A few days later, one of the defendants in the *Cruikshank* trial, seemingly emboldened by the Bradley decision, helped an armed group force five Republican officials to leave their posts. Mob terror against Republicans picked up across the South, escalating the full-throttled project of violent redemption.

THE *CRUIKSHANK* CASE was about more than abstract theories of federalism and the separate powers of Congress and the courts. The limits on the constitutional authority of Congress to control racist violence changed the balance of power in favor of state and local police, prosecutors, and courts, who could thereafter enforce white supremacy without much fear of federal oversight. As the cases described in *By Hands Now Known* underscore, the violent enactment of Jim Crow's precepts aligned with the unfettered power exercised by local police— elected sheriffs and their deputies in the rural South, police chiefs and their officers in the cities and towns.

Slavery abides in all American institutions, but its formative and enduring presence in policing during Jim Crow was particularly palpable. Indeed, the unremitting lines between violent policing, slavery, and Jim Crow were pronounced well into the twenty-first century. It could be perceived in the violence that claimed the lives of Trayvon Martin, the teenager who in 2012 violated the "white space" rule; Sandra Bland, who in 2015 defied the "never talk back to a white cop" rule; and George Floyd, the tall Black man whose mere existence was so irksome to a white officer that he felt entitled to perform a public execution in 2020. Such violence, at once calculated and casual, reconstructed the culture of policing from one generation to the next, from slavery through Jim Crow and beyond.

Performance of power and degradation, of Black otherness—this alienation of Black humanity, illegalization of Black life—is just half of the story of the parallels between modern policing and slavery. Black communities have fought back, and that militant history—the other half of the story—establishes that protest against police violence has always been central to Black social movements. From 1865 to the present, Black people have identified "law enforcement officers" as perhaps their most potent existential threat. In the first year of the twentieth century, a race riot broke out in New York City's Tenderloin district. The police force encouraged a mob intent on a lynching. New York activists who gathered the testimony of eighty victims reported that "it was the night sticks of the police that sent a stream of bleeding colored men to the hospital." Led by T. Thomas Fortune, a prominent Black journalist of the day, New Yorkers formed the Citizens' Protective League to pursue prosecutions against the officers. The league was not successful and the officers went back to their beats. That was more than a century ago, long before three Black women coined the phrase Black Lives Matter.

Lawless police acting on behalf of the state has defined how Black people experienced American law for two centuries, and concomitantly, Black struggles for citizenship and meaningful democratic participation have always included radical demands for relief from such state violence. *By Hands Now Known* explores what prevented the federal government from stepping in to control police brutality at the local level: why the Justice Department refused to craft an effective campaign to abate the terror, and how the federal courts exacerbated the problem—as had Justice Bradley in the *Cruikshank* case in the previous century. It is this pattern of non-enforcement that looks over our shoulders today. When, in current times, the Department of Justice defers to state prosecutors and juries, and when the federal courts enfeeble civil rights remedies that might make victims whole, as they do by allowing police to escape civil liability by claiming immunity, they are calling up the old playbook. Hovering all around us, in our august federal courts as much as in our county courtrooms, is the law of Jim Crow and, as well, its antecedent, the law of slavery.

THE STORIES OF the victims of Jim Crow and the communities that came to their aid anchor this account of racial violence and the legal system that fostered it. Important not only for what they teach us about Jim Crow, these stories point to an ideological debate about the American future that transcends the criminal legal system. The chapters that follow, organized in loosely chronological fashion, pursue the book's central questions by identifying specific themes, such as Jim Crow transportation during World War II, and by shining a spotlight on specific geographical areas, like Birmingham and Southwest Mississippi.

The subject of Part 1 is rendition—the legal process by which states make demands upon other states for the return of their citizens so that they may be subjected to criminal proceedings in the home state. The rendition conventions that emerged in the Jim Crow years were foreshadowed by the legal battles associated with the Underground Railroad. Together with the anti-lynching campaigns of crusaders like Ida Wells-Barnett and Walter White, rendition cases in the 1920s, '30s, and early '40s created an opportunity for southern and northern authorities to advance differing concepts of Black citizenship, states' rights, and due process. These cases also knit together a national Black community as migrants from the South reached back to help loved ones and neighbors escape the legal systems of the southern states. The cases reveal how the legal practices of slavery were reprised in the successor Jim Crow regime, and offer a perspective on cross-state campaigns to liberate Black men and women who were charged in the South and to then settle them in the growing metropolis commonly known as the "Northern ghetto."

Part 2 canvasses World War II–era cases to relate the battles between Black soldiers seeking to maintain their dignity and status as they traveled through the South and Jim Crow's gatekeepers, whether bus drivers, police officers, or white fellow riders. Like the first part, the chapters in Part 2 interrogate ideas about mobility as a feature of citizenship. The Justice Department and the War Department faced the question of whether Black soldiers had to comply with local rules regarding segregated transportation. Instead of definitive national policies protecting the soldiers, the federal government prevaricated and, with some notable exceptions, left the terrain to local authorities who were actively hostile to Black people in military uniforms. This part highlights an innovative example of politics from below—Black women's creative defiance of Jim Crow transportation, which undercut the legitimacy of the system, emboldened other Black riders, and challenged presumptions of power.

Part 3 offers an account of the establishment, in 1939, of a unit to address civil rights in the Justice Department and the challenges the department faced as it sought to reach violations buried deep in the South. To better grasp the flux and flow between federal policies and those of the states concerning civil rights criminal cases, the part follows the docket of a leading prosecutor in the federal Middle District of Alabama, which includes the capital city of Montgomery, once home to one of the country's busiest slave markets. The prosecutor began his career appropriately enough, pursuing a sheriff who visited his brutality on Blacks and whites alike, but his enthusiasm rather quickly waned as he confronted jury nullification. The part describes the suffering caused, in no small part, by this particular federal official's capitulation to local authorities, and the measures taken in Washington to address the problem.

Part 4 strips to the bone Supreme Court jurisprudence on racial violence to better appreciate the impact of the court's pronouncements on political relationships at the local level. In 1945, in the case *Screws v. United States*, the Supreme Court imposed a confusing "intent" requirement on the federal criminal civil rights statutes passed during Reconstruction that made it difficult to prove a racial homicide case. This part surveys how the *Screws* case sanctioned the Jim Crow legal system, the debates between civil rights lawyers and federal prosecutors over the meaning of *Screws*, and the impact of the case on victims on the one hand, and the nascent civil rights legal community on the other.

Part 5 features cases from the postwar era in the Birmingham region that illuminate the complex relationships that constituted the Black resistance movement. Black residents of Birmingham, one of the country's most violent cities, had no shield against police violence, but the town was also a hub of Black resistance. In Birmingham as in other large cities in the South, the NAACP and the local press collaborated to maintain a record of police homicides—in the tradition of Ida Wells-Barnett and Monroe Work—and hence this part features the work of Emory Jackson, organizer of the NAACP branch and editor of the *Birmingham World* newspaper. Active in the region as well was the Southern Negro Youth Congress, an organization of young leaders who came together to pursue the agenda put forth in 1937 by the National Negro Congress. The cases in this part suggest how police killings operated both to enforce Jim Crow and to convince whites of the need to maintain it. These killings mythified the "bad Negro" and united white opinion behind "law and order." The part explores the terms of the resistance: perceiving the police and the lynch mob as interchangeable, Black communities deemed law and legal institutions antithetical to their interests. Their opposition to each killing, and their insistence on justice, held the potential to bring these structural harms into focus and to shift the meaning of power and law. As well, the cases are profoundly compelling examples of the impulse to resist. The defiance of those who lost their lives was perhaps the most formidable and telling acts of resistance.

In Part 6, the Southwest region of Mississippi provides a site to examine how Jim Crow erased the crime of kidnapping from the codebooks where the victims were Black. Kidnapping constitutes a crime against a person, yet until well into the 1960s law enforcement practices signify that it was not illegal to kidnap a Black person. Traditionally law has conferred immunities to deprive courts of the right to adjudicate certain kinds of legal violations. Individual immunities, for example, protect judges and prosecutors from suit even when they have violated the law. In failing to prosecute kidnappers, southern states were, in effect, immunizing their acts: conferring upon them a legal right to do a legal wrong. This part explores the experiences of Black Mississippians who were abducted by whites—both police and private parties—and beaten and often banished, with no legal consequences for the perpetrators. This refusal to appreciate the criminal nature of white on Black abductions represented a form of common law, constituting a Jim Crow "Black Code."

By Hands Now Known concludes with a turn away from the Jim Crow decades to explore early twenty-first-century insights about how states should reckon with historical injustices such as those narrated in this work. Thus, Part 7 presents some concluding cases from a range of jurisdictions to probe one of the book's central questions: how amends should be made in the present to address long-buried historical harms. It examines arguments for reparations, apologies, truth proceedings, and other mechanisms that could recover this history, offer a platform for communities to confront it, and redesign legal structures that are tainted by the legacies of Jim Crow.

PART I
RENDITION

I determined I would never send another prisoner South unless I had assurances he would be protected from the mob and given a fair trial.

—*Cincinnati Common Pleas Judge Morris Lyon Buchwalter in the* Lewiston Daily, *January 1, 1895*

Shall we let Georgia, who respects no law, return a person, (even a woman) to her State where we know she will not receive "due Process of law" under our Federal Constitution? I say no. . . . I shall, if standing alone, fight to the last ditch, any effort on their part to return one of my people to their jurisdiction.

—*Attorney William T. Patrick, writing to Attorney Charles H. Houston, June 2, 1936*

1

"A New Version of the Old, Old Story"

While much has been written about the feats of escaping slaves and the Underground Railroad that shuttled them to freedom, we know far less about how the paths they forged were picked up generations later by men and women running from southern sheriffs and courts. These cases, following directly on the heels of Emancipation, were ongoing until the mid-1950s. They reveal comparable courage and creativity on the part of the runaways, and, as well, fascinating battles over sovereignty between northern and southern jurisdictions and extraordinary collaborations between northern and southern Black communities. Though the rendition cases read as a twentieth-century archive about states' rights and Black citizenship, the roots of these laws and legal practices lie in antebellum fugitive slave laws. An account of how Jim Crow's statutes and legal practices transported the norms of slavery into the American criminal justice system must begin with Civil War—era rendition.

REVEREND ANTHONY BURNS was just twenty-eight when, in July 1862, he passed away in St. Catherines, an old Loyalist city on the Canadian side of the Niagara River. Seven weeks later, Abraham

Lincoln would issue the Emancipation Proclamation. Born into slavery in the Old Dominion about four miles from the boyhood farmhouse of George Washington, Burns had in his short life traversed the continent: from Stafford County in Virginia, to Boston, to North Carolina, then on to New York City, where he took to the podiums preaching abolitionism, to Ohio for an education at Oberlin College, and, finally, to Ontario, where he died of consumption. He had been a schoolteacher, sawmill worker, tailor, minister, and lecturer. As he traveled from the South to New England, and from the Midwest to Eastern Canada, he passed in and out of slavery, bound and unbound by the hard borders of geography, bent and unbent by the fraught lines of pre–Civil War politics, sheltered and shielded by the kindness of strangers. At the time of his death millions knew Burns's story. Some fifty thousand had, eight years earlier, marched in Boston in defense of his liberty, shuttering their businesses, adorning their shops with black flags, and massing to confront the federal troops that convened to ensure his re-enslavement. African Americans, joined by the writer and minister Thomas Wentworth Higginson, armed themselves with a huge battering ram and stormed the courthouse that stood between Burns and his freedom.

Burns had been hired out by his owner to work in Richmond. One February morning in 1854, in a brazen plan, he snuck on board a ship headed to Boston. There the fugitive found work and safety in the tight-knit Black community clustered at the bottom of Beacon Hill. He had left behind in Stafford County his mother and twelve brothers and sisters. It was the young man's carelessness—and perhaps his loneliness; a letter written to one of his brothers back in Virginia—that triggered a watershed moment in US history: for Burns's owner, having intercepted the letter, went up to Boston to recover his man. In short order Burns appeared before a federal commissioner, Edward Greely Loring, whose judicial task had been, by virtue of the Fugitive Slave Act of 1850, reduced to that of a notary. Was the man who stood before the commissioner the individual named in the warrant? If yes, he was to be re-enslaved. While the matter was pending before

Judge Loring, Boston's militant abolitionists, who had a few years earlier freed the fugitive Shadrach Minkins from jail, rose to the occasion, bringing to bear outright defiance of the law, violent resistance, and negotiation in an effort to win Burns's freedom. Leonard Grimes, the first pastor of the city's Twelfth Baptist Church and an experienced Underground Railroad conductor, offered to buy Burns from his owner. The Boston Vigilance Committee held a mass meeting at Faneuil Hall at which Wendell Phillips urged the crowd to break Burns out of jail, while dozens of African Americans, accompanied by Amos Bronson Alcott and Thomas Higginson, went to the courthouse to do just that.

Anthony Burns was returned to slavery in Norfolk, Virginia, in 1854 after escaping to Boston, Massachusetts.

These militant efforts fell short. Despite Burns's expressed concerns that a full-throttled legal assault on the Fugitive Slave Act by his lawyers would, in his case, ultimately fail, inflame his owner, and thereby lead to severe retribution when he got back to Virginia, the lawyers plowed ahead, pulling out all the stops. As their client had predicted, the judge rejected their request to act contrary to the clear command of the statute, and about ten days after his arrest, Anthony Burns was rendered from Boston to Virginia. He did not go easily. As a federal military brigade marched him from the courthouse to the wharf, crowds lined the streets in protest, draping their windows in black and displaying coffins to signify the death of the man's liberty. It was the city's largest antislavery demonstration, and the last time the federal government sought to render a runaway back into slavery from Boston. And there were consequences to be meted out to those who, under color of law, had succumbed to Virginia's slaveholders: Judge Loring (whose forebears were pioneers) was removed from a state judgeship and failed to secure a professorship in law at Harvard University.

In January 1895, the *Cambridge Tribune*, in an article titled "A New Version of the Old, Old Story," recalled the Burns affair for its readers. The "new version" of the old story was also a rendition case, but this time the rights of the states battling for custody over a Black man were governed not by the laws enacted to enforce the Fugitive Slave Clause of the Constitution—the Thirteenth Amendment erased that clause— but by its constitutional neighbor, the Extradition Clause. Cambridge readers were informed about the decision of an Ohio judge to reject a rendition warrant pressed by the state of Kentucky for the return of one Reverend A. H. Hampton, an African American who appealed to the court, as had Burns, not to be returned to the South. "Oh, Judge," Hampton declared, "don't send me to Kentucky. I have got letters from my friends telling me that they would string me up." Displaying the courage that had been wanting in Judge Loring, the Ohio judge deemed it within his inherent power to prevent a man being sent back to the South where he could face a lynching. Commenting on the case, the *Cambridge Tribune*'s writer compared the new story with the old one:

> [I]f a precedent should be desired in Ohio, the noble action of Massachusetts in 1854 in the rendition of Anthony Burns had not yet quite passed into oblivion—although Burns was only flogged upon his arrival in South Carolina and not hanged, as he had a cash value of $1,500, while the Rev. Mr. Hampton, as a "free nigger" and therefore of no real value, can be comfortably lynched in Kentucky without pecuniary loss to anyone—but his church and his family.

As in the case of Anthony Burns, a titanic legal and political battle often ensued over the return of fugitives to slavery. After slavery ended, the strategies conceived to confront these challenges were reengineered to protect the lives of fugitives from southern justice, such as the Kentuckian A. H. Hampton. In the post-slavery cases, northern and southern Black communities collaborated to prevent the return of a "wanted" person, and Black lawyers played a prominent role in shaping community protest and legal strategy. These rendition cases forged ties between advocates in small southern towns and the northern metropolises to which their relatives and friends had fled, thereby knitting together a national Black community. They provided opportunities for sophisticated advocacy in state and federal courtrooms and in governors' offices. The embryonic civil rights organizations—including the National Association for the Advancement of Colored People and the International Labor Defense—took advantage of the intense drama and high stakes of the cases to build membership and fuel their campaigns for federal anti-lynching legislation.

Indeed, these cases, together with the anti-lynching crusade, were, from the 1920s through the 1940s, at the center of the national campaign to expose Jim Crow's criminal justice system. They proffered a dynamic stage upon which southern and northern authorities acted out differing conceptions of Black citizenship, states' rights, and due process. The sovereign relationships at issue—state to state, federal to state—although recodified after the war, were still very much shaped by slavery's residuals.

REVEREND A. H. HAMPTON'S CASE was one of the most important to emerge in the wake of Reconstruction. It was litigated as the South was consolidating white supremacy in the national courts with, for example, *Plessy v. Ferguson* in 1896, declaring legally required race separation constitutional, and *Williams v. Mississippi* in 1898, approving Mississippi's literacy tests and poll tax requirements despite their racially disenfranchising purpose and effect. In an 1878 case, an Ohio court had declared that the state's governor had no discretion to reject an extradition warrant once the identity of the fugitive and the validity of the warrant were determined. But seventeen years later, in A. H. Hampton's case, the Ohio court abruptly dispensed with summary review.

It appears Reverend Hampton, a resident of Marion County, Kentucky, got into an argument with a white neighbor who had accused Hampton of robbing his orchard. Hampton shot and wounded the neighbor, then fled to Cincinnati, where he was arrested. The Ohio governor and future president, William McKinley, initially agreed to send him back to Kentucky, but Hampton's lawyers, with evidence in hand that their client would probably be lynched if he were sent back, pursued a petition in state court. Morris Lyon Buchwalter, a radical Republican judge on the Cincinnati Common Pleas Court, told the Kentucky authorities that he would not allow the warrant to be executed unless he obtained personal assurances from the Kentucky governor and sheriff that Hampton would not be lynched. "Four months ago I sent . . . a fugitive from justice into Kentucky. He was lynched soon after he left the train. The authorities broke faith with her sister State of Ohio in the protection of human life. I will not send this man away from this court until I have a letter from your governor . . . that he is to be given a fair and impartial trial." The courtroom was crowded and some quiet clapping could be heard from the Black observers. More-over, the judge observed, about a dozen people had been lynched in Kentucky in the twelve months that preceded the Hampton case. In the case of Hampton, Buchwalter declared, "I determined I would never send another prisoner South unless I had assurances he would be protected from the mob and given a fair trial."

When word reached the other side of the Ohio River that radical Republicans were still making demands on the South, the Kentucky governor, John Young Brown, angrily retorted that his "self-respect and his regard for the dignity of the state of Kentucky forbid that he should ever give any such humiliating guarantee," whereupon Buchwalter, making good on his word, released Hampton. He reasoned that even though the Extradition Clause contemplated a narrowly prescribed review of a sister state's demand, the court could withhold approval if the evidence showed that the extradition proceeding was instituted "not to prosecute the prisoner for his crime . . . but to deliver him at a convenient place to kill him in the exercise of individual vengeance." In that type of case, explained Buchwalter, the duty of the judge was to "protect [the] prisoner from such unlawful death."

Buchwalter's opinion in the Hampton case affirmed that northern state court judges had a distinct duty to protect the civil rights of fugitives, prying open for scrutiny racial conditions in the demanding state. It was on this premise—that civil rights should guide the inquiries of receiving states—that the racial rights organizations constructed their rendition campaigns in the early twentieth century.

2

"Mr. Ford's Place"

In those northern states where the tracks of the fabled Underground Railroad could still be made out, and where, in the late nineteenth century, the old abolitionist cause would turn into the fight to fulfill the promises of the Civil War Amendments, the refugees' bid for freedom was enthusiastically embraced. From slavery through Reconstruction and the Redemption, continuous communities of resistance undertook highly organized military-style operations to help fugitives make good on their escape and then resettle into their new cities and towns. In places like Detroit, Chicago, and Philadelphia, triangulated historical phenomena—the Underground Railroad, the Great Migration, and Black urbanization—primed the sanctuary cities for their role in Jim Crow–era rendition campaigns.

In Detroit, Black Bottom and its neighboring streets comprised the "Negro district," where migrants from the South could find housing and a cultural embrace. This thirty-square-block area (named, like the Black Belt, for its fertile topsoil) was the heart of Black Detroit from the early decades of the twentieth century until the 1950s, when urban renewal policies and highway construction overhauled the landscape. The area swelled with migrants from the South, including many fleeing to save their lives. Detroit's larger Black community was particularly well positioned to fight on behalf of fugitives across the nineteenth and well into the twentieth century. During the antebellum years, thousands of runaways crossed the Detroit River into Upper Canada every year, with about thirty thousand making the journey between 1842 and 1862. With the abolition of slavery coming to Michigan Territory in 1835, a vibrant Afro-descendant community that included escapees from slavery alongside free Blacks settled on both banks of the river, giving rise to a Black transnational resistance tradition grounded in shared sensibilities about mutual aid and the duty to care for fugitives. These were transgressive, profoundly politicized communities living— much like the Maroon communities of an earlier time—in defiance of the laws of slavery, and tied together by the attendant risks of these clandestine missions as much as by family kinship and church.

Both before and after Emancipation these Michigan liberators had to be savvy interpreters of complex international and domestic law, using to their advantage in the antebellum period, for example, the British rules forbidding slavery in Canada, and then after the Civil War, mastering the intricacies of federal–state rendition procedures. And when the legal maneuvers ran their course, they had to know how to take direct action. One of the nation's first urban race riots, in Detroit in 1833, was ignited by the effort to protect from extradition fugitive slaves Thornton and Lucie Blackburn, a husband and wife who made their way to Michigan from Louisville, Kentucky. Thornton decided to flee with his new bride when he learned she was to be sold to the New Orleans markets. After two years in Detroit they were captured by Kentucky slavehunters, but Lucie escaped again, this time to the safety of Upper Canada. Detroit's Black community surrounded the jail where Thornton was being held and freed him, leading to the first riot over slavery in that city. Canada successfully resisted Michigan's demand to extradite the Thorntons, whereupon they settled in Toronto and started a taxi business.

Thousands of others followed the Blackburns across the river. Many were aided by the all-Black Colored Vigilant Committee of Detroit, founded in 1842 and launched from the Second Baptist Church, the city's oldest Black congregation, which in 1839 established Detroit's first school for Black children, in 1843 hosted Michigan's first Convention of Colored Citizens, and offered its pulpit to national abolitionists such as Frederick Douglass. This stream of freedom-seekers swelled after passage of the Fugitive Slave Act of 1850, increasing the Black Canadian population from 40,000 in 1850 to 60,000 in 1860. During an eight-month period from May 1855 to January 1856, the Vigilant Committee provided aid to 1,045 fugitives.

Shortly after passage of the Fugitive Slave Act of 1850, which tightened, in favor of the slave states, the legal apparatus governing fugitive cases, the matter of Giles Rose, escapee from bondage in Kentucky, came before the federal court in Detroit. Rose was recaptured in October 1850 and confined to the city jail. Unlike the Anthony Burns case four years later, the federal commissioner, faced with a militant crowd of Black and white citizens, threw in the towel and let Rose go. The Fugitive Slave Act was essentially unenforceable in Detroit. The Michigan legislature, in 1855, sought to make it even harder for slave hunters to retrieve their "bounty" in the state by passing a personal liberty law prohibiting state officials from participating in recapture operations and guaranteeing to fugitives a jury trial with legal counsel.

These were the tracks that would be dusted off by Detroit activists and lawyers when escapees from Jim Crow justice came knocking on their doors, and these were the stories they would remember as they welcomed them, reengaging the community's resources and resilience to support a new generation of freedom seekers. Detroit's history of activism during the nineteenth century, when the Black community was quite small, well prepared it to incorporate over one hundred thousand migrants from the South during the Great Migration.

In 1910 the Black population of the city was about 5,700, while by 1930 it was 120,000, increasing the relative position of the Black community from 1 percent in 1910 to 8 percent in 1930. The Black population doubled between 1940 and 1950. A second migration commenced in 1950 and proceeded through the decade, bringing in thousands of additional workers and their families, seeking, as in the earlier decades, to leave the fields behind in favor of the better paying jobs—"Negro jobs"—that the auto industry's foundries and paint departments offered. The fight for racial justice tapped into longstanding political traditions in the city. Detroit's NAACP chapter was the largest in the country, claiming, by 1943, 20,000 members. The legal expertise and national publicity these rendition cases required was easily mustered by the chapter.

In the 1940s, the Detroit, Michigan, chapter of the NAACP was one of the largest in the country. It played a vital role in assisting fugitives who were escaping unjust criminal proceedings and related mob violence in southern jurisdictions.

A key factor in the rendition battle was Detroit's militant Black working-class population. As of 1920, over 79 percent of Detroit's Black male workers were in industrial jobs, and by 1930, 14 percent of auto workers in the country were Black. By the 1930s the Ford Motor Company was one of the country's largest employers of African Americans. Word spread across the South that Ford was paying a livable wage, offering a destination for those in search of warmer suns.

> I'm goin to get me a job, up in Mr. Ford's place
> Stop these eatless days from starin me in the face

Henry Ford, and later his son Edsel, spent years cultivating relationships among the Black elite and utilized the churches as a pre-clearance hiring office for the company. These efforts would pay off in the 1930s when Blacks shied away from the nascent organizing efforts of the Congress of Industrial Organizations (CIO). Some even joined Ford's infamous strike-breaking force, the "Service Department." However, while many Black men held back from the United Auto Workers' (UAW's) organizing campaigns, indebted, they thought, to "Mr. Ford" for delivering them and their kinfolk from the plantation, thousands of others became loyal UAW-CIO men, affiliated with the largest and perhaps most militant industrial union in the country. Confined to the bottom rungs of the workforce at Ford's famous River Rouge plant and elsewhere, they fought management and white fellow workers alike, within but with equal fervor outside the union, to upgrade their jobs and improve their communities. When the union wouldn't budge they appealed to Washington, where FDR's Fair Labor Employment Practices Committee, established in 1941, might apply pressure. After the UAW-CIO won a strike against Ford and then an election in June 1941, on the eve of Pearl Harbor, African Americans became solid supporters of the UAW, although for years thereafter they were forced to fight both white chauvinism in the union and rank racism on the shop floor that prevented their access to the skilled trades.

These sophisticated organizing experiences of Black working-class men and women in the city ultimately affected the outlook and organizing capacity of the local NAACP and other advancement groups, which in different circumstances tended to be more conservative. And lawyers from Detroit's large Black middle class provided the necessary professional expertise.

So when refugees from the South made their way to Detroit during the Jim Crow era, that city—with its well-established African American community, its long history of protecting runaways, its growing Black working class and professional talent, accustomed to fighting for Black rights—was uniquely well positioned to respond.

3

"That Dusky Hospital on DeVilliers Street"

PENSACOLA TO BLACK BOTTOM

In October 1928, Detroit attorney W. Hayes McKinney heard that a sheriff from Pensacola, Florida, was in town to arrest a woman wanted on a manslaughter charge in the Sunshine State. No newcomer to extradition cases, he must have cast a prideful glance back to his much-acclaimed campaign eight years earlier to prevent Georgia from returning a Black man by the name of Tom Ray to the shame and sham of that state's courts, or equally likely, its vigilante justice. In this new case, McKinney quickly marshaled support from members of the city's NAACP branch, of which he was the president, and set out to visit his new client in a Detroit jail. Finding her to be as frightened as she was firm, McKinney quickly realized that this accomplished woman would be her own best advocate. The charges against her arose from a mournful tragedy, for which, on September 23, 1927, a jury in Pensacola had already found her not guilty.

Now, however, the Florida sheriff was on a mission. His vow was that McKinney's client—"the negress" to the readers of the *Pensacola Journal*—would be transported personally by him back to Florida to stand trial a second time on a related charge.

VIOLA WASHINGTON EDWARDS had followed a timeworn path from the South to Detroit. In her hasty departure, she left behind, like so much flotsam, a good marriage of twenty years, an adopted daughter, three stepchildren, and two prosperous businesses. Fifty-four years old when she ran for her life, she was neither a young woman nor had she any practice hiding from the law. After disappearing into Detroit's Black neighborhood on the east side of the city, she lived in constant fear that Pensacola's lawmen were close on her trail, and so she rendered herself—she who had been so prominent and in some small but significant way privileged—invisible.

William Charles Boston, an undertaker by trade, and his wife, Clara Louise Tomlinson, had lived at 961 Farnsworth Street near Black Bottom since the early 1920s, and they had a long history of helping Black southerners get on their feet in Detroit. They made no exception when Viola Edwards came along. Sticking close to a few trusted new friends, she moved quietly between her job as an assembler for Dongan Electric Manufacturing Company and her bedroom in the Bostons' home on Farnsworth Street. It was a diminished life, but it was her only one and therefore worth preserving. The howling headlines were behind her.

Or so she hoped.

Edwards was likely more terrified than surprised when one chilly October evening in Detroit in 1928 a friend whispered to her that the local police wished to see her. Such a meeting could have only one purpose. Edwards was decidedly disinclined to reveal to Detroit's chief detective exactly why she had abandoned Pensacola, so she holed herself up in her room. Detroit Chief Detective Edward H. Fox, who in fact knew the details of the alleged crimes that had turned Edwards into a fugitive, kept hunting her down, his appetite abetted by a tip and enticed by Pensacola's $100 reward. When he finally discovered her whereabouts, without a warrant but with assurance that one executed under the authority of the governor of Florida would be forthcoming, Detective Fox made the arrest. "Arrest her and hold at any cost," read the urgent wire to Fox from Pensacola's police chief. "I'll be responsible. When you get her I will send fugitive warrant."

And so he did.

Moses S. Penton, a Pensacola sheriff, arrived in Detroit to recapture Edwards with the governor's warrant in hand. He could be forgiven for thinking he would not be long delayed in the Motor City. Michigan laws on extradition were fairly straightforward: another state's request for extradition was to be honored if the identity of the person named by the demanding state was established to the satisfaction of the receiving state's decision-maker, whether that be the governor or a judicial officer. The laws appeared to leave little maneuvering room for the person named in the demanding state's warrant. However, Edwards's case was but another page in a nearly three-centuries-old unwritten legal tome on the subject of Black fugitives fleeing from the South to the North. If the Michigan governor believed it to be within his right to question the procedurally sound and seemingly routine application of a sister state for the return of a fugitive, it was on account of uncodified legal traditions that began long before Viola Edwards was born—indeed, decades before the adoption of the US Constitution in 1789. Even if the law "on the books" seemed cut-and-dried, historical experience had created a crawl space through which Edwards, and many hundreds of other Black Americans, could and did slip.

———

VIOLA EDWARDS, née Washington, was born in 1874 in Wetumpka, Alabama, one of two children of Charles and Bettie Washington. To the people of the Muscogee (Creek) Nation who named her hometown, Wetumpka translated to "rumbling waters," evoking the sounds of the Coosa River spilling over the layered rocks known as the Devil's

Staircase.* Viola learned to read and write in Wetumpka, and served as a cook in a private home. She met William (Willy) H. Edwards, who was one of only six Black employees in the US Postal Service delivering by railroad to Wetumpka. On January 12, 1908, at thirty-four years of age, she married Edwards and moved to his home in Pensacola.

Willy Edwards, a Pensacola native, was a prosperous man from a prominent family. His first wife, Lodie, also apparently from a well-to-do Pensacola family, had passed away in 1906 after a freak accident: she was kicked in the stomach by a horse. When Lodie died, the couple's three young children, Charles, Otis, and Alzata, were left in Willy's care. Viola moved into the spacious home Willy had purchased in 1893 in Pensacola's historically Black Belmont-DeVilliers district. He bought the house at a time of change for Blacks in Pensacola: in the 1880s, Blacks were relatively free from the economic and residential segregation that would begin to sequester and concentrate their communities in the first decade of twentieth century as the strictures of Jim Crow tightened. It was these new constraints that created on DeVilliers Street a typical Black "Wall Street," much like larger cities such as Miami, Tulsa, and Durham, in a town where heretofore Blacks had operated businesses across the entire city.

Although Viola worked as a cook prior to her marriage, she had trained at Tuskegee Institute's famous nursing school about forty miles from Wetumpka and would have been in one of the early graduating classes. In 1920 she worked and obtained further training in nursing at Bellevue Hospital in New York City, likely gaining valuable experience. In 1924 she founded the first maternity hospital for African American women in Pensacola. The hospital was at 513 DeVilliers Street, next door to her home. Pensacola's press announced the opening of the "Viola Edwards Hospital," with her undertaking becoming an item of note in both the Black and white communities.

---

* When the Creek were forced to leave much of their territory in Alabama, they took the sounds of Wetumpka with them, and in 1836 they gave the name to new tribal headquarters in Oklahoma.

COLORED HOSPITAL WILL BE OPEN SOON

Considerable Activity in the Local Colored Schools and Churches During Week.

The Viola Edwards Hospital located on DeVilliers street, between LaRua and Jackson streets, is expected to be open in the next few days for service. The necessary equipment which has been shipped is expected to arrive in the city soon. Much credit is due the Edwards family for constructing such a beautiful building for the benefit of the colored people, is the prevailing opinion.

Ask Contribution For New Hospital

Pensacola's new colored hospital—Viola Edwards hospital—is making an earnest appeal to the people or aid in accomplishing their desires, as the institution is not yet self sustaining. Two patients are already in the charity ward and they are without funds whatever.

Dr. E. St. Clair Thomas has been appointed field and financial agent and any funds or contributions made to him for the maintenance of the hospital will be appreciated, it is stated.

Viola Edwards, a nurse, opened an infirmary serving the Black community near her home in Pensacola, Florida, in 1922.

Applying the cooking skills she had honed in Alabama, Viola was also the proprietor of a restaurant, located near her home and new hospital. Her establishments contributed to the bustling Black commercial district on DeVilliers Street that served a rapidly growing community of native Pensacolians and Blacks migrating from rural Alabama and Florida. In the first decade of the century, when 50 percent of Pensacola's total population of about 28,000 was Black, Tuskegee University's president, Booker T. Washington, extolled the successes of its "progressive colored communities . . . [where] members of the Negro race are learning to do their own business and direct their own affairs." Indeed, Willy Edwards's achievement as one of the "six first-class clerks" was lauded in Washington's essay, "Pensacola, A Typical Negro Business Community."

———

IN AUGUST 1927, Eugene E. Tart, a white man, brought his white secretary, twenty-seven-year-old Dorothy Friederichsen, to the Viola Edwards Hospital. She was pregnant; Tart was the father. Tart was a prominent—and married—businessman; Friederichsen herself was the daughter of a well-known businessman who had recently passed away, and whose memory was still fresh in the minds and hearts of a certain group of Pensacolians. At the hospital, an abortion was performed in accordance with the wishes of both Tart and Friederichsen. Tragically, the patient succumbed to septic infection, and she died on August 5 while in the care of Edwards's hospital.

Five days later, Viola Edwards, Eugene Tart, and two Black doctors who had attended to Friederichsen, S. McGee and E. C. Moon, were charged with manslaughter in connection with her death. When the group was arrested, Tart was able to post the high bail of $5,000 while Edwards went to jail. McGee and Moon were held for two days until they could post bond. Six weeks later, the defendants, described in the local paper as "the three Negroes and Tart," faced a jury in the Escambia County courts. Astonishingly, on September 23, the jury acquitted all of the defendants.

However, the jury's verdict was just the start of Viola's travails. She became the target of a vitriolic campaign, aimed as much at abortion and midwifery as it was at Black female entrepreneurship. At the close of the trial, the prosecutor had spelled out the theme that defined the post-verdict hysteria in Pensacola: "The state has unfolded before you chapter by chapter, this sordid, subterranean story that was going on up there while you and I were going about our daily tasks," he proclaimed. "This story came to light when almighty God took a hand in the drama being enacted in the dusky hospital on DeVilliers Street." Damned in one fell swoop was Pensacola's Black "Wall Street," deemed "subterranean" (turning on its head the history of Black exclusion from white business areas), and the practice of midwifery and abortion procedures, also "subterranean" (ignoring the historical discrimination against midwives by doctors who feared competition from people like Viola Edwards).

Many in Pensacola's white community were enraged by the all-white jury's seeming betrayal of their racial interests, and their sensibilities were even more bruised by the ecstatic response of Black Pensacolians who attended the trial. In the weeks that followed, the Sunday pulpits in the white community were fiery with condemnations of the jury's proclaimed attack on "the majesty of the law," one that "[protected] thieves of anarchy, ignorance, prejudice and bolshevism." The news-papers joined the choir, with the *Pensacola Journal* pitying the plight of a "white girl fighting her greatest fight, [who] met it and lost it in the care of a group of Negroes." These particular Negroes were the pillars of the community celebrated by Booker T. Washington and others like him, but to white Pensacolians of all classes, they were ne'er-do-wells and criminals.

So fanatical was the venom aimed at Viola Edwards after the acquit-tal, and, to a lesser degree, Eugene Tart, that the prosecutor quickly brought a second case. On October 21, he obtained a criminal com-plaint charging Edwards and Tart with manslaughter again, but this time the charge was based on the fetus. Around the time of the second complaint, the Viola Edwards Hospital at 513 DeVilliers Street went up in flames, as did the Edwards home next door, which had been in the proud possession of Willy Edwards for three decades.

Viola Edwards well understood that she could not risk another trial. She packed a few belongings, bade goodbye to her stepchil-dren and husband, and abandoned any hope of rebuilding her busi-nesses in Pensacola. She fled first across the border to Wetumpka, Alabama, where she made certain her mother was in the care of rel-atives, and then proceeded northward. A sister-in-law in Detroit, she reasoned, could help her settle there until the scandal quieted down in Pensacola.

Eugene Tart, on the other hand, the man who had sought out abortion services for his mistress, had little cause to fear for his per-sonal safety. The Sunday sermons lamenting Friederichsen's fate demonized her female "abortionist," not her married boyfriend. At the time of the first trial, "Dies Among Negroes" was the headline one newspaper ran, suggesting who was blameworthy and who was not. With good reason, Edwards ran because she believed she might be lynched. Tart, on the other hand, remained in Pensacola and relied on the courts to treat him fairly, which, when all was said and done, they did.

————

IN CONTRAST TO EDWARDS, Tart's calculations about whether to flee or fight were probably not affected by a murder that filled the Pensacola headlines back in 1908—the same year Booker T. Washington's uplifting study of Black progress in Pensacola was published, and the year of Willy and Viola's marriage. In July of that year, about a mile from their home on DeVilliers Street, a twenty-eight-year-old Black man, Leander Shaw, met his death at the hands of a Pensacola mob. Charged with a fatal sexual assault on Lillie Brewton Davis, a white woman, Shaw, a widower, was abducted on July 29 from a besieged sheriff who had warned a mob gathered at the county jail that was clearly intent on a revenge killing to stand down. "Gentlemen," Sheriff James Van Pelt said, half pleading and half commanding, "here I am. You can kill me if you want to, but if you get my prisoner, it will be over my dead body. I have sworn to do my duty, and I am going to do it if I die for it."

No one, it seems, heeded the warning. A mob of men and women numbering in the thousands battered down the gate of the county jail and fired shots on the defending deputies, seriously wounding three of them. While his men were defending the front of the jail, Sheriff Van Pelt rushed to hold down the back door. With the sheriff quickly overpowered, Shaw was noosed and trussed, then dragged through the town's grand old Spanish boulevards until the crowd arrived at the historic Plaza Ferdinand VII.

Shaw was hung from an electric lamppost at the precise location where, in 1821, General Andrew Jackson pronounced new rulership of Spain's former colony, thereafter to be known as the Florida Territory, and proclaimed Pensacola its capital. The plaza, named in 1815 after the king of Spain, had not quite commemorated its centennial when Shaw's murderers desecrated its pristine European gardens by firing into his suspended body two thousand rounds of ammunition. Makeshift signs, presumably underscoring for those who may have missed the import of the bullet-infused corpse, were spread around the plaza, including one hanging from the body that read "God Bless Our Home."

Half of the "home's" population were, at that point, the children and grandchildren of slavery. Over the days that followed, white Pensacolians hoping to recover a memento from the lynching—a piece of the rope, a spent bullet, a postcard—roamed the plaza and surrounding streets, forcing Blacks living in the area to hide in their houses. It was rumored that unfortunate Black men caught off guard were for weeks thereafter beaten and murdered. Scores, if not hundreds, left town, to the perverse consternation of white businesses concerned about labor shortages.

The atmosphere—part carnival, part *damnatio ad bestias*—was memorialized by photographers whose images of Shaw's hanging body were mailed around the country within days of his death. One resident, eighteen-year-old Edward Ware, sent a postcard depicting the lynching to a friend in Jacksonville on August 1, just three days after the event. "This is the nigger brute they hung in the Plaza July 29, and riddled him with bullets. Dock, how is this for Pensacolians?" he wrote with gusto and civic pride.

Viola Edwards would have been a thirty-four-year-old new bride and stepmother of three when her neat, house-proud neighborhood was deluged by the mob that lynched Leander Shaw. Nor, most probably, would Leander Shaw's have been the only lynching haunting her as she contemplated her chances of obtaining fair treatment by Pensacola authorities in a second trial. In Wetumpka, Alabama, where Viola grew up, "nigger-killing" as sport had gotten so out of hand that in 1908 the local sheriff banished or sent to the chain gang a dozen white men who were known to have slain Black men indiscriminately in "defense of white womanhood."

When Pensacolians discovered that Edwards had taken off before she could be retried, all hell broke loose. Though the FBI had not yet adopted its "Ten Most Wanted" program, Edwards became a sought-after national fugitive, due in no small part to the unrelenting campaign of the Pensacola police to capture her. A local grand jury pronounced that "the enormity of her crime is such that the cause of law and justice in this community will suffer if she is not brought to trial for her offenses, therefore we recommend that the governor . . . offer a reward of $500 [for information leading to her capture]." Notice of another reward of $100 and a detailed description of her were broadcast across the country. In her absence, investigations into her hospital were undertaken, and the anger in Pensacola spiraled when it was revealed that more than a dozen white women had sought abortions from Edwards and her staff. No price was too high, the Pensacola sheriff must have felt, to get Edwards back to Florida.

What Sheriff Penton could not possibly have expected was the solid support for Edwards that would come from every corner of Detroit's Black community. When they learned of the arrest by Detective Fox, her friends in Detroit immediately alerted attorney W. Hayes McKinney. Born in 1877 in Coosa County, Alabama, to enslaved parents—his grandparents, both McKinneys, were the slaves of descendants of the Scottish slaveholder Harris McKinney—attorney McKinney knew well the beast of the Deep South. In 1920 the lawyer had waged a two-year battle to prevent the return of Tom Ray to Wilkinson County, Georgia.

Ray had killed his white employer in the summer of 1920 during an argument over unpaid wages. Eluding a posse for several days, Ray ended up in Detroit, only to be arrested a few months later in that city by a group that included the dead man's brother, a Georgia sheriff, and Detroit police officers. McKinney met with Michigan governor Albert Sleeper and recounted for him the lynching record of Georgia. Upon receiving assurances from Georgia's governor that Ray would be tried in a different county, Sleeper granted the warrant. About a week later, a group of armed Black men vowing to protect Ray from being kidnapped faced off with Georgia police and their white Detroit supporters.

Walter White, secretary of the NAACP, came to town and reminded Governor Sleeper that there had been 142 lynchings in Georgia since 1889, but the governer remained unconvinced. McKinney's petition to the state courts also fell on deaf ears. The Michigan Supreme Court observed that it did not favor turning the state of Michigan into a haven for the "[m]urderers and criminal classes of the southern States." As luck would have it, McKinney was able to present the matter to a new governor, Alexander Groesbeck, who would prove to be more sympathetic. The lawyer argued that there was strong evidence of self-defense that had been disregarded by prosecuting authorities in Georgia. But he also provided the governor with data on the history of lynching in Georgia. Governor Groesbeck was persuaded. He observed that "during the course of these proceedings it has been made to appear that there have been some one hundred and forty lynchings in that State."

McKinney probably knew that Ray's case was exceptional. Many northern governors perceived their role to be purely ministerial. However, appreciating as he did the growing influence in Michigan politics of Black voters and the power of organized labor, the lawyer may have also thought he could accomplish for Viola Edwards what he had done for Ray. With the help of the NAACP national office, McKinney amassed data on lynchings in Florida. It was chilling—195 persons were lynched from 1889 to 1918, of whom five, including Leander Shaw, were from Escambia County. McKinney encouraged Black civic and church organizations across Detroit to make their support for Edwards known to the next governor, Fred Green, who had just taken office. One minister, writing on behalf of "two thousand electors of northeast Detroit represented by the Pilgrim Baptist Church," reminded the governor that "no justice will be given this lady in that part of the country." Also urging Green to deny the warrant were the State Association of Colored Women and the Progressive Women's Civic Association.

Governor Green, obviously impressed by the massive support from Black and white Michiganders alike, refused to extradite Edwards. His decision was front-page news in the Black press—"Michigan Governor Saves Woman from Florida Mob," proclaimed the *Chicago Defender.* In Escambia County it came as a complete shock. Unlike Groesbeck's message to Georgia in the Tom Ray case, Green stopped short of rebuking Florida. Rather, he observed that Viola Edwards had been tried and acquitted of virtually the same charge as that in the extradition warrant, and that returning her to Florida would entail unnecessary "hardship and expense."

In the eyes of the Black press and the NAACP, the Ray and Edwards cases were comparable: each was rescued from southern mob violence, Underground Railroad style, by well-organized northern Black activists. In its annual report to the NAACP's national convention in 1930, the Detroit delegation took a victory lap, proclaiming that the chapter's "valiant Full Freedom Fighter, Mr. W. Hayes McKinney, kept Mrs. Viola Edwards from being extradited from Michigan to Florida to barbaric mob murder." For its part, the *Chicago Defender* condemned the Escambia County sheriff for playing the role of "slave-catcher." In scathing terms, it editorialized that there no longer existed "a fugitive slave law under which any backwoods county may dispatch a man with a star to arrest persons in other states."

For a few precious months early in 1929, Edwards put behind her the hysteria and terror of Pensacola and inched back into her life in Detroit. But Pensacola officials, infuriated by the governor's decision, would not be so easily deterred. The case against her codefendant, Eugene Tart, charging him with the manslaughter of the fetus his girlfriend had been carrying, was dropped without a trial, but the prosecutor kept trying to bring Edwards before the bar of justice. Sometime in 1929, months after Governor Green had rejected Florida's extradition request, Edwards was arrested in Detroit on a Florida federal charge completely unrelated to the earlier case and extradited back to Pensacola to face trial.

Upon her return to Florida, Edwards was confronted with the state manslaughter charges arising from Friederichsen's abortion and an unrelated federal case. Penniless, she could not afford to hire an attorney to defend her. The lawyer who had won an acquittal in the first trial, J. Montrose Edrehi, sought help from the NAACP's New York office, but Walter White, who had helped McKinney win the extradition fight in Detroit, saw no reason to step forward this time. White's assistant informed the Florida attorney that Edwards's case was that of "individual misfortune," and hence did not count as a civil rights matter. Edrehi eloquently defended his client:

> In my opinion this defendant would never have been brought back here for trial if she had been a member of another race; further, shortly before her first trial her hospital and home were destroyed by fire under rather peculiar circumstances. This, together with the fact that she was forced to remain in hiding for a long time, drained her of all that she had. She might also seek your aid in that she is a very intelligent woman and has been a leader in her people and has constantly administered to them in their suffering; she was a trained nurse . . . the proprietor of the only colored hospital in this city.

Walter White did not budge. Edwards was convicted on the unrelated charge in federal court and sentenced to serve sixteen months at the City Work House Prison in Cincinnati, Ohio.

In the 1930 federal census, Viola Edwards, now free and lodging back in Pensacola with two younger women, was listed as "widowed." Eventually Viola left Pensacola for good and moved back to Detroit. She was never able to resume her nursing career. Upon her return to the Motor City, she rented a room once again with the Boston family on Farnsworth Street, close to the home of her former sister-in-law, Ruth Chandler. She lived quietly among friends and family until, in 1943, she passed away at the age of sixty-six. She never regained her professional stature, her health, her good name, or her property after the Pensacola ordeal. Nor did she ever share the grief and tragedy of her story with her younger relatives or the public.

ON NOVEMBER 24, 1963, in Dallas, Texas, a local nightclub owner named Jack Leon Ruby received a telegram while he was in police custody. Earlier that day he had taken it upon himself to travel to the Dallas Municipal Building, where Lee Harvey Oswald, the assassin of President John F. Kennedy, was being transferred to a nearby jail. Ruby, in front of a live national broadcast, fired a single shot into Oswald's abdomen as he was escorted past a crowd of reporters. Oswald succumbed to his wounds that afternoon.

The telegram, sent by J. Montrose Edrehi of Pensacola, contained a proposition for Ruby:

> If you have difficulty obtaining an attorney to represent you in your case, I offer my services. During the alleged Klu Klux Days, I, a Jew, represented a negro woman charged with manslaughter, after an alleged abortion on a very high class white lady. I won the case.

ONE MIGHT SAY that the Viola Edwards case served as a bit of a training ground for the two sides in the rendition battles. The advocates for the fugitives learned how best to leverage Black political support to win gubernatorial support, while the southern states came to comprehend that the customary state house to state house courtesies would not be enough to prevail in towns like Detroit where Black people had some clout. Alabama succeeded in obtaining a warrant from a Michigan governor in 1931, but only after a bitter fight, and a case in 1933 involving an escapee from Georgia led Michigan's governor to reject extradition upon a showing of torturous conditions on the chain gang.

And then in 1938, a decade after Viola Edwards's case, Mississippi sought the return from Detroit of Washington Ellis and his wife Josie, a couple from a small town at the gateway to the Yazoo Delta. They would settle about a mile from Viola Edwards's Detroit home. Theirs was in many ways a much harder case than hers, but both sides appreciated what was at stake and adjusted their strategy accordingly.

4

Bentonia Blues

YAZOO COUNTY TO BLACK BOTTOM

Washington "Wash" Ellis's father, Robert "Bob" Ellis, was born—presumably into slavery—in 1854 near Vicksburg, Mississippi. Bob's mother, Charlotte Ellis, enslaved, was born in Mississippi in 1842 and his father, William, so far as can be determined, was born into slavery in 1825 in South Carolina. She was a laundress and he a farmer. For reasons lost to history, by 1879, Bob's parents had moved the family fifty miles east and settled on land fed by the Big Black River on one side and the Yazoo River on the other. Bob Ellis farmed on what had been known before the Civil War as the Anding Plantation, which was about three miles from Bentonia in Yazoo County. It lay at the eastern edge of the Delta, the gold coast of the South, its lush alluvial soil washed over for eons by the waters of the country's largest river, the Mississippi, and by the Yazoo, which the Choctaw called the River of Death. Once a massive swampland, it took centuries to clear out the bogs and tame the Mississippi, its tributaries, and the Yazoo and Big Black Rivers. But to the Delta planters, for whom the cotton boll was white gold, the yield made it all worthwhile.

The Ellis family farm was close to that of a family named Stuckey, and the clans intermarried from time to time. Bob Ellis married Elisabeth "Lizzie" Stuckey, his second wife, in January 1903. They were tenant farmers in Anding, about four miles, as the crow flies, northwest of the railroad in Bentonia. The couple owned an "iron gray mare mule named Beck" that they mortgaged on a yearly basis, as they did their farm equipment, for credit at the general store in town. That mortgage, setting forth the full legal name of Bob Ellis and recorded by the Yazoo County clerk, along with the couple's marriage license, evidenced the transformation of these two children of slavery to citizenship (albeit second-class) with its attendant legalities.

This case is about the Ellises' son, Washington, who was born at their home in 1893. As soon as he could carry an empty fertilizer bag, Washington was in the fields with his father, elder brother, and mother, pulling cotton. As a boy he was small and wiry—he would never grow to more than about five feet two inches—but he was fast and strong. After he learned to count, he would stand at his father's side at the end of the day to watch while the family's cotton was weighed. And he fed the hogs and raised the chickens.

Washington's early years were fettered to the deadening rhythm of the cotton field, while his young adulthood was overshadowed by the monotonous brutality of the battlefield. He was still a teenager when, to break from the plantation, Washington took a job on the Yazoo & Mississippi Valley (Y&MV) Railroad. He would later tell his grandchildren that riding the rails "all the livelong day" was hard work but never dull. In 1916, while President Woodrow Wilson pursued peace in Europe—a fool's errand in the end—the talk in the Yazoo region circled around crops, the boll weevil, and the tides of the Mississippi, Big Black, and Yazoo Rivers. It was at the top of that year, in January, that Bob passed away, leaving behind five sons, including Washington, and eight daughters.

In June 1917, as the world war swallowed up all those who could fight, Ellis—along with a group of Black men from Yazoo that included his brother, Pleas, and his cousin, the famous bluesman Henry Stuckey—enlisted. Washington bade a poignant goodbye to his sweetheart, Josephine "Josie" Winfield—a woman of extraordinary beauty and grace who had his promise that should he survive the war, they would marry—and his mother. He served for nineteen months, much of it in France, where, he would later tell his family, he nearly froze to death. Having sustained an injury at some point during the war, he was honorably discharged with a pension.

The end of 1918 found Washington once again close to the banks of the River of the Dead. Having seen what lay beyond the damnable cotton fields, other soldiers, both Black and white, believing that the world was theirs to shape, abandoned the Delta in droves and headed, usually via Memphis, north or east. But Washington Ellis stayed put. He found some acreage on a farm owned by William M. Puffer, near Bentonia, and vowed to make it provide for him and Josie, whom he married in April 1920. Their family grew quickly: Washington Jr. was born in 1921, followed by four girls. The last of the children, Dora Belle, was born in 1927. It was in that fateful year that the sprawling banks of the Mississippi disappeared, and the river's floodwaters spewed a trail of destruction from New Orleans to Cairo, Illinois, leaving Yazoo County and the Puffer lands under thirty feet of water and throwing into crisis the economic structures of the Black Belt. The Great Flood of '27 caused thousands of Black families to flee the Delta, but again, the Ellis family stayed put. Washington and Josie had what to them seemed a satisfactory relationship with Colonel Puffer, proven by the fact that Puffer gave them a small portion of land above the tenancy. Washington also had a side business making and selling good whiskey during Prohibition; folks came from miles around to buy his product. Most importantly, his mother, brothers and sisters, and cousins were within shouting distance. Yazoo was home, and had been, for three generations of Ellises.

In 1935, Wash and Josie's eldest child fell ill with tonsillitis. The parents arranged to take their fourteen-year-old son for surgery to a doctor in Jackson while the other children stayed with relatives. A friend of the family, James Allison, had an old car that he thought could make the thirty-five-mile trip, and it was settled that the three adults would travel with the boy on June 1, which was a Saturday. On that day, Washington and Josie walked from their farm into Bentonia to meet up with their friend. By the time they were to take off, however, it was late in the day, and they all thought it prudent to put off the Jackson trip for another day. Before leaving Bentonia, Josie headed off in one direction to do some shopping at Brumfield's General Store while the two men went elsewhere in town.

The sun had long dipped below the horizon when James Leon Parker (known to his friends as "Boots"), a twenty-one-year-old white neighbor, began groping Josie outside the Brumfield store. Drunk on corn liquor and perhaps egged on by the presence of his younger brother, Parker persisted despite Josie's ever-louder protests. Parker had previously made similar advances on Josie. On this occasion, Josie would later relate, he dragged her into the street and pushed her to the ground. Drawn by Josie's shrieks, Washington rushed to assist his wife. Parker drew a knife and slashed at Washington, slicing his finger. Washington also had a knife in a back pocket. When the knifework was over, Boots Parker lay prone on Railroad Avenue in Bentonia, the town that had fifteen years earlier given birth, courtesy of the blues-man Henry Stuckey, to the Bentonia blues, and through which ran the Y&MV Railroad, known to locals as the "Yellow Dog."

The Ellises knew that Parker was seriously hurt, but they did not wait around to learn whether his wounds were fatal. They all ran to James Allison's car and sped away. They stopped at the Ellis home only to drop off Josie; the two men kept going. When the gas eventually ran out, Washington ran into the swamps along the Big Black River, where he hid until he could get out of the county. In the days after Parker's death, James Allison, who had not hidden, was arrested and whipped so brutally that he never fully recovered from his injuries. Washington, Josie, and James were charged with the murder of Parker, an offense for which, if convicted, they could be sentenced to death.

A few days after her husband's escape, when Josie heard men were threatening to hang her if she did not reveal her husband's where-abouts, she, too, made plans to get out of town. She held her children tightly and then fled Bentonia. Colonel Puffer took all five of the Ellis children into his home when Josie first left town. In the months that followed, after leaving Puffer's home, the children were protected by neighbors and friends during the day. When night fell, however, they hid in the swamps, warily making their way through dense cypress groves and canebrakes, keeping their distance from the rattlers whose hiding places they were sharing.

When Washington fled Bentonia on the evening of June 1, he could not have known that Josie would also be forced to take to the road. He made his way to Detroit, while his wife settled in St. Louis, where she lived in hiding. Eventually, hearing that her husband was in Detroit, she moved to join him there. Two years would pass between Boots Parker's death and the couple's reunion. During that year the children kept hiding, resurfacing, and lying low. When it became clear that Washington Jr., the boy whose tonsillitis started it all, would never be safe in Yazoo County, the teenager, following in his parents' footsteps, left town, ultimately ending up in Detroit. The girls remained in the custody of their mother's cousin, Laura Stuckey (sister of Henry Stuckey), and her husband, Louis.

In 1937, Washington and Josie were living on Chestnut Street in Detroit's Black Bottom neighborhood. Washington held down a maintenance job at Herman Kiefer Hospital through the Works Project Administration while Josie worked as a "helper" at Trinity Hospital in Black Bottom. Although they feared desperately for their children's safety, they resisted the temptation to make contact with the family in Yazoo County. The children were told that their parents had to leave Bentonia because they had gotten into "some trouble."

———

THE ELLISES FOUND some freedom and comfort on the lively streets of Detroit. Mississippians were all around them, as were Floridians like Viola Edwards. Though their thoughts were on their four girls, they made friends and settled into their new life and neighborhood. In those days, Black life burst forth from the innards of Black Bottom.

The houses were overcrowded, as were the bars, beauty parlors, juke joints, and churches. Old-line Detroiters lived cheek by jowl alongside recent arrivals from Georgia, Alabama, and the Caribbean islands. Coleman Young, the city's mayor from 1974 to 1994, said of Black Bottom:

> [W]hile it brought on the demise of many good men, the Depression also gave life to Black Bottom. The social and economic conditions, brutal and unpitying as they were, animated the neighborhood over matters like housing and unions and communism and the Ford Motor Company. For answers—for salvation—people turned to church and politics. . . . Maben's barbershop was a left-wing caucus in the afternoon, and the nights were for meetings held in private houses behind drawn curtains. It was a climate very conducive to the nurturing of young radicals.

Then, in early May 1938, the Bentonia blues paid a visit to the Ellis home in Black Bottom. A coworker and erstwhile friend of Washington's had spotted his picture in the May 1938 issue of *Master Detective*, a popular pulp fiction magazine. Mississippi authorities were offering a reward of $500 for information leading to the capture of Washington and Josie. On May 6, just a few days after the magazine hit the stands, the couple was arrested by Michigan authorities on a federal fugitive warrant in connection with the murder of Boots Parker.

On May 7, Mississippi's governor Hugh White received a letter from Yazoo County prosecutor T. H. Campbell apprising him of the arrest, describing the legal posture of the case, and urging him to act quickly to ensure the couple's return to Yazoo:

> Leon Parker was a white citizen of Bentonia in this county and these negroes made their escape to Detroit Mich. The Sheriff of this county located these negroes . . . and had them apprehended . . . the two defendants . . . applied for a writ of habeas corpus which is made returnable May 9th next.

If Mississippi authorities were worried about their ability to win an extradition fight with Michigan, it was with good reason. Not only was there the well-publicized decision of Governor Green to refuse Florida's governor's request to return Viola Edwards in 1928, but there was also the more recent case of Jesse Crawford. Crawford had, in 1933, at the age of twenty, escaped to Detroit from a Georgia chain gang, where he had been serving a sentence for stealing a car. At a hearing presided over by Michigan executive officials, Crawford exhibited deep gashes on his wrists and legs, chilling proof of the brutality of the Georgia chain gang system. Swayed by this vivid evidence, and perhaps by Crawford's lawyer's arguments recalling Michigan's role in helping slaves flee from "the torture of Southern masters," Governor William Comstock, like his predecessors, refused to honor the warrant. Although Michigan had indeed sent another fugitive, Dove Ballard, back to Alabama in 1931, it was only after a bitter fight.

It was this history of militant opposition to extradition mounted by Detroit unionists, club women, and political activists that persuaded the Mississippi authorities who sought the Ellises' return to proceed in the federal courts rather than by way of a governor's warrant. In 1934, in the wake of the Lindbergh kidnapping, Congress had passed the Fugitive Felon Act, which made it unlawful to travel across state lines to avoid prosecution for certain serious crimes, including murder. Designed to give the FBI authority to investigate interstate kidnappings, the statute required alleged fugitives to interpose any defense to the federal charge in the district where the underlying crime took place, hence limiting the authority of the court in the detaining state to inquire into the underlying offense.* It was pursuant to the Fugi-

---

* Act of May 18, 1934, ch. 302, 48 Stat. 782: It shall be unlawful for any person to move or travel in interstate or foreign commerce from any State, Territory, or possession of the United States, or the District of Columbia, with intent either (1) to avoid prosecution for murder, kidnaping, burglary, robbery, mayhem, rape, assault with a dangerous weapon, or extortion accompanied by threats of violence, or attempt to commit any of the foregoing, under the laws of the place from which he flees, or (2)

tive Felon Act—a latter-day Fugitive Slave Act—that the Ellises were brought before a federal commissioner in Detroit.

The novel defense made by the Ellises' attorney gave the federal commissioner pause. The lawyer conceded that they had fled, but argued it was not, as required by the statute, to avoid prosecution, but rather to avoid being lynched. He requested that the matter be referred to Edward Moinet, a federal district court judge. A full hearing before a crowded courtroom ensued, at which Josie and Washington presented riveting evidence of their fight with Parker on Railroad Avenue, and of the near-certain lynching that faced them had they remained in Yazoo County. Josie proclaimed that when she heard some men say "when we catch them two we are going to hang them and burn them to ashes," she ran into the woods, where she hid until she could escape.

Judge Moinet was convinced that to return the Ellises to their home state would put their lives in danger. He condemned the Mississippi authorities for "using" the federal court to circumvent Michigan's extradition laws, and observed that the couple appeared to have an absolute defense to the murder charges pending in Yazoo County. Denying the Yazoo sheriff's request to release the Ellises to his custody, the judge released them to the custody of Michigan state authorities.

Well versed in the intricacies of Michigan's extradition battles, the NAACP moved into high gear immediately to prevent the Michigan governor from acting on the Mississippi extradition warrant. With the Ellis case, they had a sympathetic set of facts, and they made the best of it. Here was an attractive, hardworking couple forced to flee a lynch mob, all because the gallant husband defended his wife from a sexual assault by a drunk young man. Their young daughters were still pick-

---

to avoid giving testimony in any criminal proceedings in such place in which the commission of a felony is charged. Any person who violates the provision of this Act shall, upon conviction thereof, be punished by a fine of not more than $5,000 or by imprisonment for not longer than five years, or by both such fine and imprisonment. Violations of this Act may be prosecuted only in the Federal judicial district in which the original crime was alleged to have been committed.

ing cotton in Mississippi and relying on the goodwill of relatives. The director of the chapter, Dr. J. J. McClendon, reminded the governor-elect of Michigan, Frank Murphy, that "to return these people to Mississippi would be to subject them to nothing less than mob violence and death as a penalty for a man attempting to protect his own life and the chastity of his wife." William Pickens, national director of NAACP branches, followed up with his own letter to Murphy. "We blush not a bit in seeking to have this request from Mississippi denied," he wrote. "The awfuliest record of injustice to colored people in recent times has been shown by that State."

The advocates, Pickens and McClendon, knew that they would find Frank Murphy's to be a sympathetic ear. When Murphy ran for mayor of Detroit in 1929, Black support was key to his victory, and he counted heavily on these constituents, who made up roughly 9 percent of the city's population in 1936, when he ran successfully for governor. Judge Murphy's sensibilities on racial justice issues had been put to the test in 1925. That year, as a young judge on Detroit's Recorder's Court, Murphy presided over the famous trials of Ossian and Gladys Sweet. The Sweets were charged with murder after they staved off a mob intent on attacking their new home, which they had just purchased in a white neighborhood. On their second night of residency, a hostile crowd pelted the house with stones. Shots were fired from within the Sweet home, hitting and killing a man in the crowd. Clarence Darrow represented the Sweets, winning an acquittal with the help of Murphy's favorable jury instructions and evidentiary rulings. During the trial, Judge Murphy's courtroom was filled with mean onlookers whose presence portended violence, but the jurist tried the case with such evenhandedness that Walter White would later commend him: "Never had a trial been conducted with more scrupulous fairness than it was by Judge Frank Murphy." Murphy would later be appointed to the United States Supreme Court by President Roosevelt, whose bid for reelection in 1932 Murphy had vigorously championed. Black voters had eagerly supported Murphy's successful mayoral campaign in 1931, and the following year, significant numbers of former Black

Republicans switched parties to vote for Roosevelt over Hoover—
Henry Ford's candidate.

In the meantime, Mississippi authorities redoubled their efforts to
persuade Murphy to extradite the Ellises. After the federal proceedings
concluded, Mississippi governor Hugh White dashed off a telegram
warning Murphy to ignore as propaganda the claim that the Ellises
would be harmed if they were returned to Mississippi. Refusing extradition, he wrote, would only encourage "southern negroes who want
to escape trial and punishment for their crimes [by going] to northern
states where organizations and members of their race will raise the old
cry of feared mob violence."

Governor White obtained statements from nearly every public official in Yazoo County, including its mayor, every member of its board
of supervisors, three judges, two prosecutors, the chief of police, the
sheriff, and the father of Boots Parker. The letter promised that peace
would prevail and a fair trial allowed should the Ellises be returned
to Mississippi. Also weighing in with a separate letter to the Michigan governor was Mississippi senator Theodore Bilbo and congressman Dan McGehee, who represented Yazoo County. As Governor
White's lawyer put it, Murphy had "the statements of practically every
public judicial, peace and court officer of the section where the crime
occurred and where the indictment was found." White promised he
would call out the National Guard if it became necessary to protect the
Ellises. Additional assurances came in the form of affidavits from officials of two counties close to Yazoo that allegations of recent lynchings
in their areas, which were of concern to the Michigan governor, were
unfounded. Also supplied was evidence that Washington Ellis had been
convicted in the county courts on a bootlegging charge. The Mississippi state legislature weighed in as well; on July 26, 1938, it appropriated $1,000 for the use of Yazoo County to "effect the return . . . of
Wash Ellis and Josie Ellis [for the murder of] Boots Parker."

Governor Murphy stalled for time. He was up for reelection in
November, and he probably did not wish to act on the matter before
then. In August he asked Mississippi's Governor White to withdraw his

request for extradition because of the "inflamed state of public opinion [that] not only resulted in a mob pursuit of Ellis and his wife . . . but also on two occasions during the present month of July 1938 . . . resulted in the killing of negroes without the benefit of trial within a short distance from Bentonia." He also noted that he "might be severely criticized" if he granted the extradition request and harm befell the Ellises in Mississippi. White declined to withdraw the warrant, warning his Michigan counterpart that he would be opening floodgates should he provide a safe harbor for the Ellises. "It is neither your province nor mine to remove the determination of guilt or innocence from the courts vested with that duty," he chastised, and then warned, "It would be a lamentable result for Mississippi negroes to feel that Michigan offered an unconditional refuge to colored criminals of the worst type, and that precedent would certainly bring Michigan numbers of dangerous fugitives who would inevitably commit serious offenses and constitute an element highly dangerous to your native citizens."

As soon as the Michigan election was over—Murphy was defeated—White renewed his appeal. Finally, on December 7, just weeks before he left the governorship, Murphy made his decision. He referenced the "state of public feeling" in Mississippi and the favorable decision of the federal court as the reasons why he believed it would be a "grave error" to return Josie and Washington Ellis to Mississippi. The battle was over, the prize won. At long last, the Ellises could become full-fledged citizens of the state of Michigan.

Wash and Josie Ellis immediately set about reuniting their family. They bought a house in Black Bottom at the intersection of Chestnut and Dubois Streets, and sent for their four girls. Four years had passed since the daughters had seen their parents. Decades later, Ida Bessie would recall that her father had disappeared the night before her tenth birthday. Instead of the party that her mother had promised, her world descended into a chaos that would spread across her teenage years. Louis and Laura Stuckey, who took in the girls, had eight children of their own. When the burden of caring for them overwhelmed the Stuckeys, the four Ellis girls were divvied up among other relatives.

Although their father sent cash by circuitous routes, these were lean years for the sisters. Relief finally came when they boarded a Greyhound bus in Bentonia in spring 1939 and headed to Detroit. Their parents, their brother, and a new home and school were waiting for them. The house on Chestnut Street quickly filled up with the rollicking sounds of a large and busy family. They all lived there until the 1960s, when Black Bottom was destroyed by the wrecking balls of urban renewal, dispersing the Ellises and hundreds of other Black families across the city.

Washington Ellis was eighty-four years old when he passed away in 1974. A quiet man who loved a good poker game and expensive shoes, he never forgot his planting days: he grew vegetables in the side yards of the Ellis home on Chestnut Street. He retired after a long career at the same city hospital where, in May 1938, his coworker had turned him over to the police. He liked to tell his grandchildren about his life in Mississippi. He would touch on his railroad days and his time in the army, but he never said much about the "trouble," a topic they knew little about. For Ellis, the city of Detroit in 1935 became both a cloister and a container. He was a wanted man for the remainder of his life outside Michigan state lines. He and Josie made their peace with the strictures on their mobility, grateful to have escaped into the massive fold of the Great Migration, if saddened to have left behind the Bentonia blues, the "Yellow Dog" railroad, and the fields that had, in 1882 and for years thereafter, been plowed by Washington's father's multiply mortgaged "iron gray mule named Beck."

The blending of the Stuckey and Ellis families crossed into the twenty-first century: the two intermixed clans gather in Yazoo County every year for the Stuckey-Ellis family reunion. Washington and Josie's daughter Alberta Holt related the story of her parents' "troubles" at one such family reunion in 2002.

> Daddy was a farmer. He raised his own corn, greens, vegetables and cotton. He had people working in the fields and sometimes we

would work in the fields, clearing the grass and stuff from around the cotton . . . it was nice. Yes, I remember when daddy got into trouble. . . . They came that night. . . . I don't know how many people; it was a lot of them . . . a mob. Yes, it was a mob.

IN SPRING 1938, in New Orleans, Louisiana, when the sheriffs in Yazoo County decided to ramp up efforts to capture Washington and Josie Ellis, they placed a "Wanted" advertisement with a photograph and description of Washington in *Master Detective* and the promise of a $500 reward. Police officers in New Orleans' First Precinct acted quickly on this random news about a wanted couple with a nice price on their head from a neighboring state. On May 11, two of these officers arrested Loyd Dewitt Talmadge Washington, a forty-one-year-old man, at the restaurant where he worked as a cook. Undeterred by the distinct dissimilarity of the two names and the latter's insistence that he had been in the US Army when the Bentonia events took place in 1935, the officers were convinced that the New Orleans cook was the man sought in Yazoo, Mississippi.

WASHINGTON "WASH" ELLIS. *Murder.* Rewards: MASTER DETECTIVE, $100; authorities, $400. Age, 40-45; height, 5 feet, 2-3 inches; weight, 115 pounds; hair, kinky; nose, flat; two gold upper front teeth; complexion, solid black. War veteran. Occupation, farmer share cropper. Wanted with wife for murder of white man. *If located, wire Sheriff R. D. Warren, Yazoo City, Miss.*

A "Wanted" photograph of Washington Ellis appeared in the May 1938 issue of *Master Detective*, leading to his arrest in Detroit, Michigan.

His denials seemed only to enrage the New Orleans officers. Rather than make further inquiries or contact the Yazoo officials, they pulled out a rubber hose and whipped Washington nearly to death. After about an hour of the "third degree," five or six of Washington's teeth were broken, his ribs cracked, and his face transfigured to look like a piece of rotten fruit. He would later testify that his life was spared only when one of the officers at the station reminded the assailants that they should not "kill this man in here, after all he is wanted in Mississippi."

Loyd Washington remained in the First Precinct for twelve long days while the New Orleans officers waited for confirmation of his identity from Yazoo County. That would not be forthcoming, especially because on May 6, right after *Master Detective* was delivered to thousands of newsstands around the country, the real Washington and Josie Ellis were in detention in Detroit. Nevertheless, Loyd Washington was neither released nor allowed to contact his family, or to seek medical or legal help. After almost two weeks in jail, he was transferred to the Orleans Parish detention center, where, for the first time, he had a chance to write a letter to his mother, Letha Washington, in Calcasieu Parish. She paid a visit to the Calcasieu Parish sheriff, who placed a call to Yazoo County authorities and learned that the man they were looking for, one Washington Ellis, had already been arrested. Loyd Washington stepped out of the Orleans Parish jail the following morning. With his ribs broken, it felt like each step was taking him closer to his grave. A doctor at the parish detention center told him "nature was mending it."

———

NOT EVERY RENDITION case from Black Bottom was as successful as was the Ellis matter. Occasionally cases went forward before activists could muster meaningful support for the fugitive. Sometimes the crime that the fugitive left behind was such that its racial injustice was not abhorrent enough to move the public officials to action. And it was particularly difficult to persuade governors to grant relief where the critical defense was that the man named in the foreign state's warrant was not the man pleading for his life in Michigan. While rendition cases were not supposed to be about the merits of the underlying crime, judgments about accountability inevitably affected decision-makers. In 1940, two years after the Ellises won a reprieve, a man from New Orleans named Wilbert Smith sought refuge in Michigan.

5

The One-Way Ride
on Airline Highway

CRESCENT CITY TO BLACK BOTTOM

In 1933, local attorneys described John Grosch, chief of detectives of the New Orleans Police Department—an all-white shop with a reputation for corruption and brutality, visited with cruel casualness on African Americans and labor organizers—as "the 'best' third-degree artist in the United States." From there he picked up the nickname "Third Degree Grosch," boasting that he "secured over three hundred confessions." He had hired his older brother, William, in 1928 as a doorman in the department, and promoted him to detective in 1931; William swiftly became known in the Black community as the "killer twin." The policing methods honed by the Grosch brothers borrowed from the medieval rack and screw. Their belief that an innocent man would rather lie than die was deployed with vicious banality on African Americans.

Nor were Black people the brothers' only targets. John Grosch led terrorizing police raids on New Orleans workers, violently breaking up striking longshoremen and truckers during the late 1930s organizing drives by the CIO in the Crescent City. In 1938 a teamsters' strike precipitated a police raid led by Grosch on a CIO hall, with Grosch's men "beating the Negroes with clubs and cursing all of us," and resulting in the arrest of eighty-four people. John Grosch ordered the raid, he later testified, so that his men could "seize such things as Communist literature." He added that he did not need to obtain a warrant because "we do not need a search and seizure warrant in a public building." The courts dismissed the charges against most of the arrested union organizers, but Grosch was not deterred. He re-arrested the leaders, including the well-known ILWU organizer Burt Nelson, decreeing that he would "run them out of town." These CIO leaders were beaten by Grosch's men "beyond description until they were too tired to beat us any more, all to the tune of 'you son of a bitch, you're gonna leave town.'" Burt Nelson and another man were taken by police to the Huey Long Bridge and told, "if we ever see you within fifty miles of New Orleans, we'll kill you." Having illegally re-arrested and then banished the labor leaders, Chief Grosch boasted that he had rid the city of the CIO: "We have no room in New Orleans for the CIO Communist party [to travel here] from San Francisco [and] agitate among the negroes."

William Grosch was known to be even more sadistic than John, who, by virtue of his position, protected William from any real scrutiny of his handiwork. Only two weeks after his promotion from doorman to detective, William was the subject of a complaint by a suspect whom he had severely beaten; during his ten years as a detective he killed six suspects, four of them African American. Seventeen-year-old Charles Anderson, one of Grosch's victims, was shot in the back of the head as he walked down the steps of his home. So outrageous was the killing that a local affiliate of the Workers Alliance of America made a futile attempt to physically block the coroner from burying young Anderson before the death could be properly investigated. William's longtime partner, Andrew Arnold, who was equally vicious, fatally shot two additional suspects.

William Grosch favored two methods of questioning suspects. In one, he beat men to near death with a rubber hose until they "confessed." Particularly macabre was his practice of offering the destroyed men ice cream and cake after he had extracted their statements. The other was the confessional "ride," which Grosch and his partner, Arnold, perfected. After beating their prisoner within the limits permissible at the police station, Grosch and Arnold would drive the man along Airline Highway into a deserted area in Jefferson Parish, allegedly to search for evidence.* Out of the sight and earshot of those with business at the police station, including any squeamish or overly moralistic fellow officers, Grosch and Arnold would threaten to lynch their victim, and perform a mock execution. Grosch readily bragged that the "one-way" ride was his preferred method of securing trial-proof "evidence."

IT WAS ANDREW ARNOLD and William Grosch, masters of the one-way ride, who, in 1940, drove from the Crescent City to the Motor City to claim the person of one Wilbert Smith, also known by the alias Wilbert Moore. Born in 1902 in Zachary, in East Baton Rouge Parish, Wilbert Smith was the eldest of Emma Smith's four children. The African American family lived on "Back Street," which is what the road that ran parallel to Main Street was called in small Louisiana towns at the turn of the century.

If Smith attended school at all as a boy, it would have been in a one-room classroom at the Little Star Baptist Church on Church Street. Although public schools for whites in East Baton Rouge Parish dated back to 1866, it was not until 1934 that the Zachary Colored School, a Rosenwald institution, opened its doors. For Black pupils, most of whom walked to the school when Wilbert was in the elementary years, the school term was still only six months, and that lasted well into the twentieth century. The white schools, on the other hand, in both the town and rural areas, remained open at least nine months a year.

---

* This was the section of US 61 that Huey Long built to connect Baton Rouge, where he worked, to New Orleans, where he played.

The town emerged from the plantation of Darel Zachary in the late nineteenth century, and was defined by the Louisville, New Orleans & Texas (LNO&T) Railway, to which Zachary gave a right of way in 1884. The railroad ran along its Main Street. The LNO&T would ultimately become part of the Y&MV Railroad—the old "Yellow Dog"—that snaked up through Bentonia, Mississippi, where Henry Stuckey played the blues, about two hundred miles due north of Zachary. Zachary, with a population of about eight hundred in 1902, lay fourteen miles north of Baton Rouge and between two rivers—the grand old Mississippi to the east of the town and the Pearl to the west. In June 1903, a fire, rumored to be set by two fruit peddlers who were heating bananas in their Main Street wooden stands to quicken their ripening, wiped out nearly every building in town. Left standing was just the Y&MV Railroad depot.

Zachary's Black residents seeking to shop in white-owned stores on Main Street gained access through the rear shop doors on Back Street. An eclectic mix of businesses, including cafés, juke joints, lawyers' offices, pleasure parlors, and shoeshine shops sprawled up and down Back Street, delimiting the areas in which Black grocery shoppers, insurance brokers, jazz and blues musicians, and partakers in the sex trades could move freely. Wilbert's mother raised her four children alone on Back Street until she married Harvey Moore. The couple farmed cotton until the boll weevil ruined much of the crop in 1908. Mr. and Mrs. Moore would remain in the parish, but their restless son Wilbert moved on.

Following in the footsteps of many young Zacharites, Wilbert Smith left his parents' home in 1920 and got a job with Standard Oil, which ran a work train through Zachary. Wilbert later moved to Abbeville, in Vermilion Parish, where he amended his name to Wilmer Smith and married Fadra Joiner, who worked as a cook in a private home. Whether Wilmer and Fadra had any children is unknown, and whether Wilmer at some point moved from Abbeville, with or without Fadra, is also unclear. However, a death in New Orleans in 1930 would for Smith be gravely consequential.

ON JANUARY 17, 1930, at about 12:30 a.m., a rookie New Orleans police officer named Lester Johnson, not yet fully accredited and on duty a mere four months, flagged down an old Ford touring car at the corner of Esplanade Avenue and North Rampart Street and ordered the driver to get out. Johnson told the driver he was arresting him for reckless driving. The newspapers reported that when the driver alighted from the car, a fight ensued. The driver freed himself from the officer's grip, drew a pistol, shot Johnson in the abdomen, and fled the scene. The officer dragged himself to a nearby drugstore, from whence he was taken to the hospital. Four days later Officer Johnson succumbed to his wounds.

Press reports identified the registered owner of the Ford car as nineteen-year-old Sidney J. Bourgeois, who lived in the city's Seventh Ward and identified himself as a white man, but Bourgeois was not charged with the crime. The New Orleans police detained at least one other individual, but released him after the injured officer, fighting for his life in the hospital, failed to make an identification. Wilmer Smith, the erstwhile Zachary resident, was said to have been the driver of the vehicle at the time of the shooting. Although he was never identified by Johnson, Smith was charged with the murder.* At the time the accused was twenty-nine years old and living with a different partner, one Daisy Powell.

Smith did not wait around to establish his innocence in court, perhaps with good reason. In 1930 New Orleans policemen killed eight suspects, constituting 9 percent of homicides in the city that year. As notorious for its homicidal record as for its failure to hold its officers to account, there was little chance for Smith in New Orleans, so he took to his heels. Like the Ellises and Viola Edwards before him, he

---

* A news report published on the day of the shooting identified the owner of the automobile as Sidney Bourgeous. Later stories state that Smith owned the vehicle. ("Policeman Shot Arresting Negro Reckless Driver," *Times-Picayune,* Jan. 18, 1930.)

ended his flight in Detroit, that most prominent Underground Railroad venue. In his new city, Smith once again fiddled with his name, reverting to his given first name, Wilbert, and taking on his mother's married name. Thus, his formal name at the Dodge Plant where he found work was Wilbert Moore, though friends called him "Red" and "Coattail." He found a new wife for himself and became, at least subterraneously, a Michigander.

In December 1940, Smith was arrested in Detroit by local police and held for Louisiana authorities. Seeking to speedily extradite Smith, the New Orleans Police Department sent Detectives Grosch and Arnold, the impresarios of the "Airline Highway One-Way Ride," to Detroit. Michigan governor Luren D. Dickinson, a Republican, held a hearing in late December. The governor was fairly new to the job, having assumed the post in 1939 when Frank Murphy's successor died in office, and by some accounts he was far more interested in his farm in Eaton County than in matters of state. He quickly signed a warrant for Smith's return. Grosch and Arnold prepared to drive off with their prey, but the battle had just begun. Smith's coworkers at the Dodge Plant promptly raised $150 for his legal fees. The local NAACP chapter took up the case, as it had for Washington and Josie Ellis, Viola Edwards, and scores of others.

Smith's lawyers pursued a petition for habeas corpus in the Detroit Recorder's Court before Judge William McKay "Mac" Skillman. Wilbert Moore, the Detroiter, they argued, was not Wilmer Smith, the man wanted in New Orleans, and in any event if he (Smith or Moore) were returned to New Orleans, he would be lynched before a jury could hear his defense. Prescience and panic swirled around Smith's words as he beseeched Judge Skillman, "I will never be tried by a New Orleans court." Here his agonized plea to the court echoed that of Reverend Anthony Burns in 1854 and Reverend A. H. Hampton in 1895. Skillman gave Smith's lawyers an opportunity to show that their client was in Detroit at the time of the killing back in New Orleans, but the testimony did not convince the judge. He denied relief, giving Smith time to appeal to the Michigan Supreme Court. When that court declined to act, Smith was turned over to Grosch and Arnold.

The two detectives, who had bided their time impatiently in Detroit for three weeks, were eager to get back home. On Wednesday, January 15, 1941, they finally arrived in New Orleans with their prisoner. The officers drove Smith first to the Third Precinct, which covered the area where Officer Johnson had been shot in 1930, and booked him. Then, they put Smith back in their police vehicle for "the ride" down Airline Highway.* Smith did not make it back to the station. About a half mile into Jefferson Parish, right on the other side of the Orleans Parish line, he was shot to death by Grosch, the "killer twin."

When word reached New Orleans that Smith had been killed by Grosch, most Black residents, and likely many whites too, knew immediately that there had been a police lynching. The African American New Orleans Press Club met within days of the shooting, protesting the "deliberate murder." The Press Club wrote to Louisiana's attorney general Eugene Stanley and US Attorney General Robert Jackson demanding a prompt investigation, and it collected the evidence to support its claim that Smith was murdered. The undertaker who embalmed Smith, James T. Willie, reported that the body bore marks of a serious beating, including a crushed skull, and that shots may have been fired into Smith's already dead body. The Press Club dubbed the death a "streamlined lynching." At a mass meeting on January 26, 1941, at the New Hope Baptist Church, an audience of a thousand heard Reverend Gardner C. Taylor and others insist on swift action against the officers. Orleans Parish investigators initially balked at demands for a thorough investigation, but after seven weeks of local and national protests,

---

* According to Bob Dylan's lyrics, Abraham said to God, "Where do you want this killin' done?" and God said to Abraham, "Out on Highway 61." (Bob Dylan, "Highway 61 Revisited," Columbia Records, 1965.)

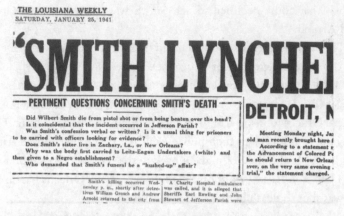

Wilbert Smith died in the custody of New Orleans police officers shortly after he was extradited from Detroit, Michigan, to stand trial on a murder charge.

the parish's district attorney J. Bernard Cocke reluctantly agreed to open a file on the matter. He ordered Smith's body exhumed. Present at the exhumation were representatives for the Press Club and Detectives Grosch and Arnold. The coroner, invariably a reliable witness for the police, concluded that Smith had not been beaten and that, as Grosch claimed, he died from a gunshot wound to the right side of the head.

Grosch and Arnold told a fantastical story of how Smith ended up dead in their custody on the other side of the parish line just hours after they arrived in Louisiana. Smith promised to take the officers to a spot where the weapon that had been used to shoot Patrolman Johnson— eleven years earlier—had been hidden, they claimed. As they drove, however, Smith asked to get out of the vehicle to respond to a call of nature. Once out of the car, the handcuffed man managed to attack Grosch, who had to defend himself by shooting his prisoner in the neck. The officers' official report averred:

Detective Grosch fired one ineffectual shot to try to stop the Negro. Grosch while scuffling with the negro struck him with his regulation revolver to try and subdue him but as Arnold and Grosch were scuffling with the Negro he managed to get his two hands over Detective Grosch's head with the handcuffs on and attempted to choke the officer, when Detective Wm. Grosch fired the second shot which struck the Negro in the neck. He fell to the ground dragging Grosch with him.

One skeptic, a white real estate broker from Shreveport named E. Clinton Hamilton, reported to the national NAACP that the detectives' story could not be credited. "Many of us saw and talked with this man when he came thru Shreveport on January 15 accompanied by two officers," Hamilton wrote to Walter White, attaching to his letter a clipping from the *Shreveport Times*. "He was handcuffed and there was a chain around his waist fastened to the handcuffs. . . . It seems highly improbable that any serious attempt to escape would have been made by him." Certainly an investigation was called for, Hamilton opined, suggesting that "[a]t least the authorities in Michigan should know how hazardous it is to deliver Negro prisoners to Southern officers for safe delivery in the South."

Grosch and Arnold did what they could to silence a woman who might have implicated them in Smith's death. On February 9, 1941, when it was evident that protests in the Black community were not subsiding, the two detained Daisy Powell, the former wife of Wilbert Smith, beat her so severely that she spent a week in the hospital, and then ordered her to leave town. She refused, seeking instead a grand jury investigation. In response, Grosch and Arnold, claiming they visited Powell to follow up on a tip that she knew of others involved in the killing of the police officer, the incident that led to the murder case against Smith, accused her of fabricating the story about the beating.

The detectives got away with what appear to be many murders. In

1940 Jefferson Parish was reputed to have some of the worst law enforcement officials in the state. There was no hope that District Attorney John Fleur or Sheriff Frank Clancy would lead a proper investigation, and thus few could have been surprised in May 1941 when a Jefferson Parish grand jury refused to indict the officers. Members of the Press Club testified before the grand jury, as did the mortician who had earlier informed the Press Club of his damning findings. All of their work, and all of the protest, was to no avail.

SMITH'S FATE may have reminded some of New Orleans' more senior Black residents that the old ways of the slave catchers still informed policing in their town. Paterollers, as they were called, were the officers, some official, some private, whose policing job was to return runaway slaves to their owners. When the Civil War broke out, leaving more women in charge of the plantation's enslaved community, it was the paterollers who recaptured and returned to their erstwhile owners Black women and men who had acted on the impulse of a freedom that was near but not yet legally enacted. Typically, if an enslaved person was caught by a pateroller before she could make good on her escape she would be severely beaten before being returned to the owner. She would not be killed, and this, a sort of blessing in disguise, she owed to her market value, as was so sardonically pointed out by the author of the article, written in January 1895 for the *Cambridge Tribune*, "A New Version of the Old, Old Story." Anthony Burns was, in 1854, more likely to survive a thwarted escape attempt than was A. H. Hampton, in 1895, upon whose life no price tag hung, or, in 1941, Wilbert Smith.

6

Resisting Rendition

LEGAL STRATEGIES AND POLITICAL ADVOCACY

The campaigns on behalf of Detroit residents Viola Edwards, Josie and Washington Ellis, and Wilbert Smith were but three of scores of cases that required northern authorities to make calculated political judgments about southern policing and judicial systems. Collectively these cases present an enduring "Red Record" of mob violence, peonage, and brutal penal practices, for they recorded stories that were not meant to leave the South. As the cases involved cross-border disputes, the constitutional rights of these Jim Crow–era fugitives should have been protected by federal statutes. That they were not had a lot to do with the legal infrastructures that sustained slavery and then cast a shadow over the post-slavery regimes. Federal law could and should have preempted state legal regimes by setting the constitutional floor, but Congress failed to act.

BEFORE THE US CONSTITUTION WAS adopted in 1789, each colony decided for itself, on a case-by-case basis, whether to turn over enslaved fugitives to a demanding colony. While most slaves were rendered, the non-slave northern colonies sometimes rejected the claims

of southern colonies and their slave owners on the theory that slavery
was so inimical to natural law that it could not be sustained except by
positive law. Put another way, the institution could only be supported
or facilitated in those jurisdictions where legislative acts acknowledged
the legality of slavery. On this reading, enslaved persons setting foot
in "free" colonies became emancipated and could not be returned to a
state of peonage.*

The Constitution's Fugitive Slave Clause eliminated these disparities
among the colonies. From 1789, the Constitution required all states to
"deliver up" escaped slaves to their proven owners. The clause provided the positive law that had been missing before 1789.† Indeed, it
was the Fugitive Slave Clause that helped sell the constitutional bargain
in the South. James Madison argued before the Virginia ratifying convention that the clause gave southern states "better security than now
exists. . . . At present, if any slave elopes in any of those States where
slaves are free, he becomes emancipated by their laws: for the laws of
the States are uncharitable to one another in this respect." The same
section of the Constitution established, in the Extradition Clause, that
states had the right to demand of sister states the return of non-slave
fugitives from justice.

But while the Constitution's Fugitive Slave Clause, and the Fugitive
Slave Act of 1793 adopted by Congress to implement it, supplied the
positive law that had been lacking before the Revolution, the non-
slave states often still balked when faced with rendition claims from
the slave states. This resistance to rendition, combined with the robust-
ness of the Underground Railroad, led slaveholding states to press for

---

* The wet foot/dry foot policy under which Cuban refugees gained sanctuary in the
United States in the twentieth century followed the same logic: if you could make it
to "freedom," you were safe.

† US Constitution Art. IV, § 2, Cl. 3: "No Person held to service or Labor in one
State, under the Laws thereof, escaping into another, shall, in Consequence of any
Law or Regulation therein, be discharged from such Service or Labor, but shall be
delivered up on Claim of the Party to whom such Service or Labor may be due."

further reforms. It was the passage of the Fugitive Slave Act in 1850, one of a set of compromises designed to forestall southern secession, that closed the legal loopholes and tied the hands of northern states by limiting the scope of their review in rendition matters. Congress made federal courts the exclusive adjudicators of rendition warrants and prescribed only summary proceedings, thereby putting an end to the defiant noncompliance of northern states' executive and judicial authorities. In the 1854 Boston case of Anthony Burns, for example, the federal commissioner, Edward Loring, who issued the warrant returning Anthony Burns to slavery, deemed his hands tied by the Fugitive Slave Act of 1850.

The Fugitive Slave Clause was, in effect, mooted by the victory in the Civil War, restoring to states the discretion they had enjoyed before the Constitution came into force. Northern antipeonage activists—those militant legatees of the abolition movement—attempted to exploit this void to press their state officials to extend sanctuary for escapees from the reprised slavery of convict leasing, chain gangs, and similar barbarisms of southern law. The Extradition Clause, constitutional neighbor to the now defunct Fugitive Slave Clause, became the point of reference for escapees from Jim Crow justice and those seeking their return. Rooted in comity and designed to provide a speedy and reliable method of extraditing persons charged with criminal offenses, the intent of the Extradition Clause was to discourage states from looking behind a facially valid warrant to explore the motives of the demanding state or its capacity to afford to the fugitive constitutional protections. But news reports and campaigns launched by northern communities were making it abundantly clear that southern states could not—or would not—protect returning fugitives from violence, and hence public officials in northern states soon began to more closely scrutinize extradition petitions from the South where the escapees were Black.

While some of these campaigns sought relief from the state's executive offices, others were played out in the courts. As to gubernatorial authority under the Extradition Clause, the US Supreme Court had decided as far back as 1861 that federal authorities could not force a state's chief executive to deliver a fugitive from justice back to the demanding state. In that pre–Civil War case, *Kentucky v. Dennison*, the governor of Ohio, William Dennison, had refused to return to Kentucky a freedman, Willis Lago, indicted there for the crime of enticing an enslaved woman to leave her owner. The case ensured that when they acted pursuant to the Extradition Clause, governors could do so without fear of federal override.

One of the most significant early twentieth-century cases to come out of a northern governor's office was the Tom Ray matter, in 1921. Jim Crow had by then tightened its grip, and migration had augmented Detroit and other Black northern communities, strengthening their resolve and power. Michigan's governor released Ray because he feared the petitioner would be lynched were he returned to Georgia. In some cases, a looming lynch mob was not the only factor causing one governor to reject the rendition request of another. Rather, the improbability of obtaining a trial untainted by racism could be a motivating cause. In another 1921 case, a Minnesota governor, Jacob Preus, refused to extradite to Oklahoma a Black man charged in connection with the infamous Tulsa Race Massacre. "A reputable black, who lives in Minnesota," the governor noted, had persuaded him that the fugitive would not be able "to secure a fair trial in the courts of Oklahoma."

Two decades later, in 1948, California's governor Earl Warren refused to return Wiley King to Mississippi. Were King to have been extradited, it would have been to complete a life sentence rendered in 1925 for the killing of another African American man. King's defense counsel argued to Warren that the sentence followed "a trial which lasted only ten minutes and denied him the service of legal counsel." King, who in California had lived an "exemplary life," argued that in 1927 he had been pardoned by the then Mississippi governor after paying a prison guard $250 to secure his freedom. An energetic campaign to keep King in California was aided by favorable political timing, with one Errol G. Gallagher excitedly writing to Thurgood Marshall that "as a candidate for Congress in Warren's home district, I am anxious to see what he will do when the Vice Presidential Candidate on the Dixiecrat ticket [Mississippi's Governor Fielding L. Wright] asks the Vice Presidential Candidate on the Republican ticket [California's Governor Earl Warren] to send a Negro back to Mississippi." Taking note, no doubt, of demonstrations of around ten thousand people, Thomas E. Dewey's vice presidential candidate, and future Supreme Court chief justice, denied the warrant, proclaiming that "the ends of justice would not be served by breaking up this family and sending its bread winner back to prison."

ALTHOUGH MANY CAMPAIGNS focused on persuading the governors of the sanctuary states that fugitives would not receive a fair trial if returned, when that failed, appeals to courts often followed. Long-term strategies suggested that such appeals to the courts were essential. While gubernatorial decisions secured important individual victories, garnered public attention, and mobilized Black northern communities, they lacked lasting precedential value in the wider effort to protect Black fugitives. However, in the early decades of the century, only on rare occasions were judicial proceedings fruitful. The NAACP achieved just five instances of successful judicial redress by habeas review throughout the 1920s.

An exception to this pattern came in a dramatic case in 1942 in Pennsylvania. Appealing to the state courts for relief was Thomas Mattox, a young man threatened with extradition back to Georgia from Philadelphia. Just sixteen years old, young Mattox was wanted in his home state for attempted murder. The teenager had escaped a near-lynching in Elberton, a small town near Georgia's border with South Carolina. Having been attacked on the highway by a young white man who beat him and his sisters with a car jack, Mattox struck back with a knife, inflicting a wound that sent the white youth to the hospital for some stitches. That night, running for his life, Mattox boarded a north-bound train. To pressure them into revealing Thomas's whereabouts, his sisters were criminally charged and his mother severely beaten. The family finally caved and told Elberton authorities where Mattox was in Philadelphia. An extradition warrant was quickly drawn up.

The well-known civil rights advocate Raymond Pace Alexander represented Mattox. Alexander offered the testimony of the boy's sisters and mother to prove that he would be seized by a mob if he were returned to Georgia. William H. Hastie, dean of Howard Law School, and Thurgood Marshall, counsel for the NAACP, participated in a "friends of the court" brief filed by the National Lawyers Guild at the state appellate level. They informed the court that there had been six lynchings within thirty miles of Elberton. Clare G. Fenerty, the trial judge, had, during his service as a Republican congressman, lent his support to anti-lynching legislation. Troubled by the complaint of the Georgia prosecutor that his anti-lynching advocacy was proof of bias, Judge Fenerty read the accusation into the record. He noted with some sarcasm that the Georgia prosecutor did not seem to want "a judge who believed in the desirability of punishing legal authorities for permitting murder," and he went on to observe that "[t]here can be no presumption of protection for the accused from murderous violence when the prosecuting attorney—charged with the duty of insuring this protection—expresses such bias and prejudice." Judge Fenerty refused to extradite young Thomas Mattox.

———————

SHUTTLING IN THIS MANNER back and forth between governors' chambers and state and federal courtrooms, advocates for the fugitives were always on the lookout for the most sympathetic forum. In 1944, for example, Judge Francis B. Allegretti of Chicago's criminal court refused to return John Catchings to Mississippi to stand trial for murder, doubting Catchings would "ever get a chance to tell his story on the witness stand." Perhaps in anticipation of this refusal, a few weeks before the judge's ruling, a Mississippi federal grand jury indicted Catchings under the Selective Service Act for failing to report to his board for a physical examination. A federal judge in Chicago, asked to render on the new federal charge, refused to go along with the ploy. Ordering Catchings's release, he observed that it would be a "mockery of justice" to put Catchings on trial for the Selective Service violation The "indictment for the violation of the Selective Service Act," he wrote, "is merely a subterfuge in order to get the defendant back to Mississippi." Five years later, Mississippi was still attempting to extradite Catchings. William Henry Huff, one of the most well-known rendition lawyers, finally brought the saga to a close by convincing Illinois governor Adlai Stevenson to reject an extradition warrant.

With the federal felony charges against Catchings also dropped, William Huff would claim that he had won his seventy-seventh straight extradition case.

7

Who Stays Up North,
Who Goes Back Down South

Attorney William T. Patrick was, like William Henry Huff, a Georgia native. A Detroit NAACP official, Patrick, too, had a healthy rendition practice. There was one case, however, that, unfortunately, Patrick could not win. He could not persuade the NAACP's Charles Hamilton Houston to come to the aid of thirty-five-year-old Mrs. Willie Fleetwood, nor was he able to convince a Detroit court to allow his client to remain in Detroit.

Long before there emerged a definition for distinctively gendered abuse, Willie Fleetwood chose to fight for her life rather than succumb to domestic violence. Around 8 p.m. on the Fourth of July in 1933, in Rome, Georgia, Mrs. Fleetwood, then thirty-two years old, was attacked at her home by a twenty-four-year-old Black man whom she knew and who, she said, came after her with a razor. Fleetwood wrested the weapon from the man and slashed him to death. She fled Rome, with her daughter, to Detroit, where, from 1933 to 1935, she lived in Black Bottom. She and her daughter made a home for themselves on Brewster Street, less than two miles from where Viola Edwards was staying with the Boston family, and worked as a domestic, until, in 1936, Georgia authorities pursued her extradition.

Arguing that constitutional fair trial rules did not apply when Black people faced criminal charges in Georgia, William Patrick tried to persuade the judge to block extradition. In a long recitation of the "Jim Crow methods" that would prevent a fair trial should his client be returned to Georgia, Patrick represented to the judge that a witness, a Black man who had been brought to Michigan by the authorities to testify against Mrs. Fleetwood, had submitted an improper affidavit. This allegation distressed the Georgia lawyers, who turned to the witness and asked him to attest to Georgia's justice: "We treat 'darkies' alright, don't we, Charley?" the lawyer asked, to which "Charley" nodded, under duress but affirmatively.

Because the man Mrs. Fleetwood killed was Black, the NAACP declined to assist. Charles Hamilton Houston explained to Patrick: "The difficulty is that unless some evidence of race discrimination appears in the case, it does not fall within our jurisdiction. We do not interfere in cases of Negroes against Negroes unless evidence of oppression can be shown. If you have any information as to danger of specific prejudice in this case, please advise us."

The "evidence of oppression" was, of course, twofold: Mrs. Fleetwood would, in 1936, have to put her claim of self-defense before a white male jury that would be blind, if not hostile, to the audacious assertion by a Black woman that she had a right to fight for her survival. Notwithstanding Houston's rejection of the matter, Patrick persevered with his argument that Fleetwood's was a "race case" because of the constitutionally inadequate procedures afforded Blacks in Georgia's criminal courts. He argued that Georgia's failure to abide by the US Supreme Court's rulings prohibiting jury discrimination was grounds to reject extradition. "Georgia has not applied to Michigan with clean hands," he proclaimed. "[Georgia] should not come to Michigan and obtain her cooperation in covering up their defects, especially where one of my people is involved." Patrick ultimately lost, but didn't drop his debate with Houston. He wrote him again, reiterating that the case was one the association should have accepted:

Shall we let Georgia, who respects no law, return a person, (even a woman) to her State where we know she will not receive "due Pro-

cess of law" under our Federal Constitution? I say no . . . I shall,
if standing alone, fight to the last ditch, any effort on their part to
return one of my people to their jurisdiction.

While the NAACP was the main organization involved in campaigns to fight extradition, it was not the only one. Often the association worked at the national level alongside the Civil Rights Congress
or its predecessor, the International Labor Defense (ILD), and with
civic and church groups locally. The association tended to be more
selective in the battles it engaged in than the ILD, as evidenced by
the dispute between the two organizations during the Scottsboro trials
in the 1930s: the NAACP was reluctant to become involved in that
defense because the accused might not have been innocent. Leery of
being charged with condoning "black criminality," NAACP strate-
gists prioritized cases that presented straightforward racial issues and
in which innocence was evident or legal responsibility diminished.
Although the search for "clean" cases left many fugitives in the lurch,
association officials, strapped for resources and attentive to fundraising
imperatives, believed their caution was warranted.

Some found support for this posture in a case that the ILD took on
while the association held back—one that did not end well. A successful campaign was mounted in 1933 to convince Michigan governor
William Comstock to prevent the return of Jesse Crawford to a Georgia chain gang. Crawford was supported by the ILD and the League
of Struggle for Negro Rights, a civil rights organization launched in
1930 by the Communist Party (CPUSA). Four months after Comstock's favorable decision, however, Crawford was arrested in Detroit
for stealing a car belonging to an official of the ILD during an address
by Mrs. Jannie Patterson, mother of Haywood Patterson, one of the
"Scottsboro Boys." In response, the two groups issued a statement,
reiterating that "in defending Crawford from extradition, the League
of Struggle for Negro Rights and the International Labor Defense were
defending a principle they will continue to defend: that of struggle
against the persecution and exploitation of the Race people." They

went on to "notify all workers' organizations that due to this conduct of Crawford's, we are severing all connections [with Crawford]." Seventeen years later, in March 1950, Crawford was extradited to Georgia from Pennsylvania to complete a sentence for larceny and burglary rendered just three months earlier.

The Viola Edwards case also revealed the association's concerns over case selection, and speaks to the association's view of what constituted sympathetic facts. After authorities in Escambia County brought new federal and state charges against her and finally succeeded in extraditing her to Florida her Florida lawyer argued passionately that Edwards was the target of a racist and sexist vendetta, the NAACP attorneys refused to become involved; the case no longer offered prospects for favorable legal precedent.

BARBAROUS PENAL PRACTICES often got the NAACP's attention in the rendition arena. Despite federal laws outlawing peonage as early as 1867, Black Codes and laws criminalizing Black unemployment provided a steady supply of labor through convict leasing. As conditions in these prison camps were inhumane, escape was commonplace, numbering in the thousands each year across the South. In 1932 the association came to the defense of Robert Elliot Burns, a white fugitive from a Georgia chain gang who won his gubernatorial appeal to remain in New Jersey. His story had received national attention in the 1932 Warner Bros. film *I Am a Fugitive from a Chain Gang*, based on Burns's memoir. Walter White's testimony before New Jersey's governor Moore made clear why the association was intervening:

> In the present instance it is a white man, not a Negro, who is sought
> for rendition, but the National Association feels that the barbarities,
> the cruelties, and the inhumanities of the Georgia prison camp and
> chain gang system have repeatedly called to the attention of the
> civilized world and . . . are such that essential justice itself protests

against the return of any human being to such conditions . . . of which Negroes in America have been the chief victims.

In September 1939, Otis and Dock Woods, father and son, and Solomon McCannon—sought by Georgia on a charge of robbery on a plantation—were taken into custody in Chicago, along with four other men wanted by three southern states. Attorney William Henry Huff, who would become the superstar of extradition cases (and was also a pharmacist, poet, and songwriter), was a relative of the three fugitives. He argued before Illinois governor Henry Horner that the three men were in fact escapees from a chain gang in Oglethorpe County, formerly under supervision of a white plantation owner, W. T. Cunningham, who had held the men in peonage. At the state capitol with Attorney Huff were five carloads of friends of the men, a number of other Georgia fugitives, and two white men—attorney Noble Lee, secretary of John Marshall Law School, and Martin Klass, deputy clerk of the Municipal Court of Chicago. Having persuaded Governor Horner to let the men remain in Illinois, Huff declared that Georgia's requisition attempt was "the 1939 edition of the 'Fugitive Slave Law.'" He went on to promise that he would "not be satisfied until Cunningham has been prosecuted for peonage and conspiracy."

While Huff was usually challenging rendition efforts by the southern states, in this instance he reversed course. He sought to force the Georgia planters and captors of his relatives to answer charges in a federal court in Chicago. In 1941, acting as counsel for the Abolish Peonage Committee, Attorney Huff saw to it that W. T. Cunningham and Hamilton McWhorter, the planter's attorney (and a former president of the Georgia State Senate), were indicted in federal court in Chicago on charges of conspiracy to deprive his clients of their constitutional rights and to impose conditions of slavery and peonage. In this pathbreaking matter, the International Labor Defense and the National Negro Congress helped Huff obtain, for the Department of Justice's case, over one hundred affidavits of support from peonage victims.

The Georgia federal district court judge, Bassom Deaver, refused to deliver Cunningham and McWhorter to Illinois to answer the federal charges. Conceding that rendition may have been justified, Judge Deaver nevertheless deemed the evidence on the peonage charges inconclusive. The Georgia attorney, Hamilton McWhorter, would not be sent to Chicago, Deaver ruled, because he was "a reputable lawyer of forty years' experience." The man's "old age" and affliction "with a serious heart ailment" militated against his removal to "a distant district for trial, without any substantial grounds for prosecution."

Ironically, when Judge Deaver released the two Georgia men from custody on the warrants Huff had obtained, the Abolish Peonage Committee protested that "the only question before Judge Deaver . . . was whether the men arrested were the same men mentioned in the indictment and whether or not there was probable cause they might possibly have violated the law." That claim roundly echoed that of Anthony Burns's owner in 1854 in Boston; of the State of Kentucky in the A. H. Hampton case in 1895; and of the State of Mississippi in Washington and Josie Ellis's case in 1938. This time, however, the shoe was on the other foot. Although Huff's argument did not prevail, he did achieve an important measure of victory. In 1942 the US Supreme Court unanimously struck down Georgia's debt law, and later that year the federal government initiated a civil rights investigation into Oglethorpe County's debt peonage system, which had followed Emancipation.

In a letter to Thurgood Marshall in March 1941, William Henry Huff described the ordeal his relatives in Oglethorpe County, Georgia, had endured after Solomon McCannon escaped. They were arrested and held as if for ransom. To Marshall he wrote:

> I would gladly go back to Oglethorpe County, Georgia, be hung to the highest pine therein, as was poor, defenseless Obe Cox, and be, as he was, tarred, feathered, gasolined, riddled and charred, and if that course would create the sentiment necessary for the abolition of peonage-involuntary servitude-slavery, for I can truly say as Cullom said in the closing chapter of "Fifty Years of Public

Service," "I have no great fear of death except for the physical pain that accompanies it, for I know that when old Charon shall come to row me across the river Styx, I shall be ready to go."

William Hayes McKinney, who won freedom for Viola Edwards and Tom Ray; William T. Patrick, who represented Mrs. Willie Fleetwood; and William Henry Huff, who boasted of succeeding in seventy-seven rendition cases: these lawyers—all three hailing from the Deep South, two of them sons of enslaved parents—and the communities they worked with transformed the old abolitionist cause into a fight to fulfill the promises of the Civil War Amendments. Their arguments ran parallel to, and supplemented, the campaign for federal anti-lynching legislation. Their tactics, in court and beyond, evinced the continuity of communities of resistance. From slavery, through Jim Crow, and on to the civil rights era, these activists stretched formal law to its outer limits and, when necessary, undertook highly organized military-style operations to help fugitives make good on their escape.

World War II would bring the radical ethos of some of these sanc-

Illinois attorney William Henry Huff is said to have successfully handled seventy-seven rendition cases.

tuary cities into contact with the Deep South in an altogether different way. Black soldiers, from Black Bottom and elsewhere, were drawn by the war back down into the communities from which their relatives—and perhaps they themselves—had fled. They went south, where they joined with thousands of Black southern men and women in uniform, to train. In the process, these young people ignited new dreams of freedom, reinforced the spirit of Black resistance, and insisted on a "Double Victory."

PART II
RACED
TRANSPORTATION

Yes, I know I'm in the South. I'm in the South because the army brought me here to fight your war for you. It's not my fight, the things I'm fighting for don't exist for me or any Negro. Poor [white people] like you have rights, but I haven't but by God I'm wearing Uncle Sam's uniform. I'll make you respect it and treat me like any other soldier. If you were any part of a man you'd be in uniform yourself.

—*Corporal Fred Edwards to store cashier, Camp Shelby, Mississippi, 1942*

There have been numerous killings of Negro soldiers by civilians and civilian police. . . . We are not aware of a single instance of prosecution or of any steps being taken by the Federal Government to either punish the guilty parties or to prevent the recurrence of these crimes against the uniform of the United States Army.

—*Thurgood Marshall to US Assistant Attorney General Tom C. Clark, New York City, 1944*

8

The Color Board

Rendition addressed issues of mobility from South to North, harkening back to the Fugitive Slave Act of 1850. During World War II, as soldiers traveled from North to South, the relationship between Black mobility and Black freedom arose in a different context, raising questions about the content of American democracy at home while a war was being waged in the name of that principle abroad.

Jim Crow's most notorious divide was perhaps the one separating two races on a streetcar. The fight to erase that marker began when the first segregated streetcar was introduced. It was a struggle waged daily, and largely invisibly, on the local stage by individuals subjected to the indignity of being forced to the back of the bus, and on the national stage by Homer Plessy. The battle was a shaping force in the over half a century's organized campaign to bury Jim Crow: the line was despised for what it represented and for the frustration it caused riders who were just trying to get someplace. The story of buses and soldiers, often not much more than a footnote in accounts of World War II's home front, recovers the dynamic tension of competing provincial, national, and international agendas. Soldiers—or veterans—brought onto a southern town's buses and streetcars their understanding of Blackness from Detroit, or of freedom from France or Burma, creating a combustible stage where national political priorities met up with local law enforcement.

BLACK RIDERS WAGED a collective crusade against the Jim Crow streetcar as far back as the late nineteenth century. There were boycotts in Atlanta in 1892, in New Orleans and Norfolk in 1902, in Savannah in 1906, and in several other cities. These early campaigns set the stage for the struggle to de-racialize the bus across the first half of the twentieth century. As commonplace as planned actions were, everyday performances of protest that might flare up on any bus at any time included cursing the driver, destroying the color board, defying commands to create space for whites, and all manner of cross-racial physical skirmishes. Such impromptu insubordination was, by the 1940s, so widespread as to be an inescapable feature of bus travel. The police records of southern cities are replete with "disorderly conduct" cases attesting to the resistance of riders. Arrests, however, were an inadequate deterrent to the guerrilla war percolating up from the bottom. Black passengers became louder and more militant as time went on, with opposition to the back of the bus finally exploding during World War II and in its immediate aftermath.

African American soldiers traveling to the South, many for the first time, insisted that they be transported with dignity, and thereby fortified the resistance of everyday Black passengers. Soldiers could afford to be outspoken in their opposition to Jim Crow. They defied the insults and mistreatment of white drivers and passengers alike, even when ordinary Black riders, whose daily survival required it, bore the mask of subservience and subordination. Soldiers, by contrast, wore the uniform of their country. They could and did resist more boldly and directly, and many paid with their lives for their protest against segregated transportation. They were met with astonishing violence. In most cases neither the US War Department nor the Department of Justice came to the soldiers' defense. Their martyrdom has yet to be recognized; the violence they endured was never fully documented. Certainly, it never made it into the sagas about the "Greatest Generation."

Black people remained segregated at the bottom rungs of the armed services during World War II. A Black labor battalion here takes a break from unloading boats in the Aleutian Islands in 1943.

IT WAS NEVER EASY to police racialized space on the buses and streetcars of southern towns. Unlike railroad waiting rooms, trains, or theatres, where space was more or less permanently partitioned, city riders had to contend with unpredictably shifting seating needs for the two races. And unlike city streets, where pedestrians could parry and thrust as was appropriate for the time and place of the mixed raced space and the disposition of the walker, there was little maneuvering space on the bus. The insults of Jim Crow were more keenly experienced in a contained space where tired strangers jostled against each other and tensions ran high. Racial rules collided with gender and class etiquette and upended generational hierarchies, requiring elderly Black women to stand if white teenagers were without seats, and middle-class Black school teachers to yield to young white toughs. Everyone—Black and white, soldier and civilian—came as who they were on the bus, whether well-clad or disheveled, sober or drunk, loud or soft-spoken, polite or ill-mannered. Jim Crow's all-powerful precepts nullified gender and class identities, privileging only the racial marker. And although some African Americans could minimize the psychic scars of segregation by driving their own cars or avoiding racialized spaces like parks and movie theatres, working-class people had to take city transportation to get to town and their jobs.

A bus driver's eyes were necessarily on the road, making it especially challenging to enforce Jim Crow laws. Southern authorities took two approaches to this vexing dilemma, one formal and the other informal. In the first approach, many southern towns enhanced the powers of the driver. Although these men were not trained in law enforcement, in many places they were authorized to carry handguns, blackjacks, and other weapons, and in some jurisdictions they had authority to make arrests. The legal history suggests that drivers were given police powers for the express purpose of enforcing Jim Crow. With armed drivers and tense passengers, the interior of the bus was like a prison yard: slights could swiftly turn into insults that could morph into violence. And as African Americans became increasingly militant during the war years, the drivers became even more wary. In Birmingham in 1942, a bus driver warned Horace C. Wilkinson, a well-known national political operative from the city and a jurist, as the two observed a group of Black people hustling to board, "Right there, mister, is where our next war will break out, and it may start before this one is over!"

In the second, less formal, approach to the enforcement problem, southern authorities relied on drivers to monitor the color line not only by managing the arrest of Black riders for violating Jim Crow laws, but also by constantly reminding all riders of the degraded status of Black people. The drivers routinely harassed Black passengers, showering insults on them and rendering palpable the race hierarchy in the signage. They would pass by Black riders at stops to save room for white passengers who might be waiting farther down the route; drive off before Black passengers who had paid the fare at the front could board at the rear; arbitrarily enlarge the no-man's-middle-rows in anticipation of white riders; and shortchange Black customers or throw them off the bus on a whim.

White riders took it upon themselves to monitor the behavior of their Black fellow passengers, and Black people, too, vigilantly guarded their allocated space, such as it was, producing a dangerously intractable contest of wills. John Howard Griffin, a white journalist who in 1959 passed for a Black man and wrote about the experience, recalled that he once rose slightly from a Black seat on the bus to offer it to a middle-aged white woman, but quickly sat back down as he caught the disapproving looks of other back seat passengers, as if to say, "this space is Black by law—and ruled by Blacks." The vexing permeability and imprecision of the race line turned the bus driver into a pigmentation expert with unpredictable consequences when light-complexioned riders boarded the bus. The idiocy of the racial rules, at once unyielding and ambiguous, spawned a war dance with its own gait and signaling that had to be mastered by newcomers.

The cases that follow relate the battles fought by African American soldiers and veterans who lost their lives on US soil at the hands of bus drivers and the police officers who backed them up. In contrast to the rendition story, they offer a vastly different setting within which to consider how Black people coalesced in the first half of the twentieth century to form a Black nation grounded in resistance, how southern authoritarianism thrived in the midst of a war for democracy, and how, often working in concert, the federal government and southern officials constructed and construed Jim Crow.

9

POB Noxubee,
POD Back of the Bus

Henry Williams was born in 1918 in Macon, Mississippi, the town from which the Confederate governor Charles Clark ruled after Jackson, the state capital, was destroyed by Union forces in the Civil War. Noxubee County—Macon is the county seat—lies along the Mississippi-Alabama state line. In the language of the Choctaw, whose land it was for many centuries, Noxubee means "stinking water." One of the most famous Choctaw chiefs, Pushmataha, was born in Noxubee in the 1760s. His tribe was deported from the area—eleven million acres—after the Treaty of Dancing Rabbit Creek was executed in 1830 in the southwest corner of Noxubee. Of the twenty thousand members of the Choctaw Nation, only four thousand remained in Mississippi after the Indian Removal Act.

Noxubee is one of the poorest counties in the poorest state in the country, and African Americans—who comprise about three-quarters of the population—remain deeply mired in a prison of low education, high unemployment, higher incarceration, and hellish health conditions. In 1970 the courts ordered Noxubee's schools integrated, but that year only twenty-five of the county's four thousand Black students attended white schools. A few months after the court order, a private school, Central Academy, was launched and accepted 88 percent of the county's white students. The school system was still rigidly segregated as recently as 2013.

As with the schools, Black and white burial grounds also maintain the color line. Noxubee had offered up hundreds of men to the Confederate army. In Macon over five hundred soldiers from both sides of the conflict occupy row upon row of unidentified graves at the all-white Odd Fellows Cemetery. By 2016, by dint of purveyors of civic pride, almost 250 of these unknown soldiers were identified and their names added to a Confederate monument erected in 1901 that now stands in front of the county courthouse, on Dr. Martin Luther King Drive. Meanwhile, Private Henry Williams remains unknown in his hometown.

Williams's maternal grandfather took his surname, Lowery, from the slaveowner John M. Lowry, on whose Noxubee County plantation he worked until Emancipation. His paternal grandparents had been slaves in Pickens, Alabama, just across the state line. Williams's mother, Maggie, married her neighbor, Watt Hood Williams, and bore five children, the youngest of whom was Henry. Watt Williams was a sharecropper. When Henry was about nine years old, the boy moved to Birmingham to live with his older sister Mary, who had married a Noxubee neighbor, Grant Robinson. Henry attended high school in Birmingham, and then in 1940 enlisted in the US Army, which sent him to Brookley Field, in Mobile. According to military records, he was employed in "warehousing, storekeeping, handling, loading and related occupations."

On Saturday, August 15, 1942, Private Henry Williams went into Mobile to do some shopping. It was a busy time in a bustling city.

Mobile was also named for the people who lived on the land before Europeans arrived in 1702: the Mobile tribe. The population of the coastal city exploded during the World War II years, when soldiers were stationed at Brookley, the supply depot for the Army Air Force. Mobile expanded with sixteen thousand civilian and military employees. They were crammed in with recent arrivals from smaller hamlets who had made their way to the regional coastal towns—New Orleans, Biloxi, Mobile, Augusta—in search of jobs in the war industry. Historically, Mobile's significant wealth rested on cotton and slaves, but in the early to mid-twentieth century, the shipping and shipbuilding industries predominated. Even before World War II, shipping had rapidly expanded in this cosmopolitan city. Unlike Noxubee County, where harsh racial codes prevailed unchecked by any outside forces, Mobile had more moderate Jim Crow rules to accommodate tourists and national business interests.

The bulging wartime population destabilized the city's customary hierarchies, in no small part because the races were quite literally bumping into each other in unavoidable ways on public streets and buses, and because Black men and women were gradually moving into war industry jobs, although not at the same rate or level as whites. Chockablock with men and women drawn there by the booming economy, Mobile had neither the housing nor the transportation to keep pace with its wartime population. Boarding rooms with "hot beds"—where workers shared beds and slept in shifts—usually associated with megapolises like New York and Chicago, were common, and many workers slept under tents in city lots. Mobile became one of the most important industrial cities in the South and the second-largest city in Alabama.

With the Black population ballooning, the community's small NAACP branch, led by the energetic John LeFlore, was all but overwhelmed as it fought back against police brutality, barriers to federal employment, inferior schools, and Jim Crow public facilities. Segregated federal public housing was particularly burdensome for the growing Black population: after the war began, the National Housing Agency built fourteen thousand new units for whites but fewer than one thousand for Black people. LeFlore tried to stay on top of the racial violence that flared up repeatedly at the new shipyards. The boomtown seemed more like a tinderbox as Black people pushed back aggressively against the white stranglehold on the good, federally supported jobs.

For Black defense workers and soldiers alike, Brookley Field, where

Henry Williams was stationed, was a hostile site. It was rigidly segregated, and Black soldiers chafed against everyday depredations small
and large: their quarters were near the mosquito-infested swamps at the
rear of the base, their rooms were dark and windowless, and their mess
hall gloomy and barely habitable. They were consigned to menial work
with little chance of promotion, while their superiors were all white,
including the MPs. Brookley reflected the worst face of the Jim Crow
army. It offered no protection from Mobile's relentless racism when the
men were off base, and it reinforced their status when they returned.
White Mobile residents feared, resented, and loathed the Black soldiers.
In 1943 a white lawyer wrote to Governor Chauncey Sparks complaining about "conditions . . . [in] Army camps with negroes and white
boys from the North." He added, "Just last week my daughter was
asked . . . to go to the hospital at Brookley Field and serve refreshments
to the soldiers confined in the hospital. When she got there she found
negroes and white boys attending the entertainment without any dif-
ferentiation whatsoever, and our finest girls in Mobile were asked to
serve refreshments to the negroes."

Black soldiers were frequently seen to be defying Mobile's ordi-
nances on segregated buses. Even without the impertinent young
energy the Black soldiers must have exuded, the city buses were easily
ignitable as wartime crowding brought strained tempers and narrowed
the customary zone of separation. One Mobile rider, Walton Craft, put
it this way in a letter complaining to Governor Sparks: "I have witnessed . . . negroes crowding rear and up aisle, hanging over the white
women and girls. Frankly, it is not pleasant . . . to have some negro
hanging over you or his body touching you from time to time, the
'Negro Odor' sometimes almost more than a person can stand." Unlike
many southern cities where the law required separation, in Mobile the
mechanics of how to do this were left to the passengers themselves,
with Blacks self-seating from the back of the bus forward and whites
doing the same from the front to the back until the bus was full. Blacks
in Mobile did not have to give up their seats for whites, as was true,
famously, for Rosa Parks in Montgomery. This caused the shared but

separated space to be fluid and more unstable than the letter writer found tolerable.

For their part, Blacks were not put off so much by the crowded conditions as they were by abusive drivers and rough policing. Although travel was onerous for everyone, the Mobile police were quick to arrest African American riders. In July 1942 alone, eleven Blacks were arrested and charged with disturbing the peace, mostly in connection with busing. Mobile mayor Charles Baumhauer wrote to Thomas Vaden, a federal official in the agency responsible for wartime mobilization, about the problem in August of that year, noting that "the crowding during peak hours when the shipyards and war industries discharge many thousands of workers is the principle trouble." Baumhauer also commented on the increased friction resulting from the soldier ridership, noting that the bus company informed him of a driver who struck a soldier for refusing to move from his seat.

———————

THIS WAS THE CITY into which Henry Williams ventured to shop and do his laundry on Saturday, August 15, 1942. Small in stature at 5 feet, 2 inches, and 141 pounds, Williams had the look of a teenager. On the day in question, he raced against the clock to meet his base curfew. The driver on the bus he boarded, Grover Chandler, was a fellow Mississippian. He had left Taylorsville, also close to the Alabama border, to find work in Mobile. Chandler stopped the vehicle to chat with a coworker, which is what prompted Williams to say that he was anxious to get back to his base on time. Chandler, angered by what he perceived to be impudence on the part of the young soldier, took out his revolver and struck Williams with it several times. A scuffle ensued, and Williams, obviously worried for his safety, grabbed his belongings and attempted to escape through the back door. Some clothing spilled out of his laundry bag in his rush, and as he turned to pick it up, Chandler fired three shots, one hitting Williams in the back of the head. He died instantly right there on Chandler's bus. An

African American man was the only other passenger on board when the driver executed young Williams.

The NAACP's John LeFlore sprang into action. Instinctively, he understood the accumulated anger of Black Mobilians who had for years waged a low-level insurrection against the back of the bus and the unchecked brutality of the policemen and drivers who patrolled it. Local support was critical, and LeFlore knew well Mobile's Black community and its white elite. LeFlore, however, was perceived by some at the national level of the NAACP to be difficult to work with. NAACP youth leader Ella Baker, reporting to the national office on her visit in 1943 to the Mobile branch, wrote, "The one thing that has not changed:—John LeFlore is still the branch [leader]." The phrase "L'etat, c'est moi" might well apply to LeFlore, but few could surpass him at grassroots organizing. Black Mobilians had staged a boycott against segregated streetcars in 1902, shortly after it was legally mandated; and four decades later, in the wake of Williams's murder, LeFlore sensed that the time was ripe for another such protest. Mobile residents were, LeFlore told NAACP assistant secretary Roy Wilkins, "deeply aroused over the killing of Williams" and "appear willing to support us as never manifested before."

Initiating the "Walk to Work, Walk to Church, and Walk to Shop" campaign, the branch set August 23 as the date for the bus boycott. A list of demands—including disarming bus drivers and hiring Black drivers—was put to the management of the Mobile Light and Railroad Company. The company eventually agreed to disarm its drivers, so LeFlore and his Citizens Committee called off the boycott. Chandler was also transferred to another route, but the drivers remained all white.

LeFlore pressed for Chandler's prosecution in state court and demanded that the army investigate the slaying. Mobile police arrested Chandler on a charge of murder, but the matter was, so far as the record reveals, never presented to a grand jury. It appears there was no federal criminal investigation into Williams's killing. As for the army, Brookley Field's commanding officer Colonel Vincent B. Dixon informed LeFlore that the army could not prosecute a civilian for a killing that occurred off the base. The army neither made an effort to apprise the Williams family of the true circumstances of the case nor did it take any steps to make travel in Mobile safer for its Black soldiers.

Whatever inquiry the army may have undertaken in Williams's case apparently did not affect its judgment on the character of Grover Chandler. Fifteen months after the shooting, Chandler returned to Taylorsville, Mississippi, and enlisted in the service. Williams is buried in an unknown grave somewhere in Noxubee County. Chandler, on the other hand, lived a full life in Taylorsville until his death in 1981. An active member of the Fellowship Baptist Church and a Mason, he never had to answer for the murder of Henry Williams.

10

A Bus in Hayti

Two years later, on another hot summer Saturday, in another town, an irritated bus driver shot another soldier.

In the 1940s, Durham, North Carolina, was slightly smaller than Mobile: 60,000 in Durham to Mobile's 78,000. Both towns were near GI training grounds, and so, in Durham as in Mobile, the bus could be a lethal space. Walton H. Craft had complained to Alabama governor Chauncey Sparks about the deteriorating "condition" on Mobile buses since the war began. A year earlier, in June 1943, an official of the North Carolina Utilities Commission, Stanley Winborne, wrote to North Carolina governor J. Melville Broughton, warning, like Craft, that Durham faced "a bad situation" on the public buses. "On the local bus line between Durham and Camp Butner," he observed, "it was utterly impossible . . . to enforce the segregation laws and . . . the police of Durham stated that they could not assist." Durham, Winborne noted, was "one of the worst places we have [in eastern North Carolina] due to the large negro population   and the Northern negro soldiers at Camp Butner."

WHILE MOST OF THE NATION endured the economic collapse of the Depression years, Durham remained relatively insulated as tobacco prices soared and Americans glorified the cigarette as a sexy symbol of personal liberty. They smoked while they listened to the radio, while they drank their coffee and liquor, and while they drove their cars, all to the joy of the North Carolina tobacco barons.

Durham was host to three large tobacco factories. Black people migrating from the moribund Deep South plantations, including large numbers of women and children, found work in these factories and warehouses, and they created an "inner city" they defiantly called Hayti after the Caribbean island of revolutionary lore. Some Black aspirants to the American dream prospered. Many more, a disproportionate number of whom were women, were the cheap labor—consigned to backbreaking menial work on the factory floor—that kept the tobacco industry humming. It was they who, working in filthy, unventilated spaces, sorted, stemmed, and folded the big dusty leaves while white workers rolled the Chesterfields and Lucky Strikes. Turning to their advantage the rigid economic segregation that denied Black people access to insurance, home mortgages, loans, and educational opportunities, a Black business elite built their own insurance companies, independent schools, churches, a hospital, a library, and a college, sometimes with the support of the tobacco giants.

At its height, Hayti was home to over a hundred Black businesses. Indeed, when the North Carolina Mutual and Provident Association (the "Mutual") became the largest Black-owned insurance company in the world, the artists and intellectuals of the Harlem Renaissance declared Durham to be the economic hub of the "Negro Renaissance." In the early decades of the century, E. Franklin Frazier, W. E. B. DuBois, and others often extolled Durham to illustrate what Negro thrift, cooperation, and entrepreneurship could accomplish. In 1910, Booker T. Washington described it as "the City of Negro Enterprise," while in 1912, DuBois noted that the economic standing of Black people in Durham was "perhaps more striking than that of any similar group in the nation." These institutions helped restrict white access to Black lives, but they also reinforced the fallacy of separate but equal. While Durham's Black Wall Street induced awe, hidden from view were the cramped and unforgiving quarters where tobacco workers, 25 percent of whom were Black, made their homes. It fell to people like Charles Clinton Spaulding, president of Mutual, and other prominent members of the upper class to hold at bay the smoldering anger of these residents.

Right after Pearl Harbor, the War Department selected this thriving New South region to locate a base. Camp Butner was situated twelve miles north of Durham on forty thousand acres of lush farmland, where tobacco would otherwise have flourished. In just six months, the War Department built the camp to accommodate thirty-five thousand soldiers, of whom roughly seven thousand were Black. As Brookley was to Mobile, so Butner was to Durham. The base transformed the area, bringing energy and industry to Bull City (named after Bull Durham Smoking Tobacco). Segregated bus routes were established to transport the soldiers from Camp Butner into Durham to shop and play. Looking for home cooking and companionship, the Black soldiers would spend their days in Hayti. And, as was typically the way of southern cities, Hayti hosted—willingly or not—many businesses for nocturnal pleasure.

With its vibrant working-class and transient soldier population, Durham in the 1940s was a center of Black musical creativity. In a three- or four-block area in Hayti known as "Mexico," at a segregated little-known theatre or at the famous Biltmore Hotel, "America's finest colored hotel," a soldier could hear great jazz bands like the all-women's (and predominantly Black) International Sweethearts of Rhythm, or the renowned ensembles led by Duke Ellington, Cab Calloway, and Eubie Blake. And there was music to be heard in Durham even if your money was short. The Piedmont bluesmen performed on street corners, where Black workers, barred from the whites-only cafeterias, would eat their midshift meals outside the factories. In the 1940s, guitarist Brownie McGhee and harmonica player Sonny Terry were Durham regulars, following in the tradition of Blind Boy Fuller and Reverend Gary Davis.

In the Piedmont style, a blues guitarist runs a base line with one hand against a fast melody picked with the other hand. One must

look to the Wolof and Mandingo tribes and the banjo traditions they
brought with them to America for the roots of this music. Slaves
who were lord of the banjo would strum with a thumb at the base of
the instrument and pick out the tune higher on the neck. It was this
instrumentation, transplanted to the guitar and designed to show off
a musician's ambidexterity on the strings, that later became known
as the Piedmont style. Because it lacks the deep brooding moans and
groans of the Mississippi blues—the kind Henry Stuckey played in
Bentonia—it has a lighter feel to it. These up-tempo ragtime sounds
coming out of the Carolinas and upper Georgia were exuberant tunes
that would make a person want to "shake a leg." In the 1930s and
early '40s, itinerant musicians would play in private spaces that turned
into juke joints on the weekends. Black men and women from the
factories around town would gather to drop the weight of a week's
grueling work, the insults flung at them by the white bosses, and
their disappointing paychecks. As Glenn Hinson, a Durham native,
described it:

> The party might be at a friend's place down in Bugs Button, or
> over at Peachtree Alley, or maybe out at Camel Grove. Or per-
> haps at one of the "houses" run by Minnie the Moocher, Big
> Mattie, or any of the other local bootleggers who worked in and
> out of Durham. The room you're in is large, with a few chairs off
> against the walls and a battered upright piano in the corner. . . .
> In a small room off to one side there's a table laden with barbeque,
> fried chicken and fish, chitlins, cakes and maybe some ice cream,
> all for sale. Behind that, a woman pours bootleg from a jar into
> small glasses. There's a one-eyed man tinkling the keys on the
> piano—that would be Murphy Evans—a guitarist picking a rag
> lead, a second guitarist playing the blues lines, and a washboard
> player rubbing his board with thimbles on his fingers . . . The
> room is crammed with people dancing the "Charleston Strut" or
> the "Hollywood Skip."

Whites in Durham worried that Blacks pushed too aggressively against the race line long before the soldiers arrived to train at Camp Butner. Segregation opened a door for Black businesses, but political representation was out of reach for the town's African American community, which was disenfranchised along with the rest of Black North Carolina. Without political clout, Black advancement depended on the persuasive talent and inclination of the community's "racial uplift" men, who, invariably, because they depended on the goodwill of white bankers and tobacco tycoons for their own prosperity, were not disposed to rock the boat.

And so Durham crawled excruciatingly slowly away from its slave roots. Its bus companies refused to transport Black passengers until the state's highest court mandated it in 1930, at which point a segregated system was installed, restricting Blacks to the back of the buses and separate waiting rooms. The city did not hire its first Black police officer until 1942. In 1941, before Camp Butner was opened for business, Durham lawyer J. Elmer Long wrote to his congressman, Harold Cooley, complaining that Negroes were demanding a better entrance to the bus station and access to the restrooms in downtown stores. "If a military camp is located near this City," he warned, "it is only a question of a very short time until we are going to have race trouble." He added, "Durham is right now being troubled considerably by some negroes who live here demanding certain equal rights with the white people." Eleven days before the Democratic Party was due to meet in 1944 in Chicago to nominate President Roosevelt for an unprecedented fourth term, that race trouble came.

BORN IN 1909 in Blackstone, Virginia, Booker Spicely was the son of Lazarus Spicely and Alberta L. Wynn Spicely. His mother raised the couple's eight children, and his father was a blacksmith. The Spicelys and the Wynns go back to the early 1800s in neighboring Dinwiddie

County; some were free and some not. Lazarus and Alberta settled in Blackstone (so named to honor the English legal scholar), where they lived on Center Street and worshipped at the Shiloh Baptist Church-Dinwiddie, established immediately after the Civil War. In the late 1920s some of Spicely's sisters and brothers moved to Philadelphia, Pennsylvania. His eldest brother, Robert, established himself as a prominent chef in the city while his younger sister, Ruth, worked as a licensed practical nurse. Active in social and business circles—Robert was a member of the Omega Psi Phi fraternity and Ruth was an officiant in the Order of the Eastern Star—the family belonged to Philadelphia's Black elite. Eventually Booker joined his siblings there. He worked as a chauffeur for a white Philadelphia family until December 1942 when, at age thirty-four, he enlisted in the army. In 1943, Spicely was sent to Camp Butner.

On Saturday, July 8, 1944, Spicely, dressed in uniform, had visited some friends in Hayti, and in the early evening he boarded a return-trip Durham-Butner bus. He sat in a rear row next to a woman with a child. About twenty minutes later, as the bus made its way through the white neighborhood of Five Points, the driver picked up a group of white soldiers—including Private Robert C. Martin—who also appeared to be heading back to the base. Herman Lee Council, the thirty-six-year-old bus driver, ordered Spicely and the woman to move farther back to make room for Martin and the other white soldiers. The young woman quickly complied, but Spicely protested, saying, according to Martin, "I thought I was fighting this war for democracy. I'm from Pennsylvania. I'm not used to seeing things like this."

Council told Spicely he would have to leave the bus if he could not "keep cool." Reluctantly, the soldier moved to the last row. The bus had traveled for a few more minutes when Spicely and the woman stood up to exit at the upcoming stop. As he got off the bus, Spicely said something like, "Hey, driver, when you get into uniform we will argue about this," infuriating Council. A few more heated words were exchanged between them, and then, as Spicely stepped onto the street, Council grabbed his pistol and also disembarked. He fired two shots, striking Spicely in the heart and stomach.

Council, who was a good deal shorter and smaller than Spicely, climbed back in the driver's seat and drove away, leaving the soldier bleeding in the gutter. Police officers from Durham and Camp Butner took Spicely, still alive, to nearby Watts Hospital, where he was refused admittance because of his race. The Watts medics, presumably on the instructions of the law enforcement officers, first drew blood to perform an alcohol test. Only afterward did they send Spicely to Duke Hospital, which had "Negro" beds. At this second hospital, Spicely took his last breath, amid strangers. The alcohol test was negative.

Four days after Spicely's death, an army intelligence officer from Camp Butner filed a report based on interviews he had conducted with five passengers on the bus. The report unequivocally established that Council shot the unarmed soldier without provocation and, leaving him bleeding to death in the street, went on to finish his route. Private Martin, the white soldier, told the investigator that he was so distressed that he got off the bus at the next stop, presumably to go to Spicely's aid. The woman who disembarked with Spicely, stunned, grabbed her baby and ran away as fast as she could. In this brief period, the army official also interviewed a few local authorities, but he did not obtain any written reports from them. It was a shoddy investigation, designed, apparently, more to conceal than to reveal.

The army's actions following this preliminary investigation hint at the true concerns of the War Department: it initiated a wide-scale intelligence operation to manage African American reaction to Spicely's murder. Colonel Willis M. Everett Jr., the director of the army's Security and Intelligence Division in the Fourth Service Command in Atlanta, took a personal interest in the investigation. Indeed, three days after the shooting, Everett chastised the intelligence officers at Camp Butner for failing to inform him immediately of the killing. Prior to his service, Everett had been a successful attorney in Atlanta; he would later become well known for defending German soldiers charged with war crimes at proceedings in Dachau. In 1944 he was in charge of the army's surveillance operations in the southeastern United States, whose mission, in part, was to monitor and contain any pro-Axis activities or protest among communists or African Americans.

Everett's office sent a Black undercover investigator from Savannah to Durham to snoop around, seeking to determine, as the investigator put it, "whether or not negroes were being influence or encourage by agitators to misconduct themselves." The investigator dutifully visited "the establishments that Negroes frequent," posing as a civilian seeking a job in the war industry. His report about activities in Hayti led the army to conclude that "Durham Negro residents are not actively interested in the occurrence," that is, the killing of Spicely. The army, not content to investigate the response of Durham's "Negroes," also snuck around to gauge the pulse of Black communities in Philadelphia and in Blackstone (where Spicely was buried), and in his segregated unit at Camp Butner.

Everett's office notified the commanding officer at Camp Pickett, in Virginia, of potential protests in his area. Another undercover investigator, having visited with Mary Collier and Jayfus Ward, two leaders of the local NAACP in Blackstone, reported back to Camp Butner and Camp Pickett that no protest action was planned. Ward did tell the investigator that Spicely's brother, Robert, had urged the funeral congregants at Shiloh Baptist Church to "join the NAACP and help stop this sort of thing."* The investigator also paid a visit to the Blackstone chief of police to obtain Spicely's criminal history. The army's files on

---

* There is no evidence that Robert Spicely was politically active before his brother's death, although he was well known in the Philadelphia business community. That changed when Booker was killed. In December 1944 Robert, then working at Tuskegee Institute, along with Louis E. Burnham and six others, represented Alabama at one of the founding conferences of the Southern Regional Council at Atlanta University.

the incident contain no information about the reputation or history of the death-dealing bus driver, Herman Council, but do note the opinion of the Blackstone police chief that Booker Spicely had a "reputation as a trouble maker" as well as a misdemeanor record.

In Philadelphia, the army relied on yet a third undercover investigator to monitor the activities of Ruth Ida Spicely, the sister with whom Booker had lived. Ruth had sought to engage the NAACP and other organizations in Philadelphia in her brother's defense. The army's investigator related in great detail Ruth's appeal to the executive secretary of the local NAACP branch. He sent on to Atlanta articles from the Black press about the case, adding to the mound of clippings, mostly from the African American papers, that already filled the Intelligence Department's file on Spicely. Ironically, several of the stories in the Black press reported that the army was "investigating" the killing, as if to suggest that findings would be forthcoming, perhaps condemning the slaying; little did the newspapers' readers know that Spicely's supporters and loved ones—not his killer—were the targets of that investigation.

Finally, the army interrogated "trusted informants from the colored organizations" at Camp Butner to monitor any plans for an uprising. The FBI followed up on a report that Black people had stored munitions on the outskirts of Durham, but an army inventory revealed that everything was in order. Army intelligence officers agreed to search through Black soldiers' mail to track what they were receiving from home about the killing and to monitor for protests. Spicely had been a driver assigned to a segregated truck company at Camp Butner. Popular, he enjoyed a good reputation on the base and, according to the army's first undercover investigator, was "considered a high type negro in his outfit." There was no one in Spicely's unit who was under suspicion for being "a trouble maker" or "agitator," the investigator wrote. Those Black soldiers who had lost their friend reported, ever hopeful, ever loyal, that they expected the North Carolina courts to mete out justice fairly.

This far-reaching intelligence operation reflected White House apprehensions that racial protests, particularly in cities hosting military bases, would erupt in the summer of 1944 as they had in Detroit, Harlem, and Beaumont, Texas, in 1943. Indeed, the army's security units were, for good reason, worried about what impact Spicely's killing would have on African American soldiers and civilians. Events shortly before the slaying showed that across the South, seething Black soldiers were not too timid to fight against what they perceived to be the "enemy at home." On February 8, 1944, over three hundred Black soldiers from Camp Sutton, near Monroe, North Carolina, clashed with military police and civilian authorities. And in April, a white civilian employee at Camp Sutton threw a thirteen-year-old Black youth from a bridge into a creek, evoking wide-scale protests.

Federal surveillance reports about Black protests and predictions about likely hot spots were generated on an almost daily basis at the direction of the FBI's J. Edgar Hoover, and the naval and army intelligence services contributed to these files. In April 1944, Walter W. Breen, the director of intelligence of the Army Service Forces, informed his superiors that "there are indications that widespread disturbance is likely to develop, within the next three or four months, in several areas." He was in turn advised to undertake "an appropriate program of measures to prevent the occurrence of overt racial disturbances." The War Department, perhaps coincidentally, had, on the day of Spicely's murder, issued an order to desegregate buses, trucks, and other vehicles operated by the government or government contractors. It also prohibited restricting Blacks to designated sections of public vehicles "either on or off a post, camp, or station, regardless of local custom."

While the War Department was investigating Spicely's past and his family members, Thurgood Marshall, in the NAACP's national office, was weighing whether to participate in the criminal trial of the bus driver. Charged with manslaughter, Council was due to be tried by a jury, and North Carolina law allowed private attorneys to associate with the public prosecutor during a trial. Asked by the Spicely family to appear in the case, Marshall sent NAACP attorney Edward Dudley to Durham in his stead. However, Spaulding, the president of Mutual and an unelected Black spokesman, persuaded Robert Spicely that the family should reject lawyers from the national NAACP—"outside counsel," he called them—in favor of "a high type white attorney in Durham" and a local African American lawyer. Spaulding argued, "We who live in the south can appreciate the all-white courts including the jurors and it is going to take evidence more than anything else to win the case. . . . A local white attorney could assist in securing evidence . . . to better advantage." Marshall eventually backed off, but not without a fight. Having dealt with Spaulding and Durham's Black elite in a desegregation case a decade earlier, Marshall was familiar with their opinion that they could best mediate between the Black community and white Durham. With the clarity and bluntness for which he was by then legendary, Marshall observed:

> whole trouble around the Spicely case is the same trouble we have around all cases in North Carolina . . . certain Negro groups in North Carolina . . . believe that the only way to handle the problem is to handle it "without outside influence." One thing is certain and that is that the NAACP will not itself be intimidated by anyone, whether he be white or Negro. One of these days, North Carolina will realize that none of us can handle our problems alone.*

In September 1944, Herman Council was tried for manslaughter. The bus driver claimed that Spicely had his hand in his pocket when he got off the bus, putting the driver in fear for his life. After two days of testimony and thirty minutes of deliberation, the jury rendered a "not guilty" verdict to a shocked (and segregated) courtroom.

The War Department rushed to get ahead of the inevitable calls for action from the Black press and the national NAACP. Camp Butner

---

* Marshall was referring to a clash between the NAACP and Spaulding on the role of the national lawyers in *Hocutt v. Wilson*, N.C. Super. Ct. (1933) (unreported), a suit to desegregate the pharmacy school at the University of North Carolina.

The cartoon above is the work of Gow M. Bush, North Carolina artist, whe here depicts the slaying of Pvt. Booker T. Spiceley, Camp Butner soldier, by Herman L. Council, white, Durham, N.C., bus driver, who was found not guilty last week by an all-white jury which deliberated only 28 minutes. Many white citizens shared in the general disgust attending the verdict. Sign at right says: ATTENTION NEGROES! 1. SEAT FROM REAR OF BUS. (STATE LAW) 2. DON'T TALK BACK TO BUS DRIVER. (HE IS WHITE). 3. NO MUTTERING OR "MOUTHING." YOU ARE NOTHING 4. DO NOT APOLOGIZE. ITS AN INVITATION TO BE MURDERED.

Private Booker T. Spicely was shot to death in 1944 in Durham, North Carolina, by a bus driver for protesting segregated seating. The *Carolina Times* covered the case and published this image.

and the quartermaster in Philadelphia renewed contact with Everett's office in Atlanta and its counterpart in Blackstone, Virginia. The North Carolina investigator assured Everett there was "no trouble or racial disturbance as a result of the verdict" in Durham or at Butner. Everett's office nevertheless took steps to ensure the Durham and North Carolina police were prepared to respond to any unrest.

THOUGH NEITHER the army's nor the FBI's probes found any evidence of Negro "belligerence" at Camp Butner, or in Philadelphia, or Virginia, some linked a strange happenstance to Spicely's slaying. At about 9 o'clock on July 8, just two hours after Spicely was shot, fires ripped through Durham's downtown warehouse district, and in less than three hours three warehouses—property valued at $250,000— were destroyed. Considered one of the worse conflagrations in the city's history, the fire was said to have started in the basement of one of the Big Four warehouses. The *Daily Charlotte Observer* reported that "other establishments burned to earth included the Central leaf redrying plant and the Dillard livery stables, where twelve cows and four horses burned to death." No one was ever arrested for arson in connection with the blazes. However, the coincidence of the conflagration and the casualty was not lost on the residents of Hayti.

Robert Spicely and his younger sister Ruth waged a long and ultimately fruitless battle to make sense of their brother's murder. Ruth had raised money among her coworkers in Philadelphia for his defense, and had persuaded the Philadelphia NAACP to launch a campaign. Robert, who had attended college, represented the family's interests. He corresponded with the well-known civil rights advocates of the day, including Charles Hamilton Houston, Thurgood Marshall, and William Henry Hastie. In one such letter to Houston, he revealed deep pain and pessimism, but also hope that the NAACP could secure a modicum of justice. "I cannot bring my brother back," he wrote. "The best that can be done now is (1) serve notice on bus drivers that they cannot murder Negro soldiers with impunity, (2) focus the eyes of the country . . . on this problem of Negro soldier treatment, (3) give the Negro courage and belief in a force that he can depend upon to fight for him." In a letter to Marshall, Robert wrote, "Nothing I or anyone else can do can erase from my memory the sight of my aged mother groping her way to me and falling upon my shoulder dry-eyed . . . as she mumbled, 'My child. My child.'" He confessed that he was confused about whether to bring in Marshall in light of Spaulding's objections. "The whole situation would be far less confusing if one had a brother murdered every day, or had to deal with the courts as intimately . . . as he dealt with the grocer or barber. My course of action would be much easier if . . . there were not so many conflicting interests, urges, emo-

In 1944, Private Booker T. Spicely, stationed at Camp Butner near Durham, was killed by a bus driver after he commented that he deserved the same treatment as the white soldiers on the bus.

tions, responsibilities and desires." And he wondered whether following Spaulding's recommendation to retain a local white lawyer was the right thing to do: "That much power is dangerous in the hands of any group so small and so far divorced from the problems of the masses and yet able to speak for them as the 'good Negroes of Durham.' . . . This holds whether the persons are Dr. Shepard and Mr. Spaulding or anyone else."

Five years after a jury freed Council, in 1949, Robert Spicely asked the NAACP to reopen his brother's case. Constance Baker Motley, who would later become a federal judge in New York City, reminded the distraught man that the NAACP's efforts to participate in the criminal trial had been rebuffed by the local lawyers. There was, she implied, nothing further to be done.

Robert Spicely and his sister Ruth Ida each passed away in 1983. They never achieved for their brother the recognition he deserved.

11

"Us Colored . . . Sat Where We Wanted To"

Black soldiers not only clashed with the color board when those from the North trained at southern camps. As a signifier of racial caste, the bus retained its potency long after Black military men and women came back to their southern hometowns. Expecting that their service would erode Jim Crow and open up opportunities that had previously been foreclosed, Black veterans returned with high hopes for a different racial order. Voting rights, equal employment, and equal access to the GI Bill were top items on their political agenda, but as well they continued to protest Jim Crow transportation and police brutality. Disheartened when their civic efforts were met with Dixie hegemony, some abandoned the South, while those who stayed intensified their activities, paving the way for the later civil rights movement.

Differing understandings of what the war was all about led to violence against veterans as it had against Black soldiers. Whites sought to shove the veterans back in their place; the ex-soldiers thought they had fought for something different. "A lot of guys . . . didn't expect to find the same situation that we left," Tuskegee veteran Otis Pinkard declared. Not only had the "situation" not changed much, but veterans became a target of white racial militancy. An official of the Southern Regional Council, writing about white residents of Fort Valley,

Georgia, observed that they would likely " 'pick on' the returning veteran to try and steer him 'back into his place.' "

TIMOTHY HOOD'S PARENTS, Israel and Daisy Hood, the children of
slaves, were born in Alabama fifteen years after Appomattox. Israel's
paternal grandparents were enslaved in the Carolinas and then sold
south. His father was born into slavery, and his mother, two years
after the end of the Civil War. One of ten children, Israel grew up
in Sumter County, Alabama, on the edge of the Tombigbee River,
which, translated from Choctaw, means "box-maker." Some have said
the name is in honor of a Choctaw coffin maker who lived on the
river's banks.

During World War I, the steel mills in Birmingham and the neighboring towns of Bessemer, Brighton, and Fairfield put out the call for
eager and adventurous Black men looking to escape the farms that held
them in an endless cycle of debt and degradation. Israel Hood, one such
man, moved with his wife and his older brother, David, to Bessemer.
Israel and Daisy had three children, of whom Timothy was the first.
Israel worked at the sheet metal plant, Bessemer Rolling Mill, first as a
shearer and then as a tonnage man. It was dangerous work, but on his
father's farm in Sumter County, he had had to wait a full year for his
pay, while the steel mills paid him every week, and in cash. David also
got a job in a steel mill when he first arrived in Bessemer. Eventually,
with his wife, Perl, David owned and operated a grocery and other
local businesses. Living a few doors apart from each other, the two
couples raised their families together.

In the 1910s, when the Hood families arrived, Bessemer was a
boomtown: the fourth-largest city in the state. Established in 1887 just
thirteen miles southwest of Birmingham on the edge of Red Mountain, Bessemer was founded by Henry Fairchild DeBardeleben, a steel
tycoon whose company in the 1880s owned one hundred fifty thousand acres of land laden with coal, iron ore, and limestone worth about

$13 million. This included the four thousand acres that would become Bessemer. DeBardeleben's father's wealth came from slavery; he had owned a large cotton plantation in Autauga County. The land on which the son chose to construct a new industrial city was once owned by the Creek Nation, but in 1814 General Andrew Jackson forced these indigenous communities to cede their territory to the United States. DeBardeleben and his investors named the new town Bessemer in honor of the British inventor Sir Henry Bessemer, whose formula for manufacturing steel from pig iron on a mass scale revolutionized the industry. The town was founded with high hopes for its success as a major industrial site—one that could compete with Birmingham. As one booster put it in 1888:

> It is a new city; a growing and developing city. One with such resources awaiting utilization, such facilities for manufacture and conversion, such immense territory for market; such superb system of transportation and distribution, such a salubrious and attractive climate, and with such a grand and beautiful country in and surrounding it. . . . The field is not crowded. It is but sparsely occupied, and labor and opportunity are abundant, and years to come will not find the channels of industry overflowing nor the demand for its products diminished.

The city expanded quickly with the demand for workers who could extract whatever wealth was buried in Red Mountain and turn it into profit for DeBardeleben and his successors. The mines and mills employed more than half of the workforce, with jobs inflexibly segregated by race. Union organizers understood that because Black and white miners were dependent on each other for safety, racial tensions were somewhat abated, and in the 1930s Bessemer was the site of major organizing campaigns. In 1934, a significant strike lasting over a month pulled a combined eight thousand Black and white men off the jobs at the Tennessee Coal, Iron and Railroad Company, a US Steel subsidiary, and the Sloss-Sheffield, Woodward, and Republic companies. When it was over, two strikebreakers were dead and many more men wounded.

In Bessemer, the Black neighborhoods were cordoned off, their streets unpaved and their shotgun houses firetraps. Housing segregation was mandated by law. As late as 1954, the zoning code provided: "It shall be unlawful for any person, other than persons of the white race, to reside within the areas described."

Timothy Hood was born in Bessemer in 1922. By 1940, his parents owned a brick multibedroom home not far from the mill. They had had little formal schooling, but taught themselves to read and write, and they wanted their son to go to college. Timothy was headed in that direction when the United States entered World War II. At the end of the school year in 1942, along with his best friend, Lorenzo Wyatt, Hood registered for the draft, and a few months later, he was called to serve as a private in the Marine Corps. He served in a heavy antiaircraft group until the end of the war, when, after being honorably discharged, he returned to the family home in Bessemer. Photographs on the walls of the Hood home reveal their profound pride in Timothy. In one picture he stands at attention in uniform, a hint of a smile on his lips and confidence in his brown eyes. A supremely good-looking man, he stood 6 feet, 3 inches and weighed 175 pounds; much of it, said those who knew him, was muscle.

The Bessemer that Hood left was not much different from the one to which he returned in 1946. Life, especially Black life, was still worth little. The violence that had given rise to the battles between labor and the mining bosses seemed stuck in the city's bones. In fact, according to some accounts, the violence swelled in the early years after the war, because competition for jobs increased. For the police and city officials, it was still sport to make Black men bow and kowtow. In 1944, Bessemer's police and firemen organized a "watermelon run" for the entertainment of whites in the town. Forcing prisoners to race while being prodded with water from firehoses, whites lined the streets, cheering and goading the Black men on. To the victor went a watermelon and reduced prison time.

Timothy Hood returned from service in World War II to Bessemer, Alabama, where, in 1946, he was killed on a segregated bus.

In 1946, Bessemer's police chief was the brutal Lawton "Studs" Grimes. The chief once appeared in a local paper's photo of a KKK rally, his police uniform peeking out from beneath his white robe. Nor was Grimes the only Klansman doubling as a Bessemer police officer: an FBI agent noted during the civil rights era that the town's police department was full of "former or present Klan members." Indeed, the Bessemer Klan was so much a fabric of the community that in 1959, the local klavern posted a "Welcome to Bessemer" sign at the town's city limits, right next to the Kiwanis Club sign. Often partnering with the Klan were union-busting gangs hired by the region's industrial tycoons. Beatings, bombings, and other forms of intimidation were commonplace in Bessemer.

One Friday night in February 1946, Hood took off for Birmingham, perhaps for fun. As with busing in Mobile, seating in Birmingham was a fluctuating arrangement left in the hands of the driver and the riders. Blacks filled from the back and whites from the front until they met at the color board, placed at the discretion of the conductor, who would move the sign as the size of the two racial groups ebbed and flowed along the route. Passengers could stand in the aisles if the conductor allowed it, but only near the seated riders of their own race. That Friday night, Hood caught a crowded bus on the South Bessemer line

A "color board" separated the races on the buses in Birmingham, Alabama, and other cities in the Jim Crow South. On some buses, the driver could move the color board, expanding and contracting racialized space as necessary.

traveling north to Birmingham, and he chose a seat right behind the color board.

A few stops after Hood boarded in Bessemer, the rear of the bus quickly filled to standing room only. Eyeing an open seat in front of the board, Hood asked a fellow Black passenger to move the sign forward to free up the seat for a Black passenger. When the man declined to touch the board, Hood moved it himself and, having seen something of the world, casually reported to all in earshot that "where I just came from, us colored had all the seat room we wanted. We sat anywhere we wanted to." The bus driver, William Ryan Weeks, must have overheard. He stopped his crowded vehicle, which had traveled just three blocks from Hood's stop, walked back to the "colored" section, and ordered Hood to put the board back. Hood shot back defiantly, "Do it yourself." Tossing him seven cents—the fare he'd paid—Weeks barked at Hood to get off the bus. The young veteran complied—walking toward the front of the bus to disembark, through the white section, testing the driver even further. "Boy, why don't you go out the rear door as you're supposed to," Weeks hollered.

What happened next is contested. There were about fifty-five passengers on the bus, many of them young people out for a good time. All but two or three riders scattered after gunshots rang out. Those few who remained told investigators that Hood and Weeks first scuffled in the street near the front door of the bus. Hood gave as good as he got, but Weeks beat Hood with a steel switch handle and fired five bullets at the unarmed veteran, hitting him three times in the side. Hood stumbled away from the bus and took refuge in a private home a few doors down the street.

Greenberry Fant, the chief of police in the neighboring town of Brighton, happened to live in the area. Aroused by the commotion, he got out of bed and hunted Hood down. Bessemer police officers arrived at the scene and tossed Hood into the back of their car. Fant leaned in and confronted the moribund veteran about the fight with the bus driver, asking him if he had struck the white man. Hood, blood streaming from his torso and hands cuffed behind his back, either could not or would not answer. "If you won't talk," Fant told Hood, "you won't talk now, you s-o-b." As Hood writhed on the floor of the police car, Fant shot him in the back of the head, killing him instantly. Fant then turned in the direction of the stunned crowd, brandished his gun, and shouted, "All of you damn niggers, leave here."

Someone alerted Hood's family, several blocks away, and Israel Hood came running. The father would later tell federal investigators that the soldier of whom he was so proud, his eldest child and only son, was handcuffed and dead when he saw him crumpled up in the back of the police car. The threats to the Black crowd, the shot, the prone body: it all reprised the choreography of a lynching. Space, citizenship, and manhood were what the veteran had claimed on the bus, only to be lynched in the public square of the police car. Trying to figure out what his son had done to get himself killed, all Israel Hood could come up with was that the war had made him a changed man. "I don't know what has come over these boys that had been fighting and come back home," he told a Bessemer army investigator.

On March 22, the African American community gathered at Bessemer's New Zion Baptist Church, twelve hundred strong, to mourn Timothy and demand that the Department of Justice prosecute his killer. They heard from the victim's close friend and classmate, Lorenzo Wyatt, also a veteran, and from leaders of the Southern Conference for Human Welfare and the NAACP. The Alabama Veterans Association, launched earlier that month by Wyatt and others, in part in response to Hood's killing, demanded a response from federal authorities.

At the direction of US Assistant Attorney General Theron L. Caudle, J. Edgar Hoover initiated an investigation. A coroner's jury ruled the case a justifiable homicide, ending the matter so far as local authorities were concerned. The DOJ also closed its files without prosecuting Fant or Weeks. Caudle informed Birmingham attorney Clifford Reeves, the Hood family's lawyer, of the department's finding that no federal law had been violated by either of those men. "It's an ugly affair," Caudle opined, but one for Alabama, not the federal government.

———————

TIMOTHY HOOD WAS NOT the only family member to enlist in World War II. His first cousin, David Hood Jr., with whom he had grown up in Bessemer, also served. After Hood Jr. got back from the war, he graduated from college, earned a law degree from Howard University, and returned to Bessemer. For decades he was the town's only Black lawyer. His long career as a civil rights attorney included lawsuits protesting segregation in the Jefferson County school systems and public services. In 1957 he took up the case of Caliph Washington, a seventeen-year-old Black Bessemer youth who was tried, sentenced to death, and locked up for thirteen years for allegedly killing a white police officer, a crime he did not commit. Hood Jr. litigated valiantly on Washington's behalf for six years. During that time, two unexploded sticks of dynamite were planted in the back of the attorney's house and on multiple occasions his home was broken into and his family terrorized. He nevertheless pursued such advocacy over a long career, ultimately becoming a staunch supporter of President Jimmy Carter and a well-regarded civic leader across the South.

Henry Gaskin, Timothy Hood's nephew, wrote to the mayor of Bessemer in 2017: "Our entire family is from the Bessemer area and have deeply seated roots in the area." Gaskin believed it was time to abandon the lie that his uncle precipitated his own death at the hands of Weeks and Fant. Gaskin's mother, he told the mayor, always spoke of her brother as if he were still present. "His life was stolen by a culture that embraces the idea that certain races should remain second class citizens," he wrote, urging city officials to introduce Hood's story in the school curriculum and to name the street where the family lived in honor of his uncle.

At the time of Henry Gaskin's death in 2018, there had been no response from Bessemer.

12

Double V on the Bus

Booker Spicely and Henry Williams, along with many others, lost their lives on the front lines of what became known as the Double V campaign: the well-known "V" for victory sign used by the Allies to defeat tyranny in Europe matched with a second "V" to represent victory for African Americans fighting oppression in the United States. As the Black press—especially the *Pittsburgh Courier* and the *Chicago Defender*—and civil rights groups insisted, victory abroad would have no meaning unless coupled with equal justice at home. An editorial in the NAACP's journal, *The Crisis*, noted, immediately following Pearl Harbor, that "now is the time not to be silent about the breaches of democracy here in our own land." The *Cleveland Call and Post* editorialized that "democracy will never survive the present crisis as a frozen or half-caste concept . . . the struggle to preserve it must on all fronts be linked with the struggle to extend it. The victory must be complete if it is to be at all. We must overthrow Hitlerism within as well as Hitlerism without." The principal target of the campaign, which gained a footing in the large urban cities in the North and Midwest, was the Jim Crow South.

Dixiecrats in Washington, DC, had lobbied successfully to garner new military installations and war-related industries even as the region sought to preserve the privileges whites enjoyed. With more than 1.1 million Black people from across the country entering the service during the war—of whom about 80 percent were trained in the

The Double V symbolized the two-pronged approach of African Americans during World War II: fighting for victory over tyranny abroad and for freedom for African Americans at home.

South, for almost three-quarters of the military's training camps for Black troops were located there—and another million newly employed in the booming war-driven economy, white southerners were confronted with ever bolder equality claims, from the Black neighbors they thought they knew and from the new arrivals importing ideas from elsewhere.

Between 1941 and 1946 at least twenty-eight active-duty soldiers lost their lives in the US for refusing to submit silently to the humiliations of Jim Crow. Hundreds more suffered nonfatal gunshot wounds, imprisonment in civilian jails, chain-gang sentences, and military sanctions. The legal response to these crimes from the army was tepid at best, and state and local civil authorities were outright hostile.

The staggering changes in southern cities during World War II tested rules that had been in place for fifty years. The police in the newly distended metropolises responded aggressively to any perceived resistance to the status quo. Local authorities took their role as guardians of southern racial norms more seriously as strangers filled formerly gracious and unhurried city centers. Federal regulators took note but did little to defuse the tinderbox. In Pascagoula, Mississippi, a federal investigator reported that "extreme overcrowding of buses and other transportation facilities has resulted in some minor racial conflicts," and a federal reporter in Mobile, Alabama, made note of an alarming increase of violence against Black passengers.

White officials fretted that "their Negroes" were becoming unrecognizable, in demeanor as much as in attire. Southerners were accustomed to seeing only whites in uniforms of authority. Certainly, Black men wore the renowned Pullman Porter hats and coats and women wore maids' uniforms, but there were no Black police officers, firemen, or judges. The soldiers' uniforms turned Black men into wielders of power and authority that had heretofore been exclusively in white hands, leaving everyone to recalibrate racial roles. In 1943, Bruce Cameron, the mayor of Wilmington, North Carolina, a small coastal town that swelled by thousands during the war, complained to Governor J. Melville Broughton that the city had been experiencing "tremendous difficulty with the Jim Crow [bus] law" and implored him to "tell [editorial writers reporting on police abuse] that as long as you are Governor the colored people will have to behave themselves." The drivers resented the soldiers who refused to defer to them, and the military uniforms signaled a status more elevated than their own. It was this incendiary mix that cost Spicely and Williams their lives.

AFTER THE WAR, one soldier recalled his time in the social minefields of the South:

> To be a black soldier in the South . . . was one of the worst things
> that could happen to you. If you go to town, you would have to
> get off the sidewalk if a white person came by. If you went into the
> wrong neighborhood wearing your uniform, you got beat up. If
> you stumbled over a brick, you were drunk and you got beat up.
> If off-post you were hungry and couldn't find a black restaurant
> or a black home you . . . would starve. And you were a soldier . . .
> out there wearing the uniform of your country, and you're getting
> treated like a dog! That happened all over the South.

Just as local riders did, Black soldiers had to make split-second decisions whether to protest or live with Jim Crow, to defy or defer. In Hattiesburg, Mississippi, in April 1944, a soldier on a bus headed to town from Camp Shelby complained about having to sit in the rear of the crowded vehicle. The driver, who said the soldier swore at him, waited until all his passengers disembarked in Hattiesburg, and then he searched the streets until he found the soldier, whereupon he whipped him. In Chattanooga, Tennessee, in August, a Black soldier who refused to give up his seat next to a white soldier was convicted of a Jim Crow violation and fined. He had told the driver (and the other passengers) that he "fought by the side of the white man and intended to sit by the side of the white man also." Also in Chattanooga, in September, the soldier James Heard was fined seventy-five dollars and given a ninety-day term in the workhouse because he sat next to a white man, became "abusive" when asked to move, and loudly proclaimed that he wished he could "get all the white people on a rock pile and mow them down with a Tommy gun." In Augusta, Georgia, in October, several Black soldiers had come to the defense of one of their own. When a Black soldier was told to sit separately from the white soldier with whom he boarded the bus, they threatened the driver, who pulled his revolver on them.

Army Lieutenant Jackie Robinson, the future Dodgers slugger, was court-martialed because in July 1944 he defied a driver's order to move to the rear of an army bus in Fort Hood, Texas. Robinson, after boarding the bus, sat next to the woman with whom he was traveling, whose skin color led the bus driver to believe she was white. "Hey you," shouted the driver, "sitting beside that woman. Get to the back of the bus." When Robinson ignored him, the driver hurtled down the aisle, stood in front of the lieutenant, and directed him, but not the woman, to "get to the back of the bus where the colored people belong." Robinson stood his ground, reminding the driver that the army had recently ordered the elimination of segregation on its buses. Robinson was taken into custody by military police and tried for insubordination and a host of other charges. He ultimately prevailed, but the incident left him so embittered that after his acquittal he terminated his military career.

White soldiers were often drawn into these conflicts, sometimes because they were traveling with Black friends, but sometimes only to do the right thing. One case involving a white soldier resulted in disciplinary measures against the driver. A Black soldier stationed at Fort Benning, in Georgia, was beaten by a driver only three days after he returned from the North African theatre of operations. He had boarded a bus in Columbus and sat next to a white soldier. He hesitated when told to move to the back, whereupon the driver yanked him out of his seat, struck him on his head, and, after other soldiers stepped forward, pulled out a pistol. A white lieutenant intervened to protect the soldier. It was no doubt the lieutenant's complaint that led the bus company to discipline the driver.

On many occasions, Black soldiers banded together to defy Jim Crow. In Augusta, Georgia, in July 1944, a group of about ten soldiers went to buy tickets at the white bus station at Camp Gordon. They were told they could board but had to sit in the rear. The bus company concluded that the soldiers knew there was a "colored bus station" where they were supposed to purchase their tickets and board, but they were "making a test case of some sort."

In October, Sergeant Aubrey E. Robinson, who would later become a federal judge, was arrested while traveling from Camp Gordon to Aiken, South Carolina, after he protected a Black woman from a beating by the driver. Robinson, a New Jersey native, boarded the bus with several other soldiers, Black and white. A Black woman boarded and asked the driver to relocate a white passenger who was sleeping in the rear so that she could sit there. The driver refused to do so, returned her fare, and ordered her off the bus. Before she climbed off the bus, however, the driver struck her on the head, causing her to tumble down the steps. All the soldiers, white and Black, told the driver to stop beating the woman, but only the Blacks were arrested. Fines of twenty-five dollars were imposed on each arrested man. In lieu of paying the fine, some of the Black men were relieved of their uniforms, placed in striped convict suits, and put on a chain gang for three days. Recalling the incident years later, the future federal judge remarked, "It shook to the very core my faith in [the] nation . . . I had to call upon every ounce of training and premilitary experience to keep from becoming bitter."

13

The Departments:
War and Justice

While military men were losing their lives in the fifty-year battle to end raced transportation in the American South, neither the War Department nor the Department of Justice properly discharged their duty to safeguard their lives or to vindicate their deaths. At the end of the day, pitted against state, local, and military police, Black soldiers agitating for their rights would find no shield in the federal government. The failure of federal law was certainly a factor here; more favorable civil rights law could have served as a counterweight to the entrenched hostility of state and local law enforcement. Equally significant, however, were institutional obstacles, poor coordination, and lack of political will.

A FEW DAYS AFTER Pearl Harbor, as troops were gathering to travel south, US Attorney General Francis Biddle responded to an inquiry from Secretary of State Henry Stimson about the impact on the armed forces of state and local laws requiring segregated transportation. Biddle informed Stimson that federal law did not require interstate or local companies to desegregate their trains and buses. Relying on the Supreme Court's decision in the 1910 case of *Chiles v. Chesapeake &*

Ohio Railway, which held that the Constitution did not bar segregation in interstate transportation if the regulations were "reasonable,"
he advised Stimson that segregation was permitted on interstate lines,
but cautioned the secretary that accommodations had to be equal. The
Supreme Court might at some future date declare Jim Crow transportation to be unconstitutional, Biddle speculated, but until then the
army was bound to comply with local segregation laws and the policies
of the interstate carriers. This legal advice from the country's top lawyer to its top military official governed War Department practice for
most of the war. (Apparently coincidental to Booker Spicely's slaying
in 1944, the department did direct the desegregation of buses, trucks,
and other transportation owned and operated by the federal government and its contractors.) Biddle evidently believed the rule of *Plessy v.
Ferguson* prevented the War Department from insisting on desegregated
state and local transportation for its troops. It was not until 1946, when
the Supreme Court decided in *Morgan v. Virginia* that segregated transportation interfered with the constitutional right to travel across state
lines, that interstate travel was nominally desegregated.

These concessions to the segregationist rules and norms of local
communities undercut the ability of the War Department to oversee
the safety of its soldiers. In some cases the department did attempt to
negotiate with the civilian officials who were responsible for the protection of off-duty soldiers, and from time to time it stationed military
police officers in towns to monitor the behavior of soldiers and local
police alike. In Montgomery in 1941, after two local police officers
beat a soldier, the commanders at Maxwell Air Field attempted, unsuccessfully, to persuade the chief of police to discipline their officers. In
Beaumont, Texas, in 1942, the army transported to Fort Crockett, in
Galveston, a wounded Black soldier, one Charles Reco, who had been
shot and seriously wounded by the local police rather than leave him in
the custody of Beaumont police. But these stopgap measures were no
match for the widespread violence.

Not only did the War Department fail to dislodge Jim Crow rules or
address the violence their enforcement entailed; making matters even

worse, the other key federal agency with jurisdiction over the problem, the Justice Department, was equally ineffectual. It narrowly construed the federal civil rights statutes that might have supported prosecution when segregated conditions led to lethal attacks. Even in cases when federal law was clear, the absence of institutional will—or, equally crippling, capacity—prevented national law enforcement institutions from safeguarding the rights of these military men and women.

The overlapping jurisdiction of these two departments further compromised civil rights enforcement. Although the War Department referred civil rights matters, including homicides, to the Justice Department, it did not seem to matter how the case reached the DOJ, for, so far as available records reveal, the DOJ did not prosecute a single case over the course of the war. In some instances, if a military investigation, even a biased one, had already been undertaken, federal prosecutors closed their files. And the reverse was also true: a referral of a case from the Justice Department to the War Department often meant its demise. In April 1944, Assistant Attorney General Tom Clark asked the army to investigate the police slaying of Private Theodore Wesley Samuels, a soldier visiting in Mobile. Truman Gibson, a civilian aide to the secretary of war, adamantly discouraged prosecution, claiming that an army investigation revealed that the shooting was justified: Samuels demanded service at a café, so the army's witnesses claimed, and on being refused, allegedly because he was drunk, got into a fight with local police and military police and broke the nose of one of them, whereupon he was shot to death. Gibson reported that the military investigating authorities concluded the soldier met his death "as a result of his own misconduct." But the DOJ file included ample evidence that Samuels had been killed in cold blood by local and military police. Samuels's sister named eight witnesses who could confirm he was shot in the back; it does not appear they were ever contacted. Reverend S. R. Lee of the Interdenominational Colored Ministerial Alliance wrote to Attorney General Biddle that he "could not understand why two civilian police and military police could not arrest an unarmed soldier without brutally killing him." But the DOJ closed the case, relying instead on the War Department's investigation clearing its own officers of wrongdoing. "We will take no further action in this case unless requested to do so by the War Department," wrote Assistant Attorney General Tom Clark.

On the other hand, in the few cases where the military urged prosecution, federal prosecutors resisted. In contrast to the Samuels case, when New Yorker Edward Green was slain by a bus driver in Alexandria, Louisiana, in 1944, military authorities concluded that there was no "moral or legal" justification for the killing. But the Justice Department refused to act. It explained to Eleanor Roosevelt, Thurgood Marshall, and others that federal law provided no criminal remedy for such a civil rights violation.

14

The "Negro Transportation" File

In January 1943 William Hastie, the civilian aide to Secretary of War Henry Stimson who would later become the country's first Black federal judge, resigned in protest of the department's snail-paced approach to racial injustices. There was, he seems to have concluded, little promise of relief from the federal domain. President Roosevelt's overarching focus on the war, his reelection in 1944, and his concerns for his own legacy meant that there was little tolerance in official Washington for Black dissent, and a preference for the repressive measures that were second nature to military leaders. Even as Congress sought to make progress on racial issues to counter foreign cynicism about American democracy, Roosevelt hemmed and hawed. In a congressional fight over a poll tax measure in 1942, for example, the president lay low, following the advice of one of his aides, who wrote that poll tax reform could "in a jumpy situation create Southern fears that the government may be moving to end Jim Crow laws in transportation in the South under the guise of the war effort. It may also lift Negro hopes only to drop them again." Containment was the watchword, as evidenced by the surveillance operation launched in the wake of Booker Spicely's murder, the failure to pursue federal remedies in the Henry Williams case, and the buck-passing in the case of Theodore Wesley Samuels. A particularly telling example of the department's effort to squelch Black protest was its Negro Transportation Survey project. This initiative, launched two years into the war, sheds light on the army's transportation policies, but it also offers a revealing picture of life at the back of the bus.

The Army Fourth Service Command, which began operations early in 1942 and was headquartered in Atlanta, comprised the southeastern states of Alabama, Florida, Georgia, South Carolina, much of North Carolina, the eastern half of Mississippi, and parts of Tennessee. The reports it was receiving about attacks on Black soldiers led it to assign Black and white undercover agents to conduct a comprehensive survey of racial incidents. After reviewing the incident reports about activity on the bases and in the surrounding areas, Army Colonel Stacy Knopf, assistant chief of staff of the command, concluded that the problems stemmed in part because "the Northern negro is unaccustomed to and resents restrictions imposed by custom and law in the South" and "the negro 'white collar' class, teachers, doctors, etc. have not hesitated to agitate for 'racial equality' contrary to the customs of the community." The colonel also noted that the local police were "quick to resent misbehavior" of Black army personnel that "might go unnoticed in a white offender."

In 1944, the Fourth Command took action. Over a period of nine months its Security and Intelligence Branch compiled a file on racial conflict in cities and towns close to facilities under its command. To implement this Negro Transportation Survey, special agents from the branch met with managers of local bus companies on a monthly basis to gather information on all incidents of a racial nature. In addition to matters concerning soldiers, the survey also addressed those relating to civilian passengers.

BLACK WOMEN, the advance guard in the war against the partitioned bus, figure prominently in the Negro Transportation files. Domestics who worked in white homes were daily customers, as were mothers with their children. These women, like practiced sharpshooters, would aim just short of the felonious zone: they sat where they were not allowed, and talked loudly to each other about the abuses of the moment. The "yes ma'ams, no sirs" of their day jobs were set to the side as they laughed freely with each other in the language of their own kitchens. Off duty, they defied the racial topography of the bus, claiming within it their no-go zone. The file reveals that they sometimes paid dearly for their resistance: they were arrested for petty violations, whether illegal or not, and it was not unusual for them to be beaten, in plain sight of other riders, by bus drivers, white passengers, and the police.

Women's resistance could be as combative as it was creative. In Mobile, Alabama, Mary White boarded a bus a week before Christmas 1944. She proceeded toward the back after paying her fare, only to have the driver order her to get off and reenter through the rear. White did step out of the front door, but not before calling the driver a "son of a bitch." Fifty-five passengers looked on while the driver picked up a fire extinguisher and hurled it at White, striking her. In Columbia, South Carolina, a white soldier got into an argument with a Black woman about who should board a crowded bus first. The woman struck the soldier with a bar of soap and scratched him. The soldier then beat up the woman. The police arrested the woman, but not the soldier. In Fort Jackson, South Carolina, in 1946, Jennie Mae Davis, who worked in the laundry on the base, got into an argument with a bus driver and struck him with her pocketbook and a pair of shoes. The driver responded by kicking her in the breast. The Negro Citizens Committee of South Carolina complained to the bus company that it "could not understand how any man (with a sense of fairness) could have kicked any woman, white or negro, as he did, in the breast."

Challenging, as it does, our clichéd narrative about the organized bus boycotts of the mid-1950s, the insurgency of individual Black women was extraordinary. Nor were men, who were equally fed up with raced transportation, silent victims. In September 1944 a Black man cursed and drew a knife on a ticket agent in Wilmington, North Carolina. His complaint was that he had waited a long time to purchase his ticket, and he was tired of having to wait "on damn white people." He paid dearly, with a four months' jail sentence, for his impromptu protest.

———————

THESE PRACTICES OF DISSENT and resistance, beneath the radar and seemingly spontaneous, render visible the vocabulary and vitality of the subaltern, the historical outsider injecting obstruction and unpredictability in the interstices of daily life. The riders echoed postures of self-determination that reprised resistance to slavery. For Black women during slavery, rebellion was quintessential, and, to the present time, stereotypes of Black female personhood are referents to this stance: insolent, defiant in the face of authority, volatile, sullen, mistrusting, not disposed to the easy smile. The practices of resistance, embedded in daily life, were a necessary counter to the deadening regularity of degradation and alienation. Women riders passed these manners on to their children, teaching them how to fight back against white domination, and sharpening their class consciousness. If the hallmarks of Jim Crow were Black liability and white impunity, these riders politicized their claims to human rights through miscellaneous acts of rebellion.

They nourished a continuum of ideology, community, and congregation from slavery through Jim Crow: a counterculture, as it were, much like the music, the inside jokes, the prayers, and the kitchen talk that held Black couples, families, and neighborhoods together. In riding the bus, they imposed terms on both the front and the back of the vehicle. They talked to each other in a volume loud enough to disturb whites, they cheated the farebox, they jostled white passengers, and they sometimes refused to yield their seats and encouraged their children to do the same. They followed their own code of conduct, testing the dynamics of white rule to uphold their own agency and honor. These women were ready for the soldiers' resistance when it arrived in town.

PART III
PATEROLLERS
AND PROSECUTORS

15

Reconstruction Statutes, Jim Crow Rules

The federal government should have protected soldiers from racial violence, especially when they were on duty and in uniform. Federal laws could well have been tapped to protect other Black citizens, too, but those laws, decimated by the courts in the aftermath of Reconstruction, remained in the closed books of the federal code until the 1940s, when they were partially restored. Protection from racial violence, the War Department and the Department of Justice asserted, was better left to state and local officials.

Indeed, along with education, law enforcement has historically been jealously guarded as distinctively local territory in the United States. While the critical constitutional revisions that followed the Civil War should have rebalanced the scales in favor of the federal government, the Confederate states quickly reestablished control over policing and prosecution. It would not be until the late 1930s that the federal government even designated a bureau for civil rights law enforcement. This federal vacuum left ample space for Jim Crow to flourish across the first half of the twentieth century.

Created in 1870, the Department of Justice was established, in part, to strengthen the federal government's hand in the battle against Klan terror. The new department's first attorney general, Amos T. Akerman, a Georgia lawyer, proclaimed that he would use recently enacted criminal statutes to "subject [Klansmen] to the vengeance of the law." The laws to which he was referring were adopted by Reconstruction legislators. One law, commonly known as Section 51, criminalized conspiracies to injure a citizen exercising federal rights.* A second, referred to as Section 52, penalized willful action to deprive someone of their federal rights where the acts were performed by someone claiming to be authorized by law, such as a police officer.† A third law made it a crime to disqualify individuals for jury service on account of their race or color. And a fourth criminalized peonage or involuntary servitude. The first two of these laws directly applied to racial terror at the hands of private conspirators or public actors. From their enactment after the Civil War through the 1960s, the checkered history of the two statutes reflected both federal race politics and, more generally, judicial uncertainty about the scope of federal criminal law enforcement.

Section 51, originally enacted in 1870 as the first "Enforcement Act," and the first national law to penalize private conspiracies to deprive individuals of their protected rights, had its origins in a statute adopted four years earlier that made it a federal crime for any person "under color of law" to deprive another person "of any rights, privileges, or immunities secured or protected by the Constitution or laws of the United States." The Enforcement Act of 1870 was designed to implement the provisions of the Fifteenth Amendment and to rein in marauders like the Klan. While Section 51 prohibited conspiracies to violate federal rights—including conspiracies by private actors—the second law, Section 52, prohibited the actual violation of federal rights by persons acting under the authority of law—what lawyers call "state actors." Section 52—which also was based on the 1866 and 1870 Enforcement Acts—was limited by its terms, therefore, to public officials—sheriffs,

---

* At one time codified as 18 U.S.C. § 51, the statute is now 18 U.S.C. § 241. The statute is referred to here as Section 51 or Section 241.

† Formerly 18 U.S.C. § 52, the statute is now 18 U.S.C. § 242. The statute is referred to here as Section 52.

police officers, or election commissioners, for example—acting with willful intent to violate a person's federally protected rights.

The Republican-controlled congress adopted the two laws as the Ku Klux Klan began to overwhelm the South in the wake of the war, threatening to ruin efforts to protect the former enslaved communities—and, incidentally, to steal votes for the Democrats in the upcoming 1870 election. Radical Republicans defended the constitutionality of federal criminal law enforcement on two grounds. As Klan terror, especially aimed at elections, consumed the South, it became apparent that the law enforcement challenge was national in nature and required a coordinated national response. Solutions limited by state boundaries would not work. The other argument was more specifically constitutional in nature. Inasmuch as Congress was charged with protecting constitutional rights, including those conferred by the postbellum amendments, it had plenary power to criminalize conduct that interfered with their exercise. Congress's authority did not depend on whether the states were meeting their obligations to protect their citizens; rather, it flowed directly from the package of rights protected by the Constitution. Benjamin Butler, the Massachusetts congressman who authored the Enforcement Act of 1871, put it this way: "[i]f the federal government cannot pass laws to protect . . . the lives of citizens of the United States in the states, why were guarantees of these fundamental rights put in the constitution at all?" This division of opinion over the constitutional source of federal power to prosecute non-interstate racist crimes is still debated today.

Attorney General Akerman kept his word. He pursued investigations of violent crimes across the South. In South Carolina, a spate of violent assaults against Black Republicans in nine counties led President Ulysses S. Grant to suspend the writ of habeas corpus and dispatch additional federal troops. These measures put federal authorities in a position to conduct investigations and make arrests. About 600 men suspected of Klan activity were detained and, based on the investigations, the federal government pursued charges against about 1,200 Klansmen, winning convictions in virtually every case it tried. In Mississippi, the federal government succeeded in getting convictions in 77 percent of the cases it pursued between 1872 and 1874. By 1874, the Klan threat was significantly diminished. In addition to the retributive and deterrent benefits of these criminal proceedings, they served as a modest model of a racially integrated federal justice system, for Blacks often served as jurors and witnesses.

By 1875 it would all be wiped out. Sections 51 and 52 would disappear for half a century until, in the 1930s, the NAACP's anti-lynching campaigners dusted them off to illustrate that there was precedent and legal support for federal intervention. The Department of Justice had refused to utilize the statutes to federalize the effort to combat lynching. In Alabama in August 1933, three young men were kidnapped as law enforcement officers sought to move them from Tuscaloosa, where they were charged with rape and murder, to Birmingham. Two of the prisoners, Dan Pippen and A. T. Harden, were wrested from the sheriff by a mob and shot to death, while the third, Elmore Clark, shot at and left for dead, survived. A local grand jury declined to indict the members of the mob. Charles Hamilton Houston, then an attorney with the NAACP, urged the DOJ to pursue the killers under Section 51, and the sheriff, for failure to protect his prisoners, under Section 52. In a nearly fifty-page brief that echoed and refined the arguments made in 1870 by Congressman Benjamin Butler, Houston reasoned that the federal government had the inherent power to protect Black people against lynching without additional legislation. "A Nation whose government can protect its citizens abroad" should not abandon them "through a lack of official courage to enforce the written law," he wrote, citing the Fourteenth Amendment as well as Sections 51 and 52. Attorney General Homer Cummings rejected Houston's arguments. In light of the ongoing legislative battle over anti-lynching laws in the 1930s, the department wanted to wait for explicit congressional authority before taking on such a "local" matter.

Houston's arguments laid seeds that did not sprout until the 1940s. In 1939, the Justice Department established a special unit to protect civil rights and civil liberties—the Department's first effort to concentrate its civil rights cases and bring on lawyers who would specialize in these matters. Initially called the Civil Liberties Unit and housed in the Criminal Division, the agency was renamed the Civil Rights Section in 1941.* The new section reinvigorated the old statutes, Sections 51 and 52, and, with limited success, sought to deploy them in the war against racial terror in the South.

A set of cases from one region in Alabama sheds light on the institutional and political challenges the new federal civil rights lawyers faced in applying these Reconstruction statutes to twentieth-century white supremacist violence. The Alabama federal court system was divided into three geographical areas—the Northern, Middle, and Southern districts. The cases that follow took place in the Middle District, an area that included the state's capital city, Montgomery, as well as Tuskegee. Comprising about twenty-three counties in the southeast quadrant of the state, the district was served by the same United States Attorney from 1942 to 1953, when he was replaced by an Eisenhower appointee, and from 1936 to 1955, by the same district court judge.

---

* Initially called the Civil Liberties Unit, the name was quickly changed to Civil Rights Section. In 1957, the Civil Rights Section became the Civil Rights Division of the Justice Department. In this book the term used to describe the entity that was launched in 1939 and was in place until 1957 is the "Civil Rights Section" or CRS.

16

"Her Hips Looked Like Battered Liver"

TUSKEGEE IN THE MIDDLE DISTRICT

The sheriff of Macon County, Alabama, Edwin Evans, was well known to attorneys of the Justice Department's Civil Rights Section before his encounter with Walter Gunn in June 1942. A former high school football star, Evans took office in 1940 and immediately earned a reputation among Black and white people alike for violence, disorder, and incompetence, but he was particularly brutal to Black residents. In May 1940, the sheriff handcuffed a Black prisoner, Louis James Hatcher, to cell bars, leaving his feet to dangle just above the floor, lynching style. As Hatcher hung there, Macon County's chief law enforcer whipped him with a rubber hose and a walking stick. In March 1942, Sheriff Evans and his deputies strung forty-one-year-old Eugene Brown to a tree in the woods, whipped him with blackjacks and tree branches, and then locked him back up in the county jail. Brown had been accused of stealing tires from the filling station where he worked. Also in 1942, Evans flogged a disabled white man. In August, the sheriff and his men took Lillie May Hendon into the woods and whipped her. And in November, they assaulted Edgar Cullen Bryant with the fan belt from a car.

A husband, father of four, and skilled auto mechanic in Tuskegee, Walter Gunn invited the ire of Sheriff Evans because he was rumored to be seeing a Black woman whom the sheriff liked. Evans first assaulted Gunn in October 1941, as a Sunday morning church service where Gunn and his family were in attendance was drawing to a close. With his deputy, Evans thrashed Gunn with his handcuffs and ripped his clothes off him, all in the presence of the parishioners at Mount Esther Church. On that Sunday Evans threatened a bleeding and half-clothed Gunn that there was more to come if he did not stay away from the woman who was, it was said, the object of the sheriff's affection, and for emphasis he locked him up.

On June 27, 1942, eight months after the incident at the church, Gunn worked a full day at his brother's filling station. On his way home he was waylaid by Sheriff Evans and his deputy, Henry F. Faucett. The lawmen claimed they were pulling Gunn over for drunk driving, but according to witnesses, Gunn had not been drinking. Gunn kept going in his Packard truck, trying to outrace trouble and reach home. When he got there, his wife came to the door to see what the commotion was all about. The couple's children were playing in the front yard. As the children looked on, Deputy Faucett shot at their father from the sheriff's car but missed. Gunn got out of his car and tried to make it to the rear of the house. He was shot at several more times. Hit in the leg, Gunn fell to the ground, whereupon the officers kicked and pistol-whipped him; then, while the family watched, frantic and helpless, they dragged him back into his own Packard. They drove his truck, with him in it, unconscious, to the filling station where Gunn worked. Once there the officers forced Gunn's brother to take him to the hospital so that they would not be seen with the dying man. An autopsy revealed five bullet wounds and a fractured skull.

So distressing was Sheriff Evans's behavior that two white political

Deputy Beats Wounded Man To Death As Wife Watches

TUSKEGEE, Ala., July 9—
A Negro mother and her four
young children are alone in
the world today, innocent victims of the tragedy that befell them
when an officer of the Alabama
law shot and killed their father
and husband, Walter Gunn.,
The reason for the shooting and
killing of Walter Gunn by a deputy sheriff named Fawcett is
clouded with mystery. Apparently
the only crime the victim committed was meeting up with Fawcett and his superior officer, Sheriff E. E. Evans, on June 27.
Gunn was shot by one of the
officers in the rear of his home,
after he had been pursued for a
considerable distance, and died in
the John A. Andrew Memorial hospital at Tuskegee Institute.

In 1942, a sheriff and his deputy
from Tuskegee, Alabama, shot
Walter Gunn at his home. His
wife and children witnessed
the killing. The lawmen were
acquitted by a federal jury.

leaders of Tuskegee, Mayor Frank Carr and State Representative Henry Neill Segrest, appealed to Alabama governor Frank Dixon to take action. But the governor, a dyed-in-the-wool racist, refused to support a prosecution. Rather, he turned the information that his state police collected about the sheriff over to federal authorities. When it was clear that neither state executive authorities nor the county would act in the Gunn murder, the Tuskegee Civic Association, under the leadership of Charles Gomillion, pressed for a federal inquiry. Gunn's family enlisted the help of two white men to investigate the killing; when Sheriff Evans heard about their involvement, he whipped one of them, Readie Glenn Huguley. The fruits of the Civic Association's investigation were shared with Edward Burns Parker, the new United States Attorney for the Middle District of Alabama, and in April 1943—four months after Sheriff Evans was elected to a second term as sheriff, and ten months after he killed Gunn—a federal grand jury in Montgomery returned an indictment against Evans and Faucett based on the Gunn slaying and several other custodial assaults. The two men were brought into federal court, charged with beating thirteen African Americans, mostly separate incidents, and the fatal assault on Gunn.

Parker, then in his second year in office, faced an uphill battle from the start. Officers Evans and Faucett obstructed the FBI investigation in the county by beating up prospective witnesses. They impersonated FBI agents to discover who was cooperating with the investigation. Proclaiming that in the Black Belt they were what stood between law and order and the rule of the jungle, the two officers warned that a conviction would lead to a massive exit of whites from majority-Black Macon County. When the chief of police in Tuskegee was interviewed by the FBI, he readily admitted that the county sheriff, Evans, "had the reputation of beating negroes unnecessarily," but he worried that "should the white people take sides against Sheriff Evans and his officers and boot him out of office . . . the negroes would give more trouble in the future than they had ever given."

When the federal government's case against Evans and Faucett finally went to trial in the neighboring city of Opelika in June 1943, over three hundred law enforcement officers from all over the state filled the courtroom and surrounded the courthouse to support the defendants. Parker prosecuted the case himself, producing more than a hundred witnesses as well as the damning autopsy report on Gunn. The defense kept apace, procuring testimony from a similarly large number of witnesses, the majority of whom sought to paint the victims as dangerous criminals, liars, and ne'er-do-wells.

The Middle District judge presiding over the proceedings was Charles Brents Kennamer, whose tenure there dated from 1936. A staunch Republican, he had enjoyed a stellar rise from a small farming hamlet on the outskirts of notorious Scottsboro, Alabama, to an education at Georgetown University, then served in succession as county solicitor and United States Attorney for the Northern District of Alabama. Where cases involving Black defendants entered into Judge Kennamer's purview, he earned an initial reputation for benevolence among white Alabamians.

One of the African American victims of the sheriff's reign of terror, Lillie May Hendon, came in for special vilification at the trial. The thirty-eight-year-old Hendon had been arrested on the phony charge of stealing $154 from a cousin and confined in the county jail for three days in August 1942. On the third day, Evans and Faucett decided to take her into the woods to knock a confession out of her. Faucett held the woman down by the neck while the sheriff whipped her with a cane until her back was "blistered and bloody." She told the FBI that "I was beaten until I knew nothing," and then she was locked back up in a sweltering cell. So serious were her wounds that Florida Segrest, wife of the state representative, declared on examining Hendon after the beating that "her hips looked like battered liver." But at the trial, Judge Kennamer gave the lawyer for the defendants free rein to impugn Hendon's morals. Sheriff Evans testified that he had indeed "slapped the hell out of Lillie May" because she had made "improper advances" toward him. During his cross-examination of Hendon, apropos of nothing of evidentiary significance, the defense lawyer commanded the victim to "pull down your skirt." To ice the cake, Sheriff Evans induced Black witnesses, by what means is unclear, to come forward to accuse Hendon's male friend of inflicting the injuries that the federal prosecutor attributed to the defendant police officers, and to disparage her as sexually loose.

At the close of the case, a defense lawyer suggested to the jury that Eleanor Roosevelt, at the time first lady, and Charles Gomillion, president of the Tuskegee Civic Association, had colluded to invent the case against the two lawmen. Edwin Evans and Henry Faucett were acquitted. Perhaps himself troubled by Evans's and Faucett's reputations, if not convinced of their guilt, Judge Kennamer concluded the case with a warning to the men not to take retaliatory action against the state's witnesses.

Evans would go on to serve as Macon County's sheriff until 1950. Judge Kennamer, meanwhile, earned a mixed reputation on civil rights cases. In one matter in 1946, he was reversed by the Court of Appeals for the Fifth Circuit for ruling against would-be Black voters in a disenfranchisement lawsuit. In another matter, in 1947, he effectively destroyed, through his jury instruction, the prosecution's case against the killers of a Black man. In 1954, a year before his death, he ruled that the Bullock County Board of Registrars had discriminated against Black voters.

The nation's legal community has long celebrated the courage of those southern judges who, in defiance of their professional communities, supported civil rights cases—jurists like Elbert Tuttle and John Wisdom. But these men were rare, particularly in the 1940s. More common were men like Kennamer, who needed only to be burned once to realize there was little to be gained by being pinned an integrationist. These jurists, who had little stomach to preside over an erstwhile battle for the "lost cause" whenever a police brutality case came their way, helped to keep the federal court door closed in places like the Middle District, stripping away the protective shield the Reconstruction Congress had in mind.

And Edward Burns Parker, the prosecutor, had learned a hard lesson, too. It would be a decade before he would bring another police abuse case to the federal court in the Middle District.

17

"A Little Quick
on the Trigger"

UNION SPRINGS IN THE MIDDLE DISTRICT

Also in the Middle District of Alabama, and in Judge Kennamer's jurisdiction, was the town of Union Springs in Bullock County. The bustling center of a prosperous agricultural region in the Black Belt, where white people lived in mansion-lined streets that attested to the wealth-generating properties of cotton, Union Springs was where Edgar Bernard Thomas, born in 1882, grew up.

Thomas's father, John Thomas, born into slavery, had been run out of Bullock County in about 1900 by whites who resented his successful business enterprises. John Thomas had owned property in Union Springs, but also sought to buy land in the rural area to rent to Black tenants. Competition from a Black landowner was more than some whites could tolerate, and so they banished him. Edgar, his son, was also a businessman. In 1945, he owned a shop and café in Union Springs. At sixty-three, Edgar Thomas had enjoyed some success in his life and was looking forward to retiring and perhaps spending more time with his only daughter, who had moved from Union Springs to Chicago. A dispute with a police officer would upend those modest aspirations.

Dewey Columbus Bradley, who was not from the area, had been

hired to serve as a police officer by the Union Springs councilors shortly before V-J Day in 1945. Witnesses dispute what motivated Bradley to target Edgar Thomas, but all agreed the assault was particularly wanton, even judged by the standards of the times. Some believe Thomas was seeing an African American woman with whom Bradley was, or hoped to be, involved. A week before the shooting, Bradley arrested Thomas to scare him away from the woman, it seems, but Thomas, who had been in Union Springs sixty-three years longer than Bradley and thought, therefore, that he could straighten the matter out, sauntered over to City Hall and complained to the mayor and the local councilors—all of whom he had known for decades—about the unlawful arrest. The officials promised to take action against Bradley, but they did nothing. Five days later, on Saturday, October 13, 1945, Officer Bradley, accompanied by Assistant Chief of Police Hollis Eugene Whittle, who was armed with a sawed-off shotgun, entered Thomas's store, on the main street in the Black business district. According to a witness later interviewed by the FBI, Bradley shot Thomas in the face once, and as the injured man ran toward the back of the café, he shot him three more times, reloaded, and kept on shooting.

A man named James L. Pinckney, a minister, operated a barbershop next door to Thomas's café. The shop was open for business that Saturday morning, and so Reverend Pinckney heard the commotion and witnessed the murder of his longtime friend. He watched the two offi-

Ala. Cop Shoots Down Prominent Citizen, 60

UNION SPRINGS, Ala. — (ANP)—Edgar Thomas, 66, was shot to death Saturday morning at his home here, by Police Officer Dewey Bradley, white. According to Assistant Police Chief Hellis Whittle, the elderly Thomas sought to disarm the white policeman but citizens here are describing the killing as "a wanton murder."

Edgar Thomas was killed in the store he owned. Thomas lived in Union Springs, Alabama, all his life.

cers approach the café and heard Bradley tell Thomas, "We're going to run this damn town. I'll kill every black son of a bitch on the street." Later that day, the Union Springs police chief visited Reverend Pinckney at the barbershop and ordered him to leave town. "You see what happened to that son of a bitch next door, the same thing will happen to you," he warned. Within the hour Pinckney grabbed his hat, locked up his barbershop, left his wife behind, and hid in the woods until he could find his way to Montgomery. From there he headed to Chicago. Reverend Pinckney lost his business. He would never reside in Union Springs again.

After the shooting, the police chief, having banished Reverend Pinckney and scared away other witnesses, detained Officer Bradley for "safekeeping," but declined to charge him. The Bullock County sheriff, however, took a different view of the situation. He arrested Bradley and placed him on a bond. While out on bail, Bradley continued to patrol in Union Springs. Less than three weeks after Bradley shot Thomas to death, he shot another man, Alger Lee Gary, in the head, causing him to lose his right eye. About five weeks later, on Saturday, December 1, Bradley killed yet another man, Jessie Hightower. Hightower and his wife had been quarreling on the street in Union Springs. Bradley approached the couple and asked the husband to surrender a silver table knife, which he did. At that point, Bradley beat Jessie Hightower on the head, leading the man to exclaim, "don't hit me anymore, there's the damn knife on the ground." Bradley pulled out his pistol, yelled, "you damned son of a bitch, don't cuss at me," and shot Hightower in the heart. He was pronounced dead on the scene.

Local authorities never prosecuted Bradley for the lethal assault on Hightower and the maiming of Gary. A county grand jury was convened in the shooting death of Edgar Thomas, but declined to indict Bradley. The chief of police did charge Bradley with "conduct unbecoming an officer" after the third shooting and discharged him from the force. The chief allowed that Bradley was "a little too quick on the trigger."

The Union Springs shootings drew the attention of the Southern

Negro Youth Congress (SNYC), which was headquartered in Birmingham. SNYC's organizational secretary, Louis Burnham, appealed directly to the mayor to address Bradley's "reign of terror." The barber who was forced to hide in the woods in the immediate wake of the slaying of Edgar Thomas, Reverend Pinckney, provided a report to the Chicago NAACP branch after his perilous escape to that city. The branch alerted the New York headquarters, triggering an investigation by the Justice Department's Civil Rights Section. The FBI's main informant on the Thomas case made clear that the victim was trapped in his own shop and shot in cold blood by Bradley and Eugene Whittle. There was no unbiased contradictory testimony.

It seemed an open-and-shut case—but three years after his defeat in the trial of Macon County sheriff Edwin Evans, who had killed Walter Gunn in Tuskegee in 1942, US Attorney Edward Burns Parker refused to prosecute. He advised the Civil Rights Section that inasmuch as a state grand jury had declined to indict, and the officer was no longer on the force, federal action would be redundant. He closed his file in Montgomery and the Justice Department's lawyers in Washington followed his lead.

18

"The Testimony . . .
of the Negroes
Seems More Probable"

A year later, another case of police brutality landed on Edward Burns Parker's desk.

Midday on May 2, 1946, found William "Pim" Lockwood in his fields in Macon County at the tail end of planting season. The plant was cotton, and Lockwood, fifty-eight years old, had cultivated the same crop with his family for fifty years. He and his wife, Mary, reputed to be "good people in the area," raised their five boys and three girls on farms they rented, first in Notasulga and then in Tuskegee. Perhaps they expected that the boys would follow their path, but one of their sons, Elijah, had served with the US Army in Europe, and when he got back to Macon County two years later, his ambitions had widened. He aspired to work at the Veterans Administration Hospital in Tuskegee. Established in 1923 by President Calvin Coolidge, the hospital was the first in the nation with an all-Black medical staff. Renowned all over the South, along with the Tuskegee Institute, the hospital transformed that city from a country town into a hub of Black professional talent.

Elijah Lockwood had been honorably discharged from the service on March 12, 1946. Not quite two months later, on May 2, he was visiting the small country store of a close relative, situated about two hundred yards from his family's fields, and was hanging out with his cousin's family, which included two young girls. John Edward "Ed" Kirby, the younger brother of a deputy sheriff, came into the store to purchase some cottonseed. The two young men had been neighbors in Notasulga; Elijah was twenty-two years old and Ed, the white man, was twenty-four. Each had served their country on the battlefield. They spoke amiably at first, but Ed became peeved when Elijah told him he would be working at the Tuskegee Veterans Hospital. "You belong in the field behind that plow, helping your daddy," the young white man rebuked. "I reckon so," responded Elijah, but he repeated firmly that he was headed in a different direction. That infuriated Ed even more, for he replied, "God damn nigger, don't give me none of your flip mouth," picked up a shovel, and threw it at Elijah.

An angry Ed Kirby got in his car and drove off. A short time later he returned, shotgun in hand, called out for Elijah, and sprayed the store with shotgun pellets, just missing one of the girls. Elijah had a weapon nearby, a prized German pistol, the eagle coat of arms crisply incised on its side, that he had brought back home from his service in Germany. He retrieved the pistol from inside the store and fired back at Ed. Both escaped injury. Relieved, no doubt, that they would live to fire another shot, the two young veterans took their guns to their respective homes and stashed them away.

Ed Kirby, however, had a trump card, and as he saw it, the dispute over Elijah's career plans to trade the tenant farm for the hospital was not over. His older brother, William ("Willie") Kirby, was Tuskegee's chief deputy sheriff. At Ed's request, Deputy Kirby drove to the Lockwood home and demanded that Elijah produce the German pistol. With the assistance of another deputy, Kirby seized the weapon and then put Elijah in the back seat of their cruiser. The two lawmen were heading toward town with Elijah when the young man's father, William, and his mother, Mary, caught up with them on the road. Mary Lockwood had been in the house when the deputy sheriff barged in, forced her son to surrender his pistol, and then tossed him in the police car. As the deputies were carrying him away, she cried out to her husband in the fields, and he had rushed up to see what was happening.

Standing by the side of the deputy's car, William Lockwood asked the thirty-two-year-old deputy sheriff where he was taking Elijah, to which Deputy Kirby responded, "I am going to put him in jail and God damn it, don't you say no." Lockwood paused, and then said, "yes." A furious Kirby spun around in his seat and shouted at Lockwood, "God damn it, don't you say yes to me, say yes-sir and no-sir." Pausing before he replied, Lockwood, who was the deputy's senior by a quarter of a century, said, "yes, yes, yes." The deputy sheriff jumped out of the car, grabbed the older man by the arm and tried to toss him into the back seat of the vehicle next to his son. Protesting that he'd done nothing wrong, Lockwood resisted the arrest. Mary Lockwood pleaded with her husband to comply with Kirby's orders to submit to arrest, but he said simply, "I haven't done anything and I haven't said anything," whereupon Sheriff Kirby pushed Mary out of the way, pistol-whipped William Lockwood and, in what seemed like an instant, shot him. Elijah sat horrified, handcuffed in the back seat of the cruiser while his mother collapsed on the road. Kirby placed a nearly expired Lockwood in the back seat with his son and dropped him off at the Tuskegee Hospital, where he died. He then proceeded to the jail with Elijah.

The charge against the younger Lockwood was attempted murder. One of Mary Lockwood's other boys, Johnnie, was arrested later that day on a robbery charge of unknown origin. It would be many years before the widow would see her two sons again.

Thurgood Marshall learned about the killing from the Tuskegee NAACP branch within days of William Lockwood's slaying and while the victim was still in the morgue. Mary Lockwood composed a heartbreaking letter explaining how, in a matter of minutes, her husband was killed and her boys locked up. Immediately recognizing its legal significance as a matter that fell within Section 52, Marshall wrote to Turner L. Smith, chief of the Department of Justice's Civil Rights Section, requesting an aggressive investigation. Within a month, the

FBI had prepared a substantial report containing statements from about a dozen witnesses in Macon County, including Mary Lockwood, her son Elijah, and the two Kirby brothers. When Deputy Kirby was interviewed, he claimed William Lockwood had attempted to snatch his son Elijah from the officer's custody, and that the fifty-eight-year-old man pulled the proverbial knife on him. He shot and killed William Lockwood—whom family members remembered as a man who was quiet as a "lamb" and who wouldn't fight or "cuss"—to defend himself, Kirby told the FBI.

Ed Kirby, who had sprayed the store with shotgun pellets earlier in the morning, stated that after his initial argument with Elijah, he went home for his gun and drove back to the store. While his shotgun was still in his car, Ed claimed, Elijah fired upon him several times. Also interviewed was a thirteen-year-old girl, a relative of Lockwood's. The girl's eyewitness testimony about the shooting at the store thoroughly corroborated Elijah's, but the FBI agent who authored the report dismissed her statements, describing her as a "typical country negro girl who is extremely shy and inarticulate."

If its file is any guide, the FBI never looked into the reputation of Deputy Sheriff Kirby or that of his brother Ed, the men who were supposed to be the targets of its investigation. It was singularly focused on discrediting the dead man, William Lockwood. Agents interviewed four white men whose names the Macon County sheriff, Edwin Evans, provided as persons knowledgeable about the character of William Lockwood. (Sheriff Evans, coincidentally, had himself been tried in a federal court in 1943 in connection with his lethal assault on Walter Gunn.)

William Lockwood had no criminal record. Like hundreds of Black men of his age in Tuskegee, he had been an unknowing subject of the US government's infamous syphilis experiment and suffered its consequences. The agents had a tough time finding damning character evidence on him. One of the white men noted he'd had trouble with the deceased seven years earlier when Lockwood accused him of cheating him over the sale of some grapes. A second white man contributed a story about a disagreement William Lockwood had had with his father, and a third recalled that Lockwood had once tried to buy some mules from him.

Several features of the Lockwood case reduced the odds that Kirby would ever face prosecution. Because the killing took place on a public street and the only witnesses were African American, the officer's self-defense claim was, in effect, unassailable. The Macon County prosecutor, Harry Raymon, sought to forestall prosecution by assuring the Justice Department that he would pursue an indictment for homicide if the department would stay its hand.

About three months after Lockwood was killed, lawyers for the Justice Department's Civil Rights Section informed Edward Parker that they were inclined to prosecute. "While it is impossible to reconcile the testimony of the two opposing groups," the lawyers noted, "that of the Negroes seems more probable under the circumstances, as they appear from the report." The lawyers in Washington sought Parker's advice on whether the Justice Department should pursue an indictment or go forward on an "information" under Section 52 without a grand jury. But Parker stubbornly refused to abide by the directives he was receiving from the Civil Rights Section. When he initially received the FBI report, he simply stonewalled, declining to respond to the repeated requests of the Civil Rights Section to take action. Finally, in October 1946—just six short months after Elijah Lockwood's return from the war—he mustered a reply. Without saying why, he urged that the matter be dropped. "Considering the facts . . . in the report, I am of the opinion that this matter should be closed." A few days later, two of the department's lawyers consulted in Washington and concluded that Parker's obduracy could not be overcome. The file was closed in November 1946.

Meanwhile, NAACP lawyers in New York, who were responding to urgent letters from their Tuskegee branch, pressed the Justice Department to learn whether a federal prosecution would be forthcoming. Finally, more than a year after the murder, the department informed the NAACP's Robert Carter that it would not be pursuing the matter because the testimony of the Lockwoods conflicted with that of the deputy sheriff who killed William Lockwood. Thurgood Marshall responded quickly, taking the section's lawyers to task for refusing to go forward on account of conflicting testimony, which, Marshall reminded the government lawyers, characterized every case of police violence. Marshall also wrote that the case illustrated the need for additional federal legislation. The case "should be brought to the attention of the President's Committee on Civil Rights to point out to them the need for adequate legislation to empower [the Civil Rights Section] to protect the ordinary Negro citizen in the South from wanton killing by police officers."

As to Marshall's inquiry whether a recent ruling in a Supreme Court decision limiting the reach of federal law in police killings—the *Screws* case—had contributed to the DOJ's decision to close the file, the federal lawyers, in their response, claimed it was not a factor; rather, they told Marshall, the significant risk that the case could not be won at trial was what tipped the scales. Much later, the NAACP would learn that the basis for the decision to close the Lockwood case was nothing other than Edward Parker's refusal to prosecute. In its report, "To Secure These Rights," the President's Committee on Civil Rights cited the case as an example of obstructionism from federal prosecutors in the South:

In another case involving the killing of a Negro by a deputy sheriff, the Civil Rights Section sought the advice of the United States Attorney on July 30, and referred him to the FBI report of its investigation in the case. On September 13, the Section again asked for the advice of the United States Attorney. On October 10, it repeated its request for the third time. On October 14, the United States Attorney wrote that he had not received the FBI report, but would express his views to the Section as soon as he obtained it. On October 17, he advised that he had received the report and he thought the matter should be closed. He gave no reason for his opinion. The Civil Rights Section closed the case, apparently because the Civil Rights Section attorney in charge reported, according to a note in the file, that "X—will not go on anything."

"X" was US Attorney Edward Parker.

In an internal memorandum on November 30, 1948—a year after it closed the Lockwood file—the Civil Rights Section informed the chief of the Criminal Division that Parker was refusing to prosecute meritorious cases, citing the Lockwood matter as well as Parker's failure to follow the CRS's instructions to obtain an autopsy in a 1947 police slaying of Amos Starr, a Black man killed by a police officer in Tallassee, Alabama. "Mr. Parker advised that he is of the opinion that as the local officials believe that the victim was killed in self-defense, the Federal Government should not require an autopsy of the victim's body. It is obvious that Mr. Parker completely ignores the aforementioned medical testimony and other evidence indicating that the victim was shot in the back as he was running away from the subject." In a third case, where an FBI investigation revealed a violation of the antipeonage statute, Parker sabotaged what the CRS deemed to be "a strong case for prosecution" because, he told his bosses in Washington, he knew the local officials and some of the other persons whose conduct was under investigation. Because of Parker, the CRS was "unable to proceed with the enforcement of the Civil Rights Statutes in the Middle District of Alabama." The CRS therefore sought advice on whether to continue to conduct investigations, for "investigations alone have no salutary effect when it is generally known that violations will not be prosecuted."

Ultimately, the only convictions in the case were of the Lockwoods. Elijah Lockwood was sentenced to seven years for the attempted murder of Ed Kirby. His brother, Johnnie, arrested on the same day his father was killed, was sentenced to four years on a robbery charge. Right after William Lockwood's murder, most of the family left Alabama and moved to the New York–New Jersey area. The elders in the family rarely talked about the tragedy.

19

"Head . . . Soft as a Piece of Cotton"

LAFAYETTE IN THE MIDDLE DISTRICT

In 1950, the spell cast over the federal prosecutor's office by the Walter Gunn case in 1942 was finally broken. It took the station-house murder of a teenager to finally motivate US Attorney Edward Parker's office.

Born on March 15, 1931, in Five Points, a tiny settlement outside the city of LaFayette in Chambers County, Alabama, young Willie Baxter Carlisle was the seventh of Jim and Ella Belle Carlisle's eight children. His father, blue-eyed and known to acquaintances as "Banjo," was likely related to the family of the well-known, wealthy slave owner William Carlisle. Willie's father, a tenant farmer, took care of him and two of his sisters after Ella passed away in 1937. In 1948 Jim Carlisle died. After that Willie, then sixteen, pretty much took care of himself. At some point the young man was forced to leave school to work. He got a job at a service station in LaFayette, the seat of Chambers County, which sits on Alabama's eastern border with Georgia. (Joe Lewis was born a few miles from where the Carlisles lived, although by 1950, the heavyweight champion was long gone from the county.) Willie was tall and handsome, hardworking and well liked. Apparently he also liked a good party.

On February 17, 1950, a Friday evening, Willie and three teenaged friends tried to sneak past the ticket taker at a dance party for high school youths at C. L. Johnson's Place in LaFayette. Two city police officers, twenty-eight-year-old James Ray "Bo" Clark and twenty-four-year-old James Doy Mitcham, responded to a complaint from the sponsors of the dance and tossed the four young men out of the party. The officers continued their patrol, but they soon discovered that the air had been let out of one of the tires on their patrol car.

The following night, Clark, who had been on the LaFayette Police Department just shy of two months before this incident, and Mitcham, who had less than a year's service, rounded up the four youths whom they had chased away from the dance. Without benefit of warrant or criminal complaints, the officers accused the teens of deflating the tire, and drove them to the county jail. While the young men waited in the car, Clark went inside the county jail to get a hosepipe. The next stop was the city jail, a foreboding two-story nineteenth-century structure known as the "calaboose." The police pushed the teenagers up the stairs to the cells on the second floor (presumably the jailer and his family were at home on the floor below). As the other three teens looked on, Clark whipped Carlisle mercilessly with the rubber hose while Mitcham struck him with a walking stick. The boy wept, and finally collapsed. Two of the other teens were also whipped, while the fourth was released. Forced to carry a barely conscious Carlisle to the police car so he could be transported to the hospital, the teens would later testify that their friend was all but dead when they left the county jail. The local undertaker, Roy Silmon, who was called in to move Carlisle's body from the hospital's white ward to the "colored" ward, would later tell an FBI investigator that the teenager's head felt as "soft as a piece of cotton." Willie Carlisle died in the early morning hours of February 19. It was a Sunday, about thirty hours after Carlisle and his friends had tried to crash the dance.

Official reaction to the killing in Chambers County was appropriately swift. The officers were charged with murder by County Solicitor Dan Boyd, arrested, and released to await action by the grand jury. Their trial in March at the county courthouse attracted a thousand people—the largest crowd in the reported history of the courthouse—with whites billowing in the halls around the courtroom and about 250 Black people clustered silently in small groups in their assigned space in the balcony. With the exception of the teens when they testified, Blacks were nowhere to be seen in the main courtroom. One of the key prosecution witnesses was a white man who, positioned outside the jail on the night in question, had heard the beating. In their defense the officers claimed that young Carlisle "pulled a knife" on them in jail, and they also argued that he sustained his injuries when he fell from a bunk bed onto a concrete floor in the cell. The prosecution's toxicologist deemed it highly unlikely that this was the cause of death. In closing, the prosecutor reminded the Chambers County jurors that the nation was watching, while the defense cautioned them that the case was being tried in Alabama and "not under the law as interpreted by some judge in New York or Michigan." When the gavel came down on the jury's "not guilty" verdict, the main courtroom erupted in the howls and shouts of a football stadium, while the spectators in the balcony made their way through the crush of the jeering, cheering crowd, buttoning up their fury.

Although the local paper accepted the verdict as "fair," commentators elsewhere in Alabama were less sanguine. The editor of the Opelika *Daily News*, the neighboring county's newspaper—it was at the Opelika federal courthouse where in 1943 the killers of Walter Gunn were tried and acquitted—opined that "the case had a regrettable ending. One man (a negro) is dead, and no one is held accountable for his death." The *Birmingham News* observed that "there will certainly be room for question if police officers who admit whipping a prisoner, the beating being followed in a few hours by death, are permitted to remain on the force." Further, the paper noted that "the South is making prog-

Willie Carlisle, the young man on the right, was eighteen years old when he was beaten to death by two police officers at the city jail in LaFayette, Alabama, in 1950. Carlisle is pictured here with his cousin, Willie Frank Shealey.

ress in control of lynching. But are we equally careful to control officers of the law in their treatment of prisoners, even those who are vicious and dangerous men?" The "vicious and dangerous men" reference was perhaps to the teens who let the air out of the cops' tire.

Mitcham resigned his police position after the trial, but Clark refused to do so, requiring the City Council to remove him. The mayor explained that if the two were not removed the city would face even more adverse publicity.

The Justice Department was made aware of the killing of Carlisle before the state criminal trial. James M. McInerney, head of the Criminal Division in Washington, wrote J. Edgar Hoover about the matter right after the acquittal. Hoover took an uncharacteristically keen interest in the case. He wrote to McInerney that the "state prosecuting attorney may not have received the necessary cooperation from the police authorities," and he assigned a young agent from Montgomery, Spencer H. Robb,* to conduct a vigorous investigation.

In September, US Attorney Edward Burns Parker presented the case to a federal grand jury, which returned indictments against Clark and Mitcham for violations of Section 52. Mitcham pled guilty and was sentenced to six months in jail by Middle District of Alabama Judge Charles Kennamer—the same judge who had presided over the Walter Gunn case in 1943. Clark, on the other hand, went to trial. His case was prosecuted by Parker before Judge Kennamer, who charged the jury that "under no circumstances [does a law officer have] any right to take the law into his own hands because he is mad and undertake to punish a person." Upon the jury's conviction of Clark, Judge Kennamer imposed a sentence of ten months. It is not known whether Clark served the full sentence.

Cop Pleads Guilty Of Beating Youth

MONTGOMERY, Ala., Oct. 12. (UP)—Former policeman Doyle Mitchum, 24, pleaded guilty in Federal court today to charges of beating a young prisoner in the Lafayette (Ala.) city jail last February. The prisoner, Willie B. Carlisle, 18, Negro, died the next day.

Mitchum, and another Lafayette policeman, James R. Clark, were indicted by a Federal grand jury for violation of Carlisle's civil rights. They had been acquitted in a State court of fatally beating the youth.

Federal judge C. B. Kennamer said he would sentence Mitchum October 30.

U. S. district attorney Burns Parker said that maximum punishment for the civil rights violation could be a $1,000 fine or a year in jail or both.

Clark faces trial on the same Federal charges later this month.

A federal prosecution followed a state jury's acquittal of the police in the Willie Carlisle matter. The Department of Justice added this news article to its files on the case.

---

* Special Agent Robb would later make something of a name for himself in connection with the murder of Viola Liuzzo, for after Mrs. Liuzzo was killed by Alabama Klansmen in March 1965, Robb circulated an internal FBI memo intended to defame her. Robb reported, falsely, that Liuzzo's body "had puncture marks in her arms indicating recent use of a hypodermic needle." (Mary Stanton, *From Selma to Sorrow: The Life and Death of Viola Liuzzo* [Athens: University of Georgia Press, 1998], 53.)

Clark spent most of his life in LaFayette, died in 1986, and is buried in the town cemetery.

Alabama's Office of Vital Records has no certificate of death for Willie Carlisle. He lies in an unknown grave somewhere in Chambers County. A great-niece of Willie Carlisle, Leslie J. King, reported that on a trip she took to LaFayette, one of Willie's sisters told her that "they beat him up so badly that you could barely recognize him," and that fear of "repercussions" kept the family from pursuing a civil case.

20

"None of
Washington's Business"

While the creation of the Justice Department's civil rights unit in 1939 suggested that federal authorities were finally taking on public safety obligations that they had evaded during the height of the lynching era, this proved a false promise. As the cases from the Middle District of Alabama reflect, the political constraints that confronted local federal prosecutors, and by extension, the reach of the lawyers in Washington, severely hampered the effort to breathe life into a project to control racial violence that harkened back to Reconstruction.

In a US Supreme Court case rejecting a petitioner's request that the federal court assume jurisdiction over a civil matter to block state criminal proceedings that the litigant claimed violated his First Amendment rights, Justice Hugo Black extolled the "ideals and dreams of 'Our Federalism,'" which he believed compelled a federal court to stay its hand in deference to the states. "'Our Federalism,'" he wrote, "born in the early struggling days of our Union of States, occupies a highly important place in our Nation's history and its future." Students of the US federal system have theorized how "Our Federalism" plays out in laws on state autonomy and immunity, federal judicial abstention, and constitutionally based allocations of congressional and executive power. Whatever their value, these complicated models do not explain how "Our Federalism" fortified and insulated local regimes of racial terror in jurisdictions like the Middle District of Alabama—even while the country saw significant expansion of the FBI and the Department of Justice. Unique and special though it may have been in the eyes of Justice Black and his colleagues, Black communities on the ground read "Our Federalism" as a national endorsement of the predilections of the local sheriff.*

Political arrangements in the twentieth-century South vested enormous power in the hands of sheriffs, who, as these Middle District cases demonstrate, were synonymous with "the law" in their small towns and the outlying countryside. These men were historically accountable only to the white electorate, with whom their relationships were close and consequential. They quickly grasped that there was little reason to fear federal intervention, for they controlled the early investigative processes in these cases, and they usually had good ties with the FBI investigators, who were also "locals." And small-town police departments—for example, those that featured in the cases of Willie Carlisle and Edgar Thomas—emulated the practices of southern sheriffs, exerting ironhanded control over Black communities.

Whether they were themselves enacting the violence, as in the Middle District cases, or collaborating with private actors, or turning a blind eye, these sheriffs and local police were the centrifugal force in the regime of racial terror. Multiple actors played a role, including prosecutors, judges, defense lawyers, and juries, but the police were the sine qua non of the system. Where these crimes were concerned, policing practices made it hard to distinguish between violence authorized by formal law, illegal police violence, and vigilante crimes, for the mob and the police used terror jointly, often collaboratively. Indeed, mob law sometimes simulated the formal legal process: during the lynching era vigilantes often would hold mock trials of their victims, replicating the gestures of justice even in the chaos of the mob. White supremacist groups and the police held common views about what

---

* Although Justice Black was writing in 1971, the term "Our Federalism" captured ideas about federal–state relationships that dated back to the founding era.

constituted breaches of the racial order, even if they did not always agree on sanctions. In short, the state did not hold a monopoly on the lawful use of physical violence; rather, it benefited from loaning out its coercive power. Moreover, the validation of terror expanded the armory and the army available to the sheriffs and small-town chiefs beyond what formal law afforded them. Neither terror nor formal law alone could hold the race line. To gain maximum control over Blacks, it was essential for terror to become law. Law needed terror, and terror needed law.

Bluesmen captured well, typically in three short lines, these sheriffs' hold over their lives. Charley Patten wearily bemoaned the absolute power of Sheriff Purvis of Belzoni, Mississippi, in 1934:

> When I was in prison it ain't no use a screamin and cryin'
> Mr. Purvis the onliest man could ease that pain of mine.

And Barefoot Bill, in 1929, recorded this verse:

> I got my babe in jail and I can't get no news
> I don't get nothing but the mean old high sheriff blues.

"OUR FEDERALISM" left these sheriffs and police chiefs completely to their own devices for the first three decades of the twentieth century. The Justice Department's efforts to change these dynamics may have begun in the late 1930s, but they did not bear fruit until the late 1960s. When, in 1939, with the support and encouragement of President Roosevelt, Attorney General Frank Murphy established the Civil Liberties Unit, it was staffed by fewer than ten lawyers. Sounding a triumphal note, Murphy, the former Detroit mayor and Michigan governor with a civil rights orientation whom Roosevelt would later appoint to the Supreme Court, wrote the president that "for the first time in our history the full weight of the Department will be thrown behind the effort to preserve in this country the blessings of liberty, the spirit of tolerance, and the fundamental principles of democracy." Congratulating Roosevelt in a tone that was at once solemn and giddy, he observed that "the creation of this unit . . . with all the emphasis it places upon protection of the civil liberties of the individual citizen and of minority groups is one of the most significant happenings in American legal history."

But Attorney General Murphy and the president he served vastly miscalculated the scale and character of the civil rights violations that would fall under the jurisdiction of the new unit, the inadequacy of the laws at hand, and the structural and political barriers to effective federal enforcement. As soon as it opened its doors, the CRS began receiving complaints from all over the country. Attorney General Francis Biddle would later recall that "[o]nce the Unit was established complaints poured in, not only from victims of the illegal acts but from their fellow townsmen, from whites as well as Negroes, often from local law enforcement officials who found themselves powerless to deal with the situations they reported, and from groups organized to protect civil liberties."

Seeking both to concentrate civil rights criminal enforcement within the CRS and to clarify the Justice Department's legal authority to handle lynching as well as police brutality, in May 1940, the section circulated a memorandum interpreting Sections 51 and 52, affirming that these two laws protected a right not to be lynched. The duty fell on state officials to protect residents "against a lynching mob or against bands attacking meetings or strikers or reds." The memorandum continued: "should the jailor . . . turn over the keys to the lynchers . . . the official's failure to protect amounts to discriminatory action in unleashing unlawful forces as a direct consequence of his unique position as an official, and both he and the private parties appear subject to Federal prosecution." But, prophetically, in the spirit of "Our Federalism," the guidelines also struck a cautionary note. CRS's leadership warned that because prosecutions of law enforcement officials under

Sections 52 "may arouse antagonism on States' rights grounds, for jury reasons, and perhaps also as a matter of constitutional law," they should not resort to the law "except in cases of flagrant and persistent breakdown of local law enforcement either in general or with respect to a particular type of case."

Nothing in the law itself limited its application to flagrant cases. This policy decision clipped the unit's wings before it made its way out of the nest. Three concerns lay behind this policy of restraint: antagonism from state political leaders; jury nullification; and murky "constitutional issues." In 1940, just a year after the CRS was established, Attorney General Robert Jackson convened a meeting of federal and state law enforcement officers from across the country. The southerners in attendance took the occasion to vociferously denounce the freshly chartered section. Seeking to mollify them, the conference confirmed in its final report that "the protection of civil liberties and the prevention of mob violence is primarily the responsibility of state and local governments." The section repeatedly acceded to these pressures to assuage local authorities, operating on the demonstrably groundless presumption that "a tactful word from a United States Attorney often persuades local police officers, who are perhaps unaware of the existence of federal criminal statutes which they may be violating, to alter their conduct."

In its early years, the CRS's work was also hampered both by its reliance for investigations on J. Edgar Hoover's notoriously antagonistic FBI and by the recalcitrance of local federal prosecutors in the South. These prosecutors were for a range of reasons not well positioned to enforce the criminal civil rights statutes. Traditionally the US Attorney enjoyed considerable autonomy, which proved to be problematic across the spectrum of the Justice Department's program. Until 1953, when they were forbidden to do so, a good many US Attorneys practiced law on the side, and virtually all of them depended, if not for their livelihoods then for their political ambitions, on close ties to the business and political power structures of the communities they served. Their

perception of what constituted "evidence" and "truth" was tightly
linked to local legal practice and the racial dynamics of their communities. Until 1946, the legal staff of the section in Washington was
all white, and not until 1961 would the first Black US Attorney be
appointed. Jury nullification was a disincentive as well, for a prosecutor's success is measured in conviction rates. It was years before Edward
Parker, chastened by his loss in the Gunn case, would go back to the
courtroom with a civil rights case.* And it appears he pursued the Carlisle case in 1950 principally because he was urged to do so by J. Edgar
Hoover.

<hr>

THE CARLISLE CASE was indeed an exception, for generally the section had to contend with the FBI's refusal to conduct thorough investigations that could support the prosecutions. The problem of having
the cases investigated by a hostile FBI surfaced as early as 1940, the
section's first full year of operation. One of the Civil Rights Section's
earliest cases of racist police violence in the twentieth century, if not its
first case, was that of an Atlanta police officer. That year, the accused
officer, W. F. Sutherland, branded sixteen-year-old Quintar South
with an electric device to force him to confess to a burglary at Clark
University's gymnasium. South's white employer reported the matter to local authorities. Officer Sutherland had a reputation for tortur-
ing Black suspects, and Atlantans, Black and white, persuaded state
authorities to initiate a criminal prosecution. But some of Sutherland's
fellow officers testified that they saw no wounds on Quintar South's

---

* In 1949 Parker's office did pursue criminal cases against six officers. Thomas I.
Gantt, ex-chief of Florala City, pled guilty on a showing that he beat five African
American men to force them to confess to crimes and conspired to kidnap three other
men. Gantt's codefendants, ex-officers Harold Kelly and Pat Grimes, were not convicted. Two former Montgomery officers, William D. Durden and Winkler Campbell, were also prosecuted by Parker's office, but with little success.

body, and after a one-day trial, a Fulton County jury acquitted. The United States Attorney for the Northern District of Georgia, Lawrence S. Camp, whose tenure had commenced in 1934, considered the case to be "as perfect as can be found for test, and certainly the Civil Liberties statutes [Sections 51 and 52] have no better friend than our District Judge." The federal trial prosecutor, R. W. Martin, thought he could prove a pattern of brutality by the Atlanta police department in general and by Sutherland in particular. He wanted to introduce evidence that Sutherland was a man of "ill repute, brutality, and petty tyranny" to counter the defendant's claim of good character. However, these lines of proof required intensive investigation by the FBI, and J. Edgar Hoover refused to allow the case to go forward on these terms. "[T]he Atlanta police department is not under investigation in this matter and . . . the only person indicted is Sutherland," Hoover wrote to the CRS. Providing damaging information about the police officer would "rupture the friendly relationship which has been reestablished between this Bureau and the Atlanta Police Department," he added.

The federal judge, Emory Underwood, ruled that Sutherland's conduct, if proven, violated Section 52. Nevertheless, the case was twice mistried and ultimately dismissed because the FBI flatly refused to investigate Sutherland's history of brutality or that of the Atlanta Police Department. The Sutherland case could have been a mere bump in the road, but J. Edgar Hoover pressed his advantage and forced the unit to back off just as it was establishing its basic operating principles. In September 1940, Attorney General Frank Murphy's assistant, Matthew McGuire, in effect endorsed the FBI's decision to torpedo the section's initiatives regarding police torture. Echoing the Supreme Court's opinion in the well-known 1876 case *United States v. Cruikshank*, wherein the court directed victims of racial violence to "look to the states," McGuire observed that while police violence was "atrocious and abhorrent," it was, in his view, "questionable whether a right not to be beaten is secured by any provision of the Constitution or any Federal Statute. It is secured by State laws." McGuire was therefore reluctant to require the FBI to vigorously investigate the Sutherland case. Attorney Alexander Holtzoff, special assistant to the attorney general, was also skeptical about the new unit's legal authority in that case; in his view the claim of federal jurisdictional authority over police brutality under Section 52 was "a little farfetched."

Not only did dismissal of the Sutherland case signal the Civil Rights Section's willingness to subordinate its long-term goals to the FBI's desire to avoid friction with local authorities, but nonintervention was elevated from one of many concerns about case selection to a principle compelled by the Constitution itself. The US Attorney who succeeded Camp, M. Neil Andrews, closed the case, contending that pursuing a third trial against the officer who branded Quintar South "would not be conducive to good race relations."

THE FBI'S DEPENDENCE ON state and local police affected the integrity of its work across the spectrum of federal law enforcement, but the consequences were particularly insidious in the civil rights arena. J. Edgar Hoover acknowledged the peculiar quandary the bureau faced in the South in connection with a 1947 lynching case from Minden, Louisiana. In 1946, John C. Jones, a recently returned veteran, was kidnapped from the Minden jail and killed by a group of men who accused him of "peeping" into the home of a white neighbor and spying on the man's wife. Snatched from the sheriff's custody, Jones was driven to a bayou, tortured, and killed. Jones's nephew, who was arrested with his uncle, was whipped and left for dead near the bayou. The NAACP's Louisiana executive secretary, Daniel Byrd, read about Jones's death in a New Orleans newspaper and, sensing that it was a lynching, sounded a national alarm. The Civil Rights Section brought charges under Section 51 and 52, but a jury acquitted the defendants. In his testimony before the President's Committee on Civil Rights that same year, the FBI chief observed that the case against the men who lynched John Jones was "the best . . . we have ever made out; we had clear-cut, uncontroverted evidence of the conspiracy." But "local hostilities," he said, posed a high barrier for the FBI investigators and the CRS prosecutors. Hoover told the committee members that

> We are faced, usually, in these investigations, with what I would call an iron curtain, in practically every one of these cases in the communities in which the investigations have to be conducted. Now we are absolutely powerless, as investigators, unless the citizens of a community come forward with information. In other words, our function is to go out and get the evidence. We have to have sources of information, we have got to be able to go to citizens and have them talk freely and frankly to us, so that we may prepare the case for the prosecuting attorney.

Despite these unusually frank remarks, the FBI's refusal to fully cooperate with the CRS in its early years, as reflected in the Sutherland case, affected the Justice Department's initiatives on racial violence for decades to come. It was commonly understood that if the FBI refused to take on a case or follow a particular lead, the section would capitulate and close down the matter. Indeed, as late as 1964, when Lyndon Johnson met with Justice Department lawyers right after the Neshoba County, Mississippi, murder of Michael Schwerner, Andrew Goodman, and James Chaney, the president remarked that the problem in solving the case with alacrity was that there were "three sovereigns" involved—the federal government, the State of Mississippi, and the FBI. The FBI's relationship with local law enforcement was generally based on voluntary compliance and deference to the local power structures, and in the South, where Black lives were concerned, this meant go slow and then go away.

J. Edgar Hoover was particularly wary of the role of the NAACP and other "pressure groups," whose "aggressiveness," he wrote to Attorney General Clark, could lead the Justice Department to accept too many cases for investigation where there was an "improbability of a violation." In 1946—the year John Jones was lynched in Minden and two couples were lynched in Monroe, Georgia—Hoover urged Clark to disregard the anti-lynching campaigns of "vociferous minority groups" because the department could not win such cases and would merely be sending FBI agents on unproductive "fishing expeditions."

In the 1940 case of Elbert Williams, an NAACP member from Brownsville, Tennessee, who was lynched because he sought to vote, FBI investigators focused more attention on whether the Black witnesses they were interviewing were associated with communism than on their accounts of the lynching. As one of Tennessee's NAACP leaders, Milmon Mitchell, put it, the federal agents seemed far more interested in whether the desire of Black people to vote in the state was being instigated by communists than with finding Williams's killers, who, Mitchell complained, could be seen on any day walking the streets of Brownsville.

The FBI and the lawyers for the Civil Rights Section were deeply distrustful of the complainants in police brutality cases. Baseless suspicions about the victims' truthfulness led the unit to require a verified complaint from the victim and a preliminary FBI investigation to obtain the complainant's criminal record before it would proceed with an investigation. (Distrusting Black victims' testimony reprised long-standing courtroom practices, the roots of which lay in the refusal, during slavery, to allow Black witnesses to take the stand. It was, for instance, once a matter of law in North Carolina that "whenever a person of color shall be examined as a witness, the court shall warn the witness to tell the truth.") Victims with police records were deemed particularly untrustworthy. As described in a memorandum from Wendell Berge, the chief of the Criminal Division, to Deputy Attorney General James Rowe, "[t]he Criminal Division thoroughly appreciates that a third-degree complaint against a victim with a bad record is a very different case from one where the victim is a first offender. We also limit investigations to cases of outright brutality." The CRS would act only upon a verified complaint from a victim without a criminal record where the injuries were grave and the evidence of a civil rights violation exceptionally strong. On this policy, the CRS and the FBI were aligned.

———————

IN ITS 1947 REPORT, *To Secure These Rights*, President Harry Truman's civil rights committee took note of the FBI's failure to include police brutality cases as part of its regular law enforcement portfolio. By 1947, federal criminal enforcement had expanded significantly since the post–Civil War period, and no longer was the rallying cry of "dual federalism" a sufficient justification for neglecting constitutional race issues. Observing that the highly sophisticated investigative tools that by then were applied by the FBI in other arenas of criminal investigation were indicative of what was possible, the committee noted the bureau's complaint that civil rights cases were "burdensome and difficult" and that the investigations undertaken were often cursory or flawed. While Truman's committee did not propose remedial steps, it made it clear that the FBI was not facilitating the work of the CRS. And it reiterated that there was no longer any merit to the argument that federal law enforcement lacked the constitutional authority to act.

Aside from the difficult relationship with the FBI and prosecutorial reluctance, there were other obstacles to effective prosecution of racist police violence in the 1940s and '50s. Federal court juries in the South were segregated. And when federal authorities tried to sanction their sheriffs, local white communities uniformly sided with the officers, even when they questioned their actions. In one case where the CRS successfully prosecuted a South Carolina sheriff who routinely beat up Black prisoners, white residents of the county paid the fine that had been imposed by the federal judge. "Are we Southerners going to sit idly by while the federal government arrests, prosecutes, fines, and sends to jail our high sheriff?" one citizen proclaimed. "If the sheriff is guilty of any wrong, the Anderson County grand jury is capable of handling the matter. It's none of Washington's business."

ULTIMATELY, the most challenging bar to effective enforcement was not structural but ideological. Whereas the tenacious confederate "states' rights" narrative outlived its usefulness in other arenas of federal law enforcement, it defined, confined, and realigned civil rights initiatives until the late 1960s. Insurance fraud, tax evasion, antitrust, labor law, and kidnapping all became subject to enhanced federal policing and enforcement. But not civil rights crimes, even though they often involved interstate activity, as with the festival-style lynching that drew mob participants from neighboring states looking for some macabre excitement. Although in the 1930s the Great Depression gave rise to the labyrinthine bureaucracy that some disparagingly term "the deep state" and a pro-federalist understanding of constitutional arrangements, Washington's politicians and government lawyers alike still deemed civil rights criminal enforcement to be the province of the states—and their county sheriffs.

For Black people whose constitutional rights were nullified, it was irrelevant whether arcane, outdated, and ahistorical theories of federalism, or the remixed "Our Federalism," or winner-take-all two-party politics explained their abandonment; abandoned they were. Festering beneath the long shadow of the Rebel defeat was an abiding antipathy for all directives on race matters emanating from Washington that simply would not be uprooted by the New Federalism of the Roosevelt era. Southern politicians eagerly embraced Roosevelt's federal farm relief programs, highway construction, and social security, but hoisted the states' rights flag on all matters involving race.

In the 1943 prosecution for police brutality, the case of Walter Gunn, the lawyer representing the defendant, Alabama sheriff E. E. Evans, argued to the jury that Section 52, the federal statute criminalizing official civil rights violations, was "a Reconstruction measure passed by a vindictive government." In apparent agreement, the jury acquitted Evans.

PART IV
THE *SCREWS* EFFECT

RACIAL VIOLENCE IN THE SUPREME COURT

You people know how the South is to Negroes. So I am asking the Supreme Court to please take it up again.

—*Ethel Davis, writing to Attorney General Tom C. Clark, July 28, 1945*

21

"Look to the States"

Perhaps the most serious blow to an effective federal prosecutorial campaign against racist police brutality was the Supreme Court's impenetrable opinion in 1945 in *United States v. Screws*. The Justice Department's Civil Rights Section was still fine-tuning the scope of its authority over local police crimes, carving out the most promising prosecutorial space between the view expressed by Assistant Attorney General Matthew Maguire in the Quintar South trial in Atlanta—that the cases were constitutionally unsound—and, at the other end of the spectrum, the logic that it was the clear purpose of the Reconstruction Constitution and statutes to address such crimes. Releasing its decision on May 8, 1945, the day World War II ended in Europe, in the *Screws* case the court sought to clarify the terms on which federal juries could convict police officers for brutality. The prosecution had relied on Section 52 of the 1870 Enforcement Act. In a dissent, Justice Owen Roberts argued that such matters were "patently local crime[s]." The majority opinion rejected that view, finding that there was a place for federal prosecutions, but it disastrously muddied the waters, leaving in its wake a baffling interpretation of federal criminal authority under the Reconstruction-era laws that would, for years to follow, handicap the efforts of the Justice Department to meet this challenge.

IN THE *SCREWS* CASE, the Supreme Court was not writing on a clean slate. The previously referenced nineteenth century case of *United States v. Cruikshank* had taken much of the muscle out of the Reconstruction-era criminal laws that were designed to redress racial violence. In that 1875 Louisiana case, the court interpreted the Enforcement Act of 1870—what would later be recodified as Section 51 of the criminal code. The statute criminalized conspiracies by private parties to deprive people of their constitutional rights. The decision in the case effectively stripped would-be Black voters in the South of federal protection. *Cruikshank* accelerated the retreat regime, unleashed the Ku Klux Klan, and would, in 1876, usher in the presidency of Rutherford Hayes. Situated at the heart of the battles that occupied the country between 1867 and 1877, *Cruikshank* dramatically shifted the scales in favor of the former confederacy, cleared a path for white supremacy in the Black-majority states of Mississippi, Alabama, and South Carolina, and paved the way for the Redemption just as definitively as *Plessy* legitimized Jim Crow.

An 1873 massacre in Colfax, Louisiana, led to the federal prosecution that was on review in the Supreme Court. After a disputed Louisiana state election in 1872, the white-supremacist Democratic candidate's supporters invaded the majority-Black Grant Parish courthouse and set upon supporters of the Black Republican candidate, killing somewhere between 60 and 150 people. Most of the dead were fresh out of enslavement. The Department of Justice brought indictments against over a hundred individuals, ended up trying nine of them (most of the remainder having eluded arrest), and, against all odds, convicted three indictees of conspiring to interfere with the rights of two Black Republicans. But in March 1876, the Supreme Court, affirming a circuit court opinion by Justice Joseph P. Bradley (which white Democrats in Colfax celebrated by slitting the throat of a random Black man), reversed the convictions.

Although the Supreme Court did not declare the federal criminal

Black residents of Colfax, Louisiana, gather their dead after a massacre at the Grant Parish courthouse in 1873.

law, Section 51, to be unconstitutional in the *Cruikshank* case, it did sow doubt about its viability to address the kind of hate crimes that had taken place in Colfax. In an opinion that made no mention of the Civil War or the pervasive violence that had motivated Congress to adopt the Enforcement Act, and barely mentioned the bloody details of the massacre itself, the court found the indictments in the case improper because they did not precisely specify which constitutional rights of the victims the killers had violated. As to the prosecutors' theory that the massacre constituted a conspiracy to violate the constitutionally protected voting rights of the Black victims, the court ruled, absurdly and disingenuously, that the prosecutors failed to charge that the perpetrators were acting out of racial animus as distinguished from mere political antipathy—even though somewhere between 60 and 150 Black men were murdered in the attack as against three whites, one of whom may have died from friendly fire. "We may suspect that race was the cause of the hostility," opined Chief Justice Morrison Waite for the court, "but it is not so averred." And the court concluded that under the Fourteenth Amendment, Congress could only protect a specific set of individual rights against violation, and only violations by state actors. In 1875, for example, the right to life was deemed a "natural right," which, according to the court, was not protected by the federal Constitution but rather by state law. Hence, the thinking went, it was for Louisiana, and not the federal government, to pursue criminal remedies for the slaughter in Colfax.

The effect of *Cruikshank* on Black political participation was immediate. Perhaps its most lasting impact was its aggressive embrace of the theory of dual federalism—the idea that the state and federal governments had distinct and exclusive spheres of regulation and influence. While the court's opinion did not prevent federal involvement in racial violence cases, it endorsed the view that states bore major responsibility for such prosecutions. Writing for the majority of the court, Chief Justice Waite declared that victims of civil and political rights violations must "look to the states" for their remedies. "The power for that purpose was originally placed there," he proclaimed, and—relying on pre–Civil War precedents—concluded that "it has never been surrendered to the United States." Black Louisianans had to depend on their former owners to protect their newly gained federal rights.

Although the Supreme Court did uphold some convictions where municipal authorities actively blocked Black voters in the early post-Reconstruction years, its commitment to dual federalism defined its approach on virtually every civil rights issue during this period, including women's suffrage. This cramped vision of the Reconstruction Amendments would limit their utility for years to come. And federal prosecutors were quick to heed the message: after Judge Bradley's circuit opinion in *Cruikshank*, the attorney general directed his deputies to cease prosecuting cases under the Enforcement Act until the conclusion of the appeal to the Supreme Court, and the local federal caseload didn't return to its pre-*Cruikshank* numbers after the high court judgment.

At the turn of the century, just a year after it had decided, perversely, in *Lochner v. New York* that bakers in New York enjoyed a constitutionally protected right to be free from state labor laws, the Supreme Court took on a case raising the question of whether the US Constitution also protected Black workers in Arkansas from violence meant to drive them away from their jobs. An inquiry in 1906 from William G. Whipple, the United States Attorney for the Eastern District of Arkansas, marked the beginning of *Hodges v. United States*. Whipple wrote to Attorney General Philander C. Knox that he was "about to enter upon an important prosecution" involving "white-capping." He elaborated that "[a]n inferior class of white men feeling themselves unable to compete with colored tenants combined to drive them out of the county. The movement is denounced by all the respectable white element irrespective of party." The attorney general granted Whipple's request to proceed and allocated funds for the case. The victims, all Black workers, had labor contracts to work for a lumber company in Cross County. A mob of whitecappers marched to the lumber yard with the intent of preventing the Black men from fulfilling their contracts. The Supreme Court reasoned that in order to proceed against the whitecappers, who were private actors, under Section 51, the same conspiracy statute *Cruikshank* interpreted, the authority Congress needed in order to adopt Section 51 had to be located in the Thirteenth Amendment. But then the court cut the legs out from under the Thirteenth Amendment, ruling that it could not be interpreted to protect people who were no longer technically enslaved from racial violence. It rejected the argument that the right to be free from racial violence was, like voting, guaranteed by the Constitution. In the view of the court, the purpose of the Thirteenth Amendment was to emancipate Blacks, not to "commit that race to the care of the Nation." Echoing *Cruikshank*, the court reasoned that rights that were truly fundamental fell under the protective wing of the states rather than the federal government.

Hence the right to due process—at stake in *Cruikshank*—and the right to enter into a labor contract—implicated in *Hodges*—were, vis-à-vis private offenders, meant to be protected by states that were still flying the Confederate flag.

While the scope of Section 51 was thus narrowed, Section 52, prohibiting state actors from interfering with constitutional rights, essentially lay fallow from the time of its enactment until the 1940s. In part, the statute was ignored because before the retreat from Reconstruction, the Justice Department was focused on violence enacted by private parties. *Cruikshank* then chilled any incentive the Justice Department might have had to utilize Section 52 against southern sheriffs. It would not be until 1941—and then by a slim majority—that the court would confirm, in a case that did not raise racial questions, that Section 52 governed a state actor's unconstitutional conduct.

———————

THE CRIMES OF A SHERIFF in Baker County, Georgia, would lead to a ruling nearly as devastating as *Cruikshank*. Sheriff Claude Screws's villainous reputation was widespread long before his case reached the Supreme Court in 1945. In 1938, the sheriff came to the attention of Thurgood Marshall, by way of a letter from Oscar Ashley and his wife, Alice. Residents of Florida, the Ashleys complained that one night when they were traveling in Baker County, Georgia, Sheriff Screws and his deputies stopped them, took them into the woods, stripped them of their clothes, and whipped them both, then banished them from the county. Marshall made inquiries, but he never got to the bottom of the matter. Five years later, Marshall, along with William Hastie, filed a friend of the court brief on the side of the Justice Department in the Supreme Court's *Screws* case. It is doubtful Marshall made the connection between the letter he received in 1938 and the famous 1945 case.

22

A "Patently Local Crime"

In late 1942, Robert "Bobby" Hall, a thirty-one-year-old Black man and the eldest of Willie and Lula Hall's seven children, angered Sheriff Claude Screws. One of the sheriff's deputies had, on a whim, or perhaps on the instructions of his boss, appropriated Hall's treasured pearl-handled automatic .45 pistol. Hall, disarmed but protected, he thought, by the Second Amendment, had the audacity to pursue legal action. A grand jury heard Hall's complaint that the pistol had been unlawfully taken from him. Sheriff Screws reminded the jurors who was in charge: if "any of these damn negroes" tried to carry pistols, he would take them from them, he testified, and, grand jury be damned, he refused to return the weapon to Hall. Hall's lawyer then wrote to the sheriff about the gun. On the day the sheriff received the lawyer's letter requesting return of the weapon, somehow, out of thin air an arrest warrant materialized charging Hall with theft of a tire. (An expert retained by the FBI would later verify that much of the warrant was written by Screws himself.)

In January 1943, arrest warrant in hand, Sheriff Screws corralled two local officers to go with him to "get the black SOB and . . . kill him." The sheriff decreed that Hall "had lived too long." The three lawmen whiskeyed up and rehearsed their plans at a local bar. Around midnight they left the bar for Hall's house, boasting to the remaining drinkers that they were going after a Black man who had "got too smart." They mentioned the lawyer, the grand jury, and the gun.

The officers roused Hall and told him about his alleged crime. They also made an offhand reference to the lawyer he had retained to get his gun back from Screws, and dislodged Hall's shotgun from its place on the wall in his home, for good measure. Then they handcuffed their prisoner and drove him to the Baker County Courthouse in Newton, where the jail was located. Working together, the three cops succeeded in getting him out of the cruiser, at which point he was pounced upon by Screws, so eager was he to get on with the night's task. The officers pummeled their prisoner with their fists and beat him with a solid-bar two-pound blackjack. Neighbors, aroused by the commotion, heard the police shouting profanities and hollering to one another, "Hit him again, damn him, hit him again." Hall lost consciousness after twenty or thirty minutes, at which point witnesses heard a gunshot in the courthouse yard. The officers dragged the man's limp body across the

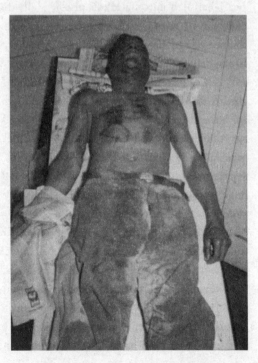

Robert Hall was killed on the courthouse lawn by Sheriff Claude Screws and his deputies in 1943. Screws was successfully prosecuted in a federal court in Georgia, but the Supreme Court reversed the conviction. The NAACP shared this image of Hall with the Department of Justice.

courthouse lawn and threw it onto the jailhouse floor. The prisoner's hands were still cuffed behind him when he took his final breath.

An undertaker would later testify that the skin was scraped off Bobby Hall's long body—he was 6 feet 3 inches and 175 pounds—his right ear was mutilated, and his head was smashed in. Asked to explain the slaying about a month after Hall's death, Sheriff Screws told local reporters that the prisoner had come after him with a shotgun. He elaborated: "I went to work on him with my fists and one of the deputies struck him with a blackjack." The local county prosecutor took no action against Screws and his accomplices. He left the investigation to be conducted by Sheriff Screws himself; neither law school nor life had taught him about foxes and henhouses. "I am an attorney," he later testified in federal court, "not a detective . . . [t]he sheriffs . . . generally get the evidence and I act as the attorney for the state."

The NAACP secured afffidavits from Hall's family members and sent them, along with photographs of the dead man, to the Justice Department, which then prosecuted Screws and the other two officers under Section 52, the Reconstruction-era statute making it a crime for a public official intentionally to violate a person's constitutional rights. A federal jury in Georgia convicted the three of violating Hall's civil rights, and they were each sentenced to three years in jail and a $1,000 fine.

To clarify an important issue of criminal law, the US Supreme Court granted review in the *Screws* case. The court addressed an obscure but deeply consequential legal question: whether Section 52—a law that one of the justices in *Screws* characterized as "for all practical purposes . . . a dead letter" because it had been used so infrequently—required the decision-maker, either jury or judge, to find that the accused had the willful intent to violate a right of the victim that was specifically guaranteed by the Constitution. In a meandering opinion, Justice William O. Douglas concluded that to sustain a conviction under Section 52, the prosecutor had to prove that the accused acted with the specific intent to contravene a specific constitutional protection—in this case, the right to a regular judicial proceeding, rather than, as Justice Douglas put it, "trial by ordeal." The Supreme Court overturned the conviction in the *Screws* case because the trial judge had failed to adequately instruct the jury on what "willful intent" meant.

Three of the dissenting jurists, Owen Roberts, Felix Frankfurter, and Robert Jackson, would have even more thoroughly demolished Section 52. They argued that public officials who violated state law—like the officers in *Screws*—could not be said to be operating under "color of law," as Section 52 required.* In tune with the Confederate narrative, Justice Roberts queried whether federal prosecution of a "patently local crime" was consistent with constitutional federalism and condemned the entire project of federal protection against racial police crimes. Taking aim at the Reconstruction project—and hence at the initiative to uproot the vestiges of slavery—Roberts wrote, "[i]t is familiar history that much of this legislation was born of that vengeful spirit which to no small degree envenomed the Reconstruction era. Legislative respect for constitutional limitations was not at its height and Congress passed laws clearly unconstitutional."

Justice Wiley Rutledge, concurring in the court's decision, could hardly suppress a laugh. The dissenters' argument "comes to this," he wrote. "Abuse of state power creates immunity to federal power. Because what they did violated the state's laws, the nation cannot reach their conduct." It is a defense, he proclaimed, that was neither "pretty" nor "valid," and he forcefully reminded the dissenters that the history of the statute belied any confusion about its aims. "Vague ideas of dual federalism . . . do not nullify what four years of civil strife secured and eighty years have verified. For it was abuse of basic civil and political rights, by states and their officials, that the [Fourteenth] Amendment and the enforcing legislation were adopted to uproot."

Only Justice Frank Murphy—the former Michigan governor who had denied Mississippi's demand to return the Ellises to that state for

---

* The three dissenters also argued that even if state action could be established, the statute was unconstitutionally vague because it did not give adequate notice of what specific constitutional rights were secured from infringement by state officials.

trial, and in 1939 launched the Justice Department's Civil Liberties Unit—voted to sustain the conviction of Screws, noting in full-throttled prose that at stake was the court's duty to protect the "obvious and necessary" right to due process. The arguments in the Supreme Court in the *Screws* case, on October 20, 1944, took place nine days after the court heard *Korematsu v. United States*, the case upholding the executive order mandating the internment of "persons of Japanese ancestry." Justice Murphy, dissenting in *Korematsu*, also scolded his colleagues there for approving an order that "falls into the ugly abyss of racism."

The *Screws* case would define the terms of federal engagement with racially motivated police crimes for decades. (In 1994, Congress finally adopted a law authorizing the Department of Justice to investigate patterns of police abuse.) In effect, *Screws* put CRS prosecutors in the position of having to theorize a constitutionally protected right that the offending officer probably knew nothing about—then teach a jury about it and persuade that jury that it was the motivating factor in the homicide. As Leo Meltzer, the acting chief of the Civil Rights Section, observed in 1950, "[t]he garden variety of police brutality cases . . . are actually occasioned by and result from either a sudden burst of passion on the part of the police officer, or because of some personal revenge or feelings between the officer and the victim. We cannot seriously believe nor sincerely urge in most of these cases that the police officer in question was actually thinking about any Federal right or civil right the victim might have when he was hit." He could have added that where African Americans were concerned, the "garden variety" cases were also actuated by race hatred, which is what should have brought them within federal purview.

An acquittal followed the second trial after the *Screws* case was returned to the federal district court in Georgia. Claude Screws would go on to win election to the Georgia State Senate in 1958. Time and again, in cases all across the country, federal prosecutors asserted that the Supreme Court's opinion in the *Screws* case prevented them from pursuing police slayings. Even before *Screws* came down in 1945, the CRS policy had been to encourage state prosecutors to take these cases, not only because such prosecutions might "arouse antagonism on States' rights grounds" but also because the penalties under Section 51 and Section 52 were far less severe than the state laws criminalizing the same behavior. Claude Screws, for example, could have been tried for capital murder in state court, whereas the maximum penalty under Section 52 in 1943 was a $1,000 fine, a year of imprisonment, or both.* Indeed, federal juries could be forgiven for inferring that no murder could be proven since a state prosecution would, in practice if not in theory, preempt the less severe federal remedy. A vote to convict on the federal charges might, to some jurors, seem to be a vote contradicting the judgment of their local prosecutor that the killing did not contravene the state's laws against criminal homicide.

Judge Bradley, writing in 1874 for the federal circuit court in *Cruikshank*, explained why the federal government had no duty to contain certain forms of racial violence, and *Screws v. United States* reinterpreted his approach for the Jim Crow era. Bradley opined: "The war of race, whether it assumes the dimension of civil strife or domestic violence, whether carried on in a guerrilla or predatory form, or by private combinations, or even by private outrage or intimidation, is subject to [federal jurisdiction]; . . . but any outrages, atrocities, or conspiracies, whether against the colored race or the white which do not flow from this cause . . . are not within the jurisdiction of the United States [unless a state's laws explicitly deny racial equality]."

The reverberations of the *Screws* decision were immediately apparent in the case of Willie Lee Davis, a soldier whose hometown was Summit, Georgia.

---

* In this case, initially Screws and the other officers were each sentenced to 3 years because there were additional federal charges.

23

"Victim . . . of a Quarrelsome Nature"

Born in 1918, near where the Canoochee and Ogeechee Rivers run together in eastern Georgia, Willie Lee Davis (known to his friends as "W.L.") served for two years as an army corporal in World War II. Having returned home on furlough to visit his widowed mother, Davis had ventured out one evening to catch up with friends whom he had not seen since he enlisted in 1941. Dressed snappily in his army uniform, on July 3, 1943, he was enjoying the company of a childhood female friend, twenty-four-year-old Cleo Cotton, at a local juke joint when he was approached from behind by James Bohannon, Summit's police chief. Bohannon would later claim he was responding to a call about a disturbance at the café. Bohannon asked no questions but rather immediately searched Davis, who protested. As the young woman stood by, the police officer slapped the soldier, who quickly made a vain attempt to regain the dignity to which he thought his uniform entitled him. He proclaimed to the police chief that he had no right to assault him because "I'm not your man; I'm Uncle Sam's man [now]." As the scuffle between the soldier and the officer heated up, Davis broke away from the chief's grip and fled into a dark alley near the roadhouse. It was a disastrous miscalculation, for the alley was closed off at the other end, leaving the soldier no escape path. On the scene was the chief's son, who illuminated the alley with a flashlight.

Spotting Davis, now cornered prey, Bohannon shot him in the chest. Midnight struck, bringing with it the nation's birthday. Cleo cried out for help, and Willie Lee Davis lay dead in the uniform of his country on the streets of the town where his mother and her ancestors had lived and labored for generations. He was twenty-five years old.

The deceased soldier's mother, Ethel Davis, a widow, was not a timid person. Her son's slaying transformed her into a tireless civil rights advocate. Prior to this tragedy, Ethel Davis worked as a maid for a white family in Summit; after her husband's death, she was the sole source of support for the couple's four children. Her employer, James Leonard Roundtree, was a state senator, having served six terms in the Georgia House of Representatives. In 2013, Roundtree's grandson, Marvin Roundtree Cox, shared his memories of Mrs. Davis, who had taken care of him during his childhood summers in Summit. She was, he said, a strong-willed and brilliant woman who was singularly fixated on vindicating her son's death.

Although Senator Roundtree's family had lived in Emanuel County for generations (his grandfather, James A. Roundtree—a lieutenant in the Confederate army—gave the town of Summit its name and owned just short of 4,000 acres in the county), he was apparently powerless to assist Mrs. Davis with local authorities. According to Marvin Cox, the town's white citizens allowed Bohannon to retain public office after the incident. Within three months of her son's death, Ethel Davis moved out of Emanuel County. She would devote the remainder of her life to seeking justice in her son's case.

The War Department typically did not vigorously investigate assaults on Black soldiers in the South by local police officials, leading civil rights advocates like William Hastie and Thurgood Marshall to complain bitterly. Within days of Davis's death in July 1943, however, the department launched an investigation. While local authorities had unhesitatingly accepted Chief Bohannon's claim that he shot Davis in self-defense, the army's investigators were convinced that the killing was unjustified, and they urged the Justice Department to prosecute. Initially, an FBI agent based in Georgia, William Kimbrough, con-

Willie Lee Davis was on furlough from the Army when he was killed by the police chief in Summit, Georgia. "I'm not your man, I'm Uncle Sam's man [now]," Davis protested when the chief slapped him. Moments later, he was dead. His mother, Ethel Davis, devoted her life to vindicating her son's murder.

cluded, in effect, that the county authorities had reached the right conclusion; he reported that his "investigation reveals victim to be of a quarrelsome nature." This would have meant the end of the road for any ordinary case in which a police officer claimed self-defense, but Tom Clark, then head of the Justice Department's Criminal Division, refused to close the file. He asked the Georgia-based agents to investigate further, because, he observed, "this is a case of the killing of a negro soldier, [and] I feel we should take special precautions to make sure we have received all relevant testimony."

On October 9, 1944—fifteen months after Davis was killed—the Department of Justice filed a criminal charge under Section 52 against Bohannon in the Southern District of Georgia. But Washington's efforts to pursue the case continued to be thwarted in the state. The US Attorney for the district, J. Saxton Daniel, who served in that position for twenty years, wrote Clark that the case should be dropped because FBI agent Kimbrough's evidence corroborated the defendant's claim of self-defense. Now the assistant attorney general, Clark persevered without local support, and a trial date was set.

But the case never went forward. Once the US Supreme Court agreed to hear arguments in the *Screws* case from Baker County, the Justice Department asked for a delay in the Davis matter, for that case, too, raised the question of what proof satisfied Section 52's "willful intent" requirement. When the opinion came down in *Screws*, reversing the conviction in a case where the facts were arguably more favorable to the prosecution than in the Davis matter, the department dropped the criminal complaint against Police Chief Bohannon. Clark, by then just a month away from assuming the top position in the Justice Department under the new Truman administration, reasoned that although "[t]here was considerable evidence to lend color to the idea that the shooting was an act of discrimination against the Negro [Willie Davis] and not one of self-defense on the part of the policeman . . . we do not believe we could prove . . . specific intent." In sum, racist police brutality was not actionable unless it could be proven that the brutality was performed with the intent to deprive the victim of a federally protected right—and the right to be free from racist violence was not a federally protected right.

After her son's death, Ethel Davis moved to New York to be closer to Thurgood Marshall and others at the NAACP who were assisting her on the case. She wrote directly to Truman Gibson, an aide to the secretary of war; Eleanor Roosevelt; and Attorney General Clark about her son. In one of her letters, she reported that Police Chief Bohannon had beaten her and several other women in Summit. She expressed fear for the life of another son, who had followed in his brother's footsteps and joined the army. She refused to abandon her campaign even after the federal case was dismissed. In July 1945, she received a letter at her home on Long Island from Archibald B. Lovett, the federal judge in

Georgia to whom the case against Chief Bohannon had been assigned. Judge Lovett explained to "Dear Ethel" that the Department of Justice was not confident it could meet the test set forth in *Screws*, but that the county could still prosecute Bohannon for murder. Seeking, perhaps, to quell her repeated claims that race explained the federal authorities' decision-making in her son's case, the judge wrote, "[y]ou may be very sure that in this court the question of race or color had no influence upon the actions of the officers."

In October, well after the Justice Department closed its file, Ethel Davis wrote to Attorney General Clark once again. Willie Davis, she wrote, had been shot to death "for no reason at all." Of Bohannon, she noted that "he has beat us poor old Negroes. . . . it was cold blood murder . . . he was never about nothing . . . he has got some Negroes selling liquor for him . . . he is a crook and all know it." And she reminded Clark that "you people know how the South is to Negroes. So I am asking the Supreme Court to please take it up again."

THE CASES FOLLOWING *Screws* had to bend to its inscrutable rules—and also meet the high bar the department set as to the worthiness of the victim, the probity of the facts, and the extremity of the crime. A Florida case met that test. In a 1947 opinion, a federal appeals court judge waxed eloquently about the setting where a killing took place and the Stephen Foster minstrel song that made it famous: "The beautiful Suwannee River—the mention of which calls to memory a plaintive melody of strumming banjos, humming bees, childhood's playful hours, a hut among the bushes, and a longing to go back to the place where the old folks stay—was the scene of the cruel and revolting crime that provoked the gesture of dealing out justice that is this case." The defendant's cruelty was visited upon Samuel McFadden, who was severely beaten and then forced to jump from a bridge into the Suwannee River by a town marshal named Tom Crews. McFadden's body was pulled from the river by fishermen sometime later. The

Justice Department won its case against Crews and—miraculously, it seemed—held on to the conviction after an appeal.

While a disproportionate number of the Justice Department's police brutality cases addressed crimes against people of color, incidents involving white victims also reached the courts. In 1951, the Supreme Court took the opportunity to revisit its opinion in the *Screws* case in another Florida matter, *Williams v. United States*, this one involving four white workers beaten by a private detective and his associates, hired by their employer, in the course of an interrogation about thefts from the lumber company where they worked. The detective, flashing a badge, took the men to a shack at their workplace and with his associates beat them over the course of three days, using a rubber hose, a pistol, and a sash cord. The ordeal was graphically described in an opinion by Justice Douglas—the author of the court's opinion in *Screws*. "One man was forced to look at a bright light for fifteen minutes; when he was blinded, he was repeatedly hit with a rubber hose and a sash cord and finally knocked to the floor. Another was knocked from a chair and hit in the stomach again and again. He was put back in the chair and the procedure was repeated. One was backed against the wall and jammed in the chest with a club. Each was beaten, threatened, and unmercifully punished for several hours until he confessed." Federal prosecutors in Florida won convictions against some of the assailants on some of the charges. In an unusual exception to the court's interpretations of Section 52, Justice Douglas affirmed the conviction.

Notwithstanding the surprising result in the Williams case, the high bar that *Screws* set alerted federal prosecutors and civil rights activists alike that the Supreme Court could not be relied upon to safeguard constitutional rights in the face of racialized police murder. Nor could federal statutory remedies or state reforms be expected. Organized protest and spontaneous uprisings continued across the South, even when—or especially when—legal claims were maddeningly unavailing. In the 1940s, these activities began to foster alternative theories of change, solidify national Black political consciousness, and spawn a deep cynicism about legal remedies and reform. Though some reforms were put in place—the advent of constitutional criminal procedures, for example—lawless law enforcement persisted. In the 1960s, that cynicism was at the heart of a political journey that would lead people to take to the streets in radical uprisings, North and South, against police violence.

PART V
BLACK PROTEST
MATTERS

24

"Bad Birmingham"

While Thurgood Marshall and others appealed to the Justice
Department to pressure local prosecutors to enforce the federal statutes addressing racial violence, communities across the country
expressed their resistance in other ways. In the South, the practices
of these resistance movements were grounded in the here and now of
daily life, drawing upon concepts of mutuality and racial solidarity,
and bringing together journalists, civic leaders, and creative voices.
Birmingham, Alabama, in the 1940s—at the height of Jim Crow—was
home to one such resistance movement.

The Birmingham civil rights movement that most people know is
the famous one: Bull Connor's dogs; jail cells stuffed to the rafters
with demonstrating children; the lives and deaths of Addie Mae Collins, Cynthia Wesley, Carole Robertson, and Carol Denise McNair
in their Sunday school shoes; the magnetic leadership of Fred Shuttlesworth; Martin Luther King Jr.'s "Letter from a Birmingham Jail."
Television brought this story into American living rooms in the late
1950s and early 1960s, and with it, images of a tinderbox town peopled
by Klansmen and their police allies on the one hand, and a determined
freedom movement on the other. There is a backstory here, on both
sides of this coin. Connor's dogs were on a well-worn path when they
attacked children in 1963, and the people rallying at the 16th Street
Baptist Church that year were the near relations of those who had

participated in protest demonstrations ever since the Great Depression brought Magic City to its knees.

Their stories matter, too, as does their protest, but time and neglect have taken their toll. Set against the mythical, defaming, and exhausting "Negro with knife" stories that filled the white newspapers of the 1940s, and marshaled against the slapdash lies casually tossed about by coroners, medical doctors, prosecutors, and judges—all of whom at one time in their lives submitted to a professional oath—were Black citizens in motion, people who risked their livelihoods and often their lives to create a movement that rivaled, in scope, ambition, and grit the well-known campaigns of the 1960s. It was a movement that circulated deep in the cultural crevices of Black life: it was what they read about in their "colored" newspapers, what they prayed over in church, what their blues were about, and what, in carefully chosen words, they passed on to their children. The organizing tools of these earlier Birmingham activists, yesteryear's Black Lives Matter movement, would be familiar today: mass meetings, strikes, petitions, editorials, appeals to Washington, funerals that assuaged grief and swelled grievance, boycotts, lawsuits, and, too, flash street demonstrations where the fury and frustration of the city's outcasts, people at the bottom, often exploded and overtook the efforts of preachers and professionals to channel and contain Black anger.

Like the threat of violence itself, resistance was ever-present. It was as individual as it was communal, as spontaneous as it was methodical: a veteran, having had enough, moves the color bar on a bus; thousands of miners, in a volatile rage, stage a wildcat strike; a father sues the police to vindicate the shooting death of his fifteen-year-old child. It was this resistance that reinforced both collectivity and identity, re-inscribing events otherwise seen as the accidental encounter between a random victim and perpetrator, and exposing the social order's ubiquitous dependency on anti-Black violence. In Birmingham in the 1940s, a Black person—any Black person—could have been killed by a white person—any white person. And thus every Black person had to make peace with the burden and duty of resistance, reckon with premature death, determine their personal point of no return, and countenance the politics of Black revolt, whether or not they wanted to. Hence the resistance, in its content and continuity, stood as a commanding counterstructure, although each action might have appeared to be a singular blow against a single antagonist. As a cultural phenomenon, the resistance borrowed from and informed Black devotional practice, while its radical cognitive threads linked Ida B. Wells-Barnett to Mildred McAdory, the Birmingham native who marched on miners' picket lines and got arrested for sitting in the front of the bus more than a decade before Rosa Parks did so.

A GOOD DEAL OF the violence in mid-twentieth century Birmingham reflected the battles between Black labor and the companies they worked for, a longstanding combat zone dating back to before the Depression that seems to have intensified at the end of World War II. By the early 1910s, beatings and abductions—arising both from labor disputes that targeted white and Black unionists alike and from the efforts of white workers to secure their racial advantage—were everyday affairs in the mills and mines around Birmingham, making it one of the most violent cities in the country. Putting aside the violence tied to labor organizing, Birmingham was a heartless town for working people, with volatile class and racial divides that could, at the snap of a finger, lead to a man's death. In the 1930s, "Bad Birmingham" recorded the fourth-highest homicide rate in the country, with over 50 murders per 100,000 people. And in the fifties and early sixties, the town was dubbed Bombingham, so commonplace were the blasts that blew up homes and places of worship.* Bull Connor, the town's infamous and long-serving commissioner of public safety, added fuel to these fires, adroitly manipulating the chauvinism and economic insecurities of

---

* There were fifty bombings between 1947 and 1965 in Birmingham, usually against Black families breaching the whites-only neighborhoods.

whites to eviscerate the progressive politics and cross-racial labor solidarity that had begun to take root during the Depression years.

The Ku Klux Klan, which officially resurfaced in 1946, worked
hand in hand with Connor to transform a region that could have been
a center of southern progressivism into a hard-core antilabor, anti-
Black town. Birmingham had always been a Klan town; in 1924, there
were 18,000 Klansmen in a city of 200,000. But the Klan fell out of
favor in the 1920s and '30s, only to be revived by the racial tensions
of the postwar era. By 1947, the Birmingham klaverns boasted 7,000
members. Two related factors contributed to the Klan's revival in the
mid-1940s: Black disenfranchisement thwarted, in one fell swoop,
half of labor's potential vote; and the managing white elites—the
"Big Mules," as Birmingham's industrial and plantation tycoons were
known, and their allies—convinced the white working class to choose
white supremacy over economic empowerment. Not until the climactic Selma-to-Montgomery March in 1965 did the Klan release its grip
on Birmingham.

WHILE THE KLAN CLAIMED its victims, so, too, did the Birmingham
police. In the decade between 1938 and 1948, only one year would pass
without a police killing. Over these ten years, fifty-four Black men
were slain by white police officers. Police killed one lone white man
in that same period—in a city that was about 60 percent white and 40
percent Black. Women, Black and white, were spared until 1949, when
a Black mother and her son were shot to death in their home. There
are many accounts of the mid-twentieth-century protest movements
that took on racist policing in cities like Detroit and New York, but
these campaigns have not generally been associated with Birmingham
and other southern cities. Black people rallied to rein in the police in
urban centers across the South in the Jim Crow era, struggles that often
served as the basis for campaigns around other political and economic
issues. Assaults by the "law" were so endemic, normalized, senseless,

and absurd that they brought Black people together despite their political or economic differences. A well-publicized police shooting caused people to take to the streets, tapping into the rage and trauma engendered by the daily slurs, the abusive language, the threats, the sexual taunts, the racial profiling, the jailhouse beatings, all of it criminalizing a community seeking to be seen as legitimate and worthy. What followed the gunshot or billy club was, on the one hand, an assault on truth, as the white perpetrators rallied around a contrived, shamelessly flimsy fig leaf of a justification and crashed through legal rules, and on the other, an attack on the reputation of the dead person and a terrorizing campaign to silence his family and supporters.

The subsequent protests put thousands in motion in Birmingham, preparing the community for later struggles, and illuminating the common threads knitting together Klan bombings, police violence, prosecutorial racism, and judicial abdication. In this sense these 1940s-era anti–police brutality demonstrations were the formidable precursor to the campaigns of the 1960s, and later, the Black Lives Matter movement.

25

Negroes Are Restless

That the Birmingham police would have unrestricted latitude to harass Black citizens was made clear with the 1939 passage of a local ordinance that made loitering a crime. Birmingham was bustling at the time, with the run-up to the war affording job opportunities and putting cash in the hands of workers previously tied to rural areas. Whites felt threatened by free-roaming, congregating Blacks, particularly in white areas of town. In a white suburb, East Lake, in fall 1939, Black people assembled en masse to protest the shooting death of Junior Watson, an eighteen-year-old Black teenager, by a white dentist. The crowd was angry and frustrated, and one protester brandished an ax. Several people were arrested, but convictions were not forthcoming. Bull Connor, explicitly referencing the demonstration in East Lake, successfully lobbied for the loitering ordinance to address what he suggested was a dangerous gap in the law. A latter-day Black Code, it was, like the turn-of-the-century vagrancy laws, used to remove Black people from public spaces and to give police power to detain protesters.

In April 1941, the ordinance had deadly consequences in Fairfield, a town on the outskirts of Birmingham. John Jackson, a thirty-year-old steelworker, was standing in line with his girlfriend near the Negro entrance to the Fairfield Theatre when police officers arrived to clear the sidewalk on which the moviegoers had congregated. Jackson, apparently not hearing the order to "move on," continued to laugh at something his girlfriend was saying. One of the officers yelled to

Jackson, "What are you laughing at, boy?" and Jackson, still oblivious
to the order to clear the street, responded, "Can't I laugh?" That was
enough to turn on the officer's kill switch. He shoved Jackson into the
back of his car and began pummeling him. Jackson did not make it to
the police station. At the funeral parlor, the mortician took note of four
bullet wounds to the chest and forehead, a broken arm, and a gash in
the head. In his pocket the mortician found draft papers, for, it being
1941, Jackson was scheduled to be called up for duty. The dead man
had drawn a knife in the back seat of their vehicle, the officers claimed.

Jackson's death prompted a boycott of the Fairfield Theatre by Black
patrons, forcing the business to close its balcony. The family retained
a lawyer to pursue prosecutions against the officers. Though the grand
jury declined to indict them, one officer was dismissed from the force,
an unusual exception to the customary disposition of such cases in the
early 1940s.

———

A YEAR AFTER Jackson's slaying, Black protesters assembled again, this
time in the thousands, in the wake of yet another police killing, on
April 8, 1942. In the interim, no fewer than five Black people had been
killed by Birmingham officers, but the slaying of Henry Mathews was
a match in a dry forest. Thirty-seven years old, Mathews had had an
afternoon off from his job as butler and chauffeur to a doctor and his
family, and he spent a good part of it getting a haircut and then hanging
out at the barbershop in downtown Birmingham. Around 6:30 in the
evening on April 8, he ventured onto one of the busiest intersections
in the Black section of town, where a traffic officer, C. W. Hopkins,
stopped him, accusing him of jaywalking. Moments later, Mathews
was on his hands and knees in the middle of the street, having been
knocked to the pavement by the pistol-wielding officer. The bullets,
four or five of them, came next, into Mathews's back. There was no
saving him. There were scores of witnesses, all of them Black, including a postman and two ministers. The officer's claim: after he stopped

Mathews, a struggle ensued, in the course of which Mathews "made a strenuous effort" to grab Hopkins's weapon, requiring him to shoot in self-defense.

The reaction to Mathews's death was swift and furious, in no small measure because his employers, Dr. Frank E. Nabers and his wife, Braxton Bevelle Nabers, disputed Hopkins's account of the murder. The Naberses were white upper-crust Birmingham through and through, Frank's father having been a lieutenant in the Confederate army and Braxton's father, Braxton Comer, an Alabama governor and US senator. It was reported that Dr. Nabers, together with another white doctor, examined Mathews's body and identified five bullet wounds to the back and none in the front. While her husband conducted that second autopsy, Braxton Nabers gathered eyewitness testimony to the effect that Officer Hopkins had slapped Mathews, then tripped him, throwing him to his knees, whereupon he shot him. Mrs. Nabers added her personal endorsement of Mathews's character: "he was very intelligent, honest and a superior servant . . . He never touched [liquor]." Ministers also attested to Mathews's sterling reputation.

A week after the slaying, a mass meeting drew 3,000 protesters. A Baptist Convention, comprising 108 churches with a constituency of 30,000—"of the best people of our race," the petitioners proclaimed—submitted a petition to the city commission demanding an investigation. The ministers reminded the white civic leaders of their patriotism, noting that "we have always been loyal and even in this present crisis we are . . . going to continue to do so." But they also had a warning: in the wake of the "brutal treatment" of which the Mathews murder was but one example, Black people were "restless."

In this case the district attorney responded, perhaps because with a pending visit from a national civil rights agency—the Fair Employment Practices Committee, appointed by President Roosevelt in 1941—the eyes of the nation would shortly be on Birmingham. He brought thirty-five witnesses before a grand jury—which refused to indict the officer. It was a deafening message for Blacks and whites in the city. Black protest, even hat-in-hand petitions and mass meetings, brought no relief to the Black community, and yet such protests were all that availed them where the ballot box was shut tight. And whites took notice of the alacrity with which white witnesses, along with Blacks, were dismissed when it came to police brutality. The city's law enforcement establishment closed ranks so tightly that even highly respected white citizens like Dr. and Mrs. Nabers could not get through. As the war propaganda machines pumped out missives about the fight for democracy, avenues for redress in Magic City seemed to be narrowing.

Two months after the killing, in June 1942, the Fair Employment Practices Committee held its first hearing in the South in Birmingham. The town's industrial leaders joined forces with political figures to condemn what they saw as federal intrusion. Seemingly ignorant of the interracial workspaces belowground, where coal was collected, Governor Frank Dixon claimed the federal government was trying to "force negroes and white people to work together, intermingle with each other," and went on to pledge that "I will not permit the citizens of Alabama to be subject to the whims of any Federal Committee and I will not permit the employees of the State to be placed in a position where they must abandon the principles of segregation or lose their jobs."

———————

THE NEGROES WERE restless in 1942, and also bitterer in their judgment that no remedies would be forthcoming from public officials in Birmingham, if an incident four months after Henry Mathews's slaying was any indication. The headline in one of the city's two Black newspapers, the *Birmingham World*, was both alarming and wearily familiar: "Negro Shot Six Times by White Bus Driver." Why six times? What was it about the Black body that invited that much firepower? And what was the "crime?"

The victim was B. J. Butcher, a twenty-three-year-old janitor at a local paper company. On August 20, he put his fare in the wrong change box on a city bus. When he asked for change, the driver, Sam Truitt, told him, "I ain't gonna give you nothing back. Git it." Butcher sighed and said to no one in particular but within the driver's earshot, "Ah, white folks. I just forgot." When he got off the bus, the driver shut off the motor and left the passengers, mouths agape, behind. He drew the gun he was authorized to carry as a bus driver.

Writing in 1918 about slavery, the white supremacist historian U. B. Phillips observed that "all white persons were permitted and in some regards required to exercise a police power over slaves." It was a frame of mind that hung around through Jim Crow—and put a gun in a bus driver's hands. Truitt chased Butcher down the street for half a block and then shot him six times. The dirty work done, the driver climbed back up in his seat and turned the engine back on. According to news reports, several hundred people poured into the streets immediately following the shooting. When, on subsequent days, the driver passed through the neighborhood where the incident occurred, demonstrators threw rocks at his bus, breaking the windows.

Butcher survived the shooting, and as soon as he could make his way out of Birmingham, he did. Leaving behind his mother, whom he had been supporting, he moved to Detroit and got a job working in the kitchen on the SS *South American*, one of the majestic passenger steamers working the waters of the Great Lakes.

26

"Mr. Van"

In Birmingham, the "Pittsburgh of the South," it was not just county
and city employees and bus drivers who wielded police power: the
big mining companies maintained private police forces to keep workers in line. These units figured in two cases from towns established by
the US Steel Corporation's southern subsidiary, the Tennessee Coal,
Iron and Railroad Company (TCI)

Predominantly Black Westfield started as a mining camp in 1906
and was later turned into a company town in what was known as the
Birmingham District. US Steel prided itself on offering its workers a
"model mining village" in keeping with its policy of "welfare capitalism." Located just south of Birmingham and next to Fairfield, site of
the movie theatre boycott, Westfield was where the civil rights lawyer
and federal judge U. W. Clemon and the Giants outfielder Willie Mays
grew up. Mays's father, Cat Mays, worked in the mines and played
baseball for the Birmingham Industrial League. It was a tight-knit
community, and tightly controlled by TCI.

An encounter between the company police and a local Westfield
resident in 1946 followed the same time-worn, wretched script: an
aggressive Black man, a "white" space, a "molested" white woman,
and a valiant police officer defending his community. William Daniel, twenty-one years old, and his new wife, Ruby, eighteen, were
doing some Christmas shopping on December 21, in the Westfield TCI
commissary, where customers made their purchases with company

scrip. William Daniel had been in the mines only six months, having returned to Alabama earlier that year after two years in the army. On this particular day, a white female clerk who waited on Daniel reported to a store manager that Daniel had insulted her. Called to the scene by the manager, officer J. A. Vanderford ("Mr. Van") ordered Daniel to follow him out of the store. It is not clear what the men said to each other, if anything, but within minutes, Vanderford shot and killed Daniel on the sidewalk in front of the commissary.

The *Birmingham News* offered an account of the event that positioned Daniel as the threat, both to the white woman and to Vanderford. E. L. Allman, chief of the Fairfield Police Department, reported that Vanderford ejected Daniel from the store "for questioning in regards to a complaint made by a white woman employee [. . . that he] made some insulting remarks . . . toward her." The officer shot Daniel because, he said, when he tried to question him, Daniel put his hand into his pocket. While the actual precipitant leading to Daniel's death remains unclear, it may well be that Daniel, a recently returned army veteran, chafed under the rules of the commissary, which subjected Black customers to constant surveillance and required them to make their purchases at long, segregated checkout lines, fortifying the hazardous Jim Crow terrain that had been cracked, if ever so slightly, in the mines where he worked side by side with white workers, and on the battlefields he had left behind him. It did not matter to Vanderford that Daniel had committed no crime: even in Alabama, there was no law against "insulting a white woman." But while the insult (if there was one) was not a crime, the implication was that every Black man was a potential rapist, and therefore a criminal. This, then, was anticipatory racial policing, which the French philosopher Michel Foucault so incisively defined: those "supervisions, checks, inspections, and varied controls that, even before the thief has stolen makes it possible to identify whether he is going to steal."

The Southern Negro Youth Congress took up the Daniel case and retained Birmingham's only Black private investigator, Frank Hunter, to conduct an inquiry. Hunter interviewed Ruby Daniel, who told the

SNYC's investigators that she and her husband had made some pur-chases and were headed out of the store when another customer told them that a white clerk was accusing Daniel of "brushing up against her." The customer urged Daniel to leave quickly, but her husband protested that he had done nothing wrong. Responding to the man-ager's request, Officer Vanderford came into the store almost imme-diately and ordered Daniel to leave. Just as Daniel reached the door to leave, his wife related, Vanderford shot him several times. Other witnesses recalled that Vanderford told Daniel he was under arrest, although at the time Vanderford likely did not yet know what he had been called to the scene for. Daniel, some said, protested that he had not done anything, at which point "Mr. Van" told him to take his hands from his pockets, and then shot him. As Daniel lay dying amid the Christmas decorations and shoppers, he moaned that he "had been shot for nothing," and prophesied that "God would punish" the man who shot him.

The Southern Negro Youth Congress gathered statements from Ruby and several other witnesses and succeeded in obtaining a grand jury investigation. However, the "William Daniels Defense Com-mittee" was no match for TCI. The witnesses who could have been helpful either worked for the company or lived in company housing, and Vanderford, it appears, kept them away from the proceedings—or, failing that, forced them to testify in his favor. The grand jury declined to indict Vanderford. William Daniel's family fled to Chi-cago. Ruby, his young bride, remained in Westfield, but her life was in ruins. She passed away at the age of twenty-three, five years after her husband's murder.

Longtime Westfield resident Demetrius Newton knew William Daniel. In 2013, he recalled that, as usual, gossip abounded among whites about how the victim's own behavior got him killed. "There were two or three rumors that the white folks was saying that he was feeling on the white woman." A different story circulated among Black people. "The other one being that the white woman asked him some-thing and he forgot to say 'yes, ma'am.' And I don't know which rumor is correct. Knowing him I would doubt that there is any credence to the first rumor."

Demetrius Newton's recollection captures how whites and Blacks, living in separate universes, thought about incidents of police brutality, and how they interpreted them to make sense of white aggression and Jim Crow rule. For whites, narratives of Black transgression—"feeling on the white woman"—made police violence necessary where otherwise it might be considered excessive, just as Black criminality and sexual aggression made lynching, chain gangs, convict labor, political disfranchisement, educational deprivation, and residential segregation necessary. For Blacks, the rumor about the failure to address the clerk as "ma'am" tapped into a resistance narrative, reflecting what today might be seen as a line in the sand against the microaggressions of white supremacy. Maintaining the narrow spaces that Jim Crow consigned to Blacks—back of the bus, back of the store, back of the line—depended on the servile obedience of grown men who, particularly after the war, were acting in unscripted and unexpected ways. And whites were pushing them back, anxiously and violently. These clashes played out in public spaces in towns like Westfield, where Blacks who crossed into racially restricted areas—perhaps unwittingly, perhaps not—were judged unruly, out of place, and criminal. White women were vectors for this racial disease, but they were also at the heart of white innocence. Their purity, their whiteness, their virtue—all, supposedly, the object of Black desire—constructed at once the Black demon and the white defender.

———

IF YOU SEARCH FOR the name of Captain "C.T." Butler, Birmingham social justice activist, in the massive literature chronicling the mid-twentieth-century labor and civil rights movements, you will be disappointed. Nor does his life story appear in any of the copious feminist literature deconstructing the linked mythologies of the Black male sexual aggressor and the passive white female victim. *Jet* magazine and the

Black press, particularly the *Birmingham World*, reported on Butler's case, but for the most part it survives as one name among seventy on an NAACP list created in Birmingham in the 1940s. His absence from history reveals the lacunae, in some ways intentionally created, in our knowledge about Black militancy in the age of Jim Crow. Two thousand miners risked their jobs to protest his fate. What was in it for them?

C.T. Butler grew up on a farm in Alabama. He moved with his family to Edgewater, another company town four miles north of Westfield, in about 1923. He would have been twenty-eight years old. The mines had for years been sucking men off the plantations, and, following thousands of other Black men, Butler heeded the call. By the time he arrived in Birmingham, the United Mine Workers had already launched several campaigns to organize miners like him. Having lost a bitter campaign in 1921, the union retreated from Alabama, but Depression-era legislation strengthened the hand of labor across the country, and in 1934, the UMW was able to force TCI to recognize it as the bargaining agent for all of its Alabama mines. Butler's local, Edgewater #6256, was launched that year. In Birmingham the union's constituency was largely Black, for those were the men digging up the coal. Although whites and Blacks worked side by side and depended upon one another in the mines, the color line defined their relationships both to the union and to the company. Relegated to the dirtiest and most dangerous jobs, Black miners lived with their families in the least desirable parts of the company's towns.

Captain "C.T." Butler, a miner and organizer for the United Mine Workers, was killed by security guards in Edgewater, Alabama.

During the 1930s, Birmingham was, according to one historian, "like a stirred ant bed," with the "specter of tens of thousands of Birmingham area unionists constitut[ing] an apocalyptic vision capable of throwing the Big Mules into full scale panic." By the end of the 1930s, almost 50,000 workers in the Birmingham region were in the union. Fully two-thirds of that number were African Americans. Without leaders like Butler advocating for the union in Black churches and neighborhoods, the UMW would not have won the 1934 election.

A pastor as well as a miner, Butler was a gifted organizer. Of compact build, good-looking, and usually traveling with a pipe hanging from his mouth, he was an inspiring speaker who could rouse a union meeting as easily as a Baptist congregation. He served as vice president of the UMW's Edgewater Local, which was the highest position a Black man could attain (notwithstanding the local's majority Black membership). In the mines six days a week, on Sundays Butler pastored the First Baptist Church of Ensley, also a position of considerable achievement in the Birmingham community. Father of thirteen and grandfather of eight, Butler was a member of the Parent Teacher Association at his children's school and participated in the activities of the Birmingham NAACP. One of his children, Vida Rouse, recalled in 2019 that her father "cared a lot for the school and the teachers. He believed in us being well educated, and the whole community, educated." Her father enjoyed calling out the names of each of his children, one after the other, from the thirty-year-old to the four-year-old. She remembered, as well, that her father drew a crowd whenever he spoke about union matters. At community barbeques "he would stand on the porch and speak to the surrounding community about the union. . . . All the people . . . would come and hear him . . . it would be large crowds."

In the early 1940s, wary of Butler's organizing prowess, TCI retaliated by evicting him from his home in Edgewater Village, where the family rented a small house and garden plot. At the time, TCI was trying to oust the UMW and install a company union in its place. The family was forced to move to Capstown, another Black mining community on the outskirts of Edgewater, also owned by TCI. There Butler got right back to his organizing work. Capstown was known as a widows' village, for many of the families were headed by Black women whose husbands had been killed in the mines or succumbed to black lung disease. Butler launched a campaign to get the UMW to demand that the company pay widows' pensions to aid these families.

On June 5, 1948, around six o'clock in the morning, Butler, dressed for the mines and with his pipe in his mouth, was walking to work, as was his daily custom, through a white residential section of Edgewater Village, when he was accosted by Mr. Van—J. A. Vanderford and another TCI police officer, Paul B. Thomas. Also present were two Jefferson County sheriff's deputies. While the Jefferson County officers stood by and watched, within minutes, the TCI officers shot Butler four times in the back, two shots per man.

What happened next came as a complete surprise to TCI—and to the UMW. Two days after the slaying, more than half of its 4,500 coal miners across the Birmingham District, apparently convinced that TCI was covering up an assassination, quit the pits. The wildcat strike forced TCI to close all six of its mines. The strikers, some of whom

Brutality In Ala. City Probed

BIRMINGHAM —(ANP)— One case of police brutality, another of a sheriff's lynching of a Negro preacher and a third involving a mob taking an NAACP worker out and beating him, were being investigated by the Birmingham branch of the NAACP here.

1. The NAACP has reports that Mrs. Minnie O'Neal, case worker for the Traveler's Aid Society was "grabbed, shoved and pushed" by a police officer at the Birmingham Greyhound Bus station on June 7.

2. Rev. C. L. Butler, 53, in the community of Cappstown, was killed in the presence (and by one) of two sheriff's deputies and two company policemen about 6 a. m. Saturday, June 5.

Rev. Butler was an ardent union man and carried a card with the United Mine Workers. He had 13 children and 8 grand children. Funeral services for him were held last Sunday.

Five TCI mines were on strike Saturday through Wednesday, namely, Edgewater, Docena, Wylam, Short Creek and Concord.

Coroner J. T. McCollum returned a verdict o justifiable r turned a verdict of justifiable homicide.

3. Another report said that a "mob of four white men posing as Tarrant City policemen" came to the home of Henry Howard of Tarrant City June 3, took him out and beat him so severely that Howard is still in the hospital.

The death of fifty-three-year-old union organizer Captain Butler at the hands of the company's security guards led to a wildcat strike that pulled two thousand workers out of the mines.

must have recalled Vanderford's slaying of William Daniel two years earlier, stayed off the job for four or five days and insisted on a fair investigation. Although the workers tried to garner UMW support for the work stoppage, the union refused to condemn Butler's murder. To the contrary, it urged the men to go back to work as "no contract dispute [was] involved," thus reinforcing the UMW's reputation among some of its membership as a union as likely to break a strike as it was to initiate one.

A few days after Butler was killed, with the strike ongoing, the officers told newspaper reporters that they had been responding to a complaint by a white family in Edgewater that the fifty-three-year-old minister had been "molesting" or "annoying" one of their seven children, a fifteen-year-old girl, early in the morning on his way to the mine. The officers alleged that Butler had leered at the girl and had dropped a letter over her fence asking to see her. They had the girl leave a blank piece of paper near her house to trap Butler, and claimed they saw him pick it up, at which point they accosted him. Butler, they said, pulled a gun from the front of his shirt, causing them to fire their weapons. The coroner promptly ruled the matter one of self-defense—even though the bullets entered Butler's body from the back.

Although the union for which he had given his life forsook Butler, his family fought for years to clear his name. At the time of the incident, his brother, Peru Butler, told the *New York Amsterdam News* that "Reverend Butler never in his life carried a pistol." The *Pittsburgh Courier* characterized Butler's murder as part of "Birmingham's wave of terror . . . alike in every respect to Hitler's Nazi inquisition," and reported that Butler was "the seventh colored citizen killed by police in the Birmingham area within 70 days, or an average of one every 10 days in Jefferson County."

Allie Glass Butler, Captain Butler's widow, enlisted the help of an attorney, whose efforts to vindicate her husband's death in court were supported by the Birmingham branch of the NAACP, of which Butler was a leader. She sued the US Steel Corporation, at the time the largest private employer in the state of Alabama, accusing the company's two officers of an unprovoked and unjustified killing. There was no support for the testimony of the TCI officers that Butler had pulled a gun, and no gun was ever produced for the jury. There was no evidence of any relationship between the white girl Butler was accused of "molesting"—no conversation, no touch, nothing except the alleged note that triggered the investigation—which Butler himself never had the opportunity to testify about. After deliberating for seven minutes, an all-male, and likely all-white jury brought in a $10,000 verdict for Mrs. Butler. It was not much, certainly not enough to stretch over the needs of thirteen children, but it was sufficiently vindicating to be covered in *Jet* magazine.

The Alabama Supreme Court twice considered US Steel's appeal of the case, and twice sustained the jury's decision in opinions that close readers could reasonably interpret as confirming the verdict that had come in the immediate aftermath of the killing by the 2,000-plus miners who walked off the job: Butler was slain in cold blood by TCI's policemen, either at the behest of or with the knowledge of TCI's bosses, as he walked to the mine where he had labored six days a week for a quarter of a century. The Jefferson County deputies declined to testify that Captain Butler had a gun, or to corroborate the TCI story about Butler's attempt to date the white teenager. Nor did the coroner support Mr. Van's claim

Husband Slain by Alabama Whites

Pastor's Widow Wins $10,000

Labor Leader-Coal Miner Shot in Back In '48; Killing Caused Mine 'Walkout'

BIRMINGHAM, Ala.—Mrs. Allie Glass Butler, widow of the late Rev. Captain L. Butler, who was shot in the back and killed by sheriff's deputies at the Tennessee Coal and Iron Company, June 6, 1948, was awarded damages of $10,000 by an all-white jury here during Holy Week. She had sued the U. S. Steel subsidiary for $50,000.

The then 53-year-old Baptist pastor, father of thirteen children and grandfather of eight, coal miner and vice president of the Edgewater Local of the United Mine Workers of America, was the eighth Negro killed in the Birmingham area in a period of seventy days when the four white men shot him in 1948. At that time a coroner's jury ruled the shooting was "justifiable homicide.

The white deputies were employed by the T. C. and I. firm

(Continued on Page 4, Col. 8)

A civil jury returned a damages award in a case brought against Tennessee Coal, Iron and Railroad by Allie Glass Butler, the widow of Captain Butler, who was shot to death by TCI security men.

that Butler had a gun. Rather, the jury appears to have credited the testimony of Mrs. Allie Butler, and that of the dead man's son: Reverend Butler did not own a pistol, nor did he have one on his person as he headed to the mine that morning.

After the trial, the Butler family completed its migration to Michigan. Vida Rouse recalled that the loss of their father meant that the teenaged and young adult Butlers either "got jobs or got married," while the older children helped raise their brothers and sisters. Eventually all but one member of the family abandoned Alabama and moved to Detroit or Saginaw. In part, fear of retribution after the civil case drove them away, but jobs in the coal industry were also drying up for Black workers. Mechanization favored whites, who had a lock on all the skilled jobs. In the 1950s, over 70 percent of Black miners in the Alabama mines lost their jobs. Though they had made up the majority of the workforce in the 1940s, by the close of the twentieth century, Black miners constituted just 13 percent of miners in the country.

Vida Rouse maintained that her father was killed because he organized the union and wanted to ensure that "the widows and their children received black lung money." He was a man bound to his time and ahead of his time. Two years after his death, UMW got TCI to establish a retirement fund under the control of the union. Described as "the single most important change in the coal industry since the New Deal," the fund provided pensions for miners and their families and screenings for black lung disease.

27

"Negro Youth, Shot Near White Residence, Dies"

The *Birmingham World*, a potent weapon in the fight against racist violence across the 1940s, reported on the C.T. Butler case, among many others. It was edited by Emory Jackson, who joined the paper in 1934 and rose to editor in 1941. While his views tilted conservative during the mass mobilizations of the 1950s and '60s (the direct action protests led by Martin Luther King Jr. in 1963 got short shrift in the paper, although they took place within blocks of the *Birmingham World*'s offices), tainting his legacy, his coverage of police killings, Klan bombings, and voting campaigns propelled the Black agenda in the 1940s. Jackson worked long hours, reporting, editorializing, and keeping those outside the city alerted to the violence. As he lectured around the country, he would describe his beloved city as the "capital of violence." He spoke not just to his Black constituents but also to his white readers, aiming at their better angels and always hopeful that the right word at the right time would strike a chord. In no small measure because of his leadership, the Birmingham NAACP branch won the coveted Thalheimer Award in 1941, the highest award the association conferred on its branches, partly in recognition of its work battling police brutality. The branch had also grown its membership to 1,000 by 1940.

Although the 1940s were a bloody decade, there was surely something in the water in 1948, the year of C.T. Butler's death. By year's end, according to the *Birmingham World*, sixteen men, all Black, had died at the hands of police. Perhaps relatedly, it was a momentous year in national politics. Birmingham was contending for the title of capital of the new confederacy that had emerged from the revolt of the Dixiecrats, providing, in July, a meeting place at its stately Municipal Auditorium and a gracious host in Bull Connor. And it was a critical year for the Big Mules, who were determined to finally oust from the area the national unions that had for two decades been making remarkable inroads in the city. These events exposed the fundamental vulnerabilities of the Black community as well as of labor in Alabama, notwithstanding the enlightened solidarities of the post-Depression years. Without Black access to the polls, politicians did not have to win over Black voters, but rather were free to use them as fodder in campaigns to entrench white supremacy. Stoking fears of "Negro crime" was a proven winner at the polls. Perhaps the spike in the death toll could be attributed to these factors.

In April 1948, the Negro Citizens Defense Committee of Birmingham gathered to respond to "the alarming and increasing . . . terrorism" against Blacks in the city. Describing "this police terrorism" as a "new pattern of racial suppression . . . in the South," the NAACP conveners of the group compared the police to a paramilitary white supremacist organization in Georgia. With Jackson and others attributing the steep rise in anti-Black violence to backlash following President Truman's national civil rights agenda, the committee sent a petition to the governor and city officials, calling urgently for action and proclaiming that "Negro citizens are greatly alarmed, incensed and gripped with almost paralyzing fears" because of the police killings. It appears that Bull Connor was the only public official to respond to the petition; he claimed the allegations of abuse were standard "communist-line stuff," leading the *Pittsburgh Courier* to retort that the red-baiting was an "overworked and weak-kneed" response to the committee's demands.

Also in April, Jackson admonished the city's police chief, Floyd

Eddins, that "the Negro community" was weary of the attacks that touched businesspeople and working-class men and women alike. "The breaking point is near," he warned, writing of citizens wantonly shot on the streets and in their homes and those complaining that their NAACP buttons were making them marked targets for police vitriol. Even for Bad Birmingham, the numbers were shocking—six Black men were killed in the two months preceding the petition—and each case was more alarming than the last. Nor did the petition slow the pace of the deaths.

- On March 27, 1948, Ike Madden, forty, was shot to death in the back of a cruiser because, the officers claimed, he "attempted to grab the police driver."
- On April 16, 1948, Atmas Shaw, forty-two, arrested for disorderly conduct, died in police custody after his "head hit the base of a stone building."
- On April 26, 1948, Marion Franklin Noble, just nineteen years old, was shot to death during his arrest for "drunk and disorderly" behavior. The officer who killed him reported that the young man "pulled a knife" on him.
- On April 30, 1948, Eugene Ward, a thirty-seven-year-old veteran, was shot to death because, reported the Bessemer officer who claimed to be investigating a "prowler," he "reached in his pocket for a knife."
- On May 8, 1948, Dave Wilson, fifty years old, alleged to have been "disorderly" at his own home, was shot when he "came out of his house with a knife."
- On May 29, 1948, Walter Weston, thirty-six, was shot three times in his bedroom (by an officer who, in the course of his career, had shot to death three other Black men) when he "cursed and drew an icepick" on police.
- On June 4, 1948, C.T. Butler was shot four times because police said they thought he was about to draw a gun from his shirt, an allegation a civil jury later rejected.

- On June 17, 1948, Willie Mack, thirty-three, was shot to death during a burglary investigation because he "refused to halt and attempted to pull a pistol."
- On August 11, 1948, Joe Perkins was shot and killed when he "sought to flee" from a business he was accused of breaking into.
- On September 5, 1948, Charles Wright, thirty-five, charged with resisting arrest, was shot and killed on the street in Birmingham for "pulling out a straight razor." He was one of four men killed by this officer over his career; the officers reported that "this boy [Wright, the thirty-five-year-old] had been drinking pretty heavy."
- Leroy Whatley, thirty-four, was stealing batteries from a salvage yard when a watchman killed him on January 15, 1949.
- James Davis Thomas, thirty, was killed by police on April 23, 1949, because "he attempted to get a knife after resisting arrest."
- Daniel Hunter, the twenty-one-year-old son of Frank Hunter, the-Black detective who investigated Birmingham police officers on behalf of, among others, the SNYC, was shot on May 30, 1949, after he "lunged by a detective and knocked him down." Hunter later died from his wounds.
- Susie Dandridge, sixty years old, and her son, Walter Dandridge, thirty-two, were shot to death by Birmingham police in their home on July 28, 1949. The two were accused of selling illegal lottery tickets.
- Thomas Patterson, a twenty-eight-year-old veteran, was killed on July 4, 1951, by a police officer on the street. The Department of Justice closed its investigation into the death without bringing charges. Its conclusion: "[a] preponderance of the evidence indicates that Patterson attacked the officer with the knife and that the officer thereupon struck Patterson with his revolver, which was discharged upon contact with Patterson's head."

The list is representative, not comprehensive. In virtually every case, if there was a coroner's inquest, the ruling was "justifiable homicide." In all but one or two cases, the officers kept their jobs. In only one

1949 case was there a prosecution, and in that matter the jury acquitted the officer. In one case in 1948, a Black man killed a deputy sheriff and died for it.

Nor was the typical coroner's judgment of "justifiable homicide" reserved for police slayings. Emory Jackson covered a 1950 incident in which a white civilian slipped by Birmingham prosecutors after he shot a teenager to death. For Jackson, the case illustrated both the resilience and the futility of the Black claim to citizenship. One evening in January, fifteen-year-old Robert Sands found himself in the city's Northside district, where he was working for a white family. His presence walking near her home startled a woman, who alerted her husband. She would later say Sands was peering into a neighbor's home, while the teen explained that dogs had chased him off the street and in between the two houses. The woman's

Robert Sands, fifteen, was shot in 1950 as he passed through a white neighborhood in Birmingham, Alabama. He died from the wounds he sustained.

husband, R. L. Meyers, grabbed his gun and, within minutes, shot Sands in the back. The bullet lodged in the youth's spine. After six months, he succumbed to his injuries, which had left him wheelchair-bound and deaf. Sands's father's dogged efforts to obtain justice for his son were for naught. The local prosecutor refused to take the matter before a grand jury, and the police and coroner heaped blame on the teenager, concluding that the killing was a justifiable act of self-defense "to prevent escape after the commission of a crime." The crime, apparently: walking in a white neighborhood after dark. Again, it was Emory Jackson whose coverage supported the family's legal campaign.

THE LAWS PROHIBITING HOMICIDE simply did not apply to Birmingham police. They had a license to carry and a license to kill, both bestowed by the executive and judicial officials of Magic City. Activists in Birmingham, including Emory Jackson of the NAACP and Louis Burnham of the Southern Negro Youth Congress, maintained records on police killings throughout the 1940s and '50s, and circulated the data to the Southern Conference Educational Fund, the National Council of Negro Women, and other civic and civil rights groups. By 1951, the national Black community was well aware of Birmingham's bloody reputation. In that year, Emory Jackson took his case to the Justice Department in Washington and demanded a federal investigation into police violence across Alabama. At a meeting with the deputy attorney general, he and Clarence Mitchell, director of the NAACP's Washington Bureau, submitted a report documenting fifty-two Black men and women killed by police in Alabama in the three previous years. Half of that number were Birmingham cases. The two men urged a thorough investigation of the matter, but to no avail, so far as the extant records reveal.

The chroniclers of the Birmingham Police Department's war on Black people in the Jim Crow era walked down the road paved by the journalist and anti-lynching crusader Ida B. Wells–Barnett as they compiled this "Red Record"—the term Wells–Barnett coined—of police murder. When, in 1892, Wells–Barnett published *Southern Horrors: Lynch Law in All Its Phases*, she pioneered a multifaceted method of critique.* At the heart of her work was forensic investigation: collecting the facts in order to effectively dispute the official stories. By compiling a significant record of such cases, she revealed the continuities across time and unmasked the political mechanisms at work. She unraveled

---

* *The Red Record* was Ida B. Wells–Barnett's book containing statistics on lynching. (Ida Wells–Barnett, *Southern Horrors: Lynch Law in All Its Phases* [New York: New York Age, 1892].)

the interlocking state, federal, and local practices that sustained what she called "Lynch Law," and named it as a national blight rather than a regional problem. She affirmed the connection between slavery, Black resistance, and Lynch Law, writing, "[i]t is now, even as it was in the days of slavery, an unpardonable sin for a Negro to resist a white man, no matter how unjust or unprovoked the white man's attack may be." She urged forceful resistance on the part of Black people, called for structural remedies, and reminded whites that their devotion to law and order was hypocritical so long as Lynch Law reigned.

These are precisely the tools that activists combating police violence in Birmingham applied in the 1940s. They counted, compiled, and critiqued. Lynching has, since the Civil War, been the touchstone for American racism: the noose, the tree, the "black charred object on the black charred ground." Americans have built monuments condemning lynching culture and asked counties to take back their history in the form of plaques and jars of dirt. But we have yet to fully account for police killings, which were, because they bore the endorsement of the state, in a sense more insidious than lynching. The activists in Birmingham—and elsewhere—did not call police killings lynchings, but they grasped the tight relationship between the two.

———

IF THE INTENT OF these attacks on Black people in Birmingham—by both private actors and the police—was to criminalize and demonize "the Negro," rendering him fungible and indistinct, then habits of resistance established the diversity, particularity, and ingenuity of Black people, expanding and revamping earlier postures of struggle, guarding their reputation as a race even as they sought to prevent harms to their individual spiritual and physical lives, even as they revered Stagger Lee and crowned him their alter ego. More urban than Jackson, Mississippi, more rural than New Orleans, more working-class conscious than Atlanta, and undeniably more southern than Harlem, Birmingham offered the thousands of Black people who lived inside Jim

Crow an opportunity to imagine a future that was vastly different from anyplace else; resistance whetted the appetite, and refusal honed the psyche, for just such a transformation. White men and women would always be there, but not as the engineers of race, the purveyors of Black death. Their police cars would not be crypts for the bodies of Black men, their kitchens tombs for the minds of Black women, their coal mines cemeteries for the souls of Black workers. What Black Birmingham created in the 1940s was not a full-fledged dismantlement project, but neither was it mere reform, for it was widely understood that the pollutants were too deeply saturated in the bones of the city to give way to small fixes. There would, it seemed, have to be ashes before the rebirth.

Black political resistance operated close to the ground while it fed and bred grand utopic gestures, in Birmingham as elsewhere. It also offered a double meaning. For Blacks, it was the space within which to critique the fraudulence and barbarism of the American legal system, while, simultaneously, the resistance reminded whites of the need to square their actions with their law's purported neutrality. The total system was illegitimate; resistance was meant to remind whites, who had a monopoly on law, that it was for them to prove otherwise. Resistance also stripped law of its false majesty; it lay bare the link between the vigilantism of the Klansmen who bombed Black homes in the late 1940s and the Birmingham police who refused to investigate those crimes. It exposed the Klan robes, literal and figurative, that covered police uniforms, making plain the continuity between extralegal anti-Black violence and official policing.

Police killings, like lynching, were a form of marketing, selling whites on why Jim Crow had to be sustained. Indeed, as signification they were more effective than lynching, for they consolidated white opinion on the basis of law and order, whereas lynching, while in effect the cutting edge of formal law, was at the same time putatively unauthorized by the state. Lynching was cast by upper-class whites in class terms; police violence was not. Regardless of the individual ideologies it encompassed, the resistance showed the interchangeable thuggery of the mob and the police, and hence held the potential to radically upend the entire belief system.

This was a collective affair, and yet the victims of police violence were then, and should be now, individuals, distinguished by the lives they led. Indeed, often they *did* do something to get themselves killed. Some were labor leaders while others simply faced down the gratuitous slaps of armed white men, and still others tried to protect their family members. What they did, and how they died, drew people together and propelled them, together, in struggle. Their stories illuminate a Birmingham movement as vital and historic in the 1940s as it was in the 1960s.

THE BIRMINGHAM MOVEMENT against law enforcement lawlessness linked freedom from police abuse to genuine citizenship and animated Black resistance, but—as evidenced by Bull Connor's long reign in that town—it was only marginally effective in reforming police practices. Police remained, by design and for decades after the 1940s, ubiquitous servants and symbols of a state devoted to Jim Crow, undeterred by liberal concepts of due process. It was the police who exercised the sovereign power to draw the line between law and lawlessness. The violence they wrought was an incident of that sovereign power as opposed to, as it should have been, a breach of it. If, in the view of the police, violence was required, as was often the case when dealing with "dangerous classes," the resulting harms were, ipso facto, not unlawful. The Birmingham movement chalked up small victories—the disciplining of John Jackson's killer, the jury award in the C.T. Butler matter—but in general the law's incorporation of police violence remained constant. What adapted was the nature of law, not the nature of policing.

Likewise, in their discretionary decisions to charge some individuals but not others, for certain crimes but not others, police, together with prosecutors, exercised an unchecked sovereign power to define what the law was. Southern police and prosecutors rarely pursued cases of kidnapping where the victims were Black, although the crime was severely punished when the victims were white. Here again, their charging decisions were the last word, separating the legal from the lawless, in the process enacting an unwritten Black Code sitting in the long shadow of slave law, compelled by Jim Crow imperatives, and effectuating popular as well as official concepts of what the law meant.

PART VI
"HE THAT STEALETH
A MAN"

—Exodus 21:16

This negro was beaten while tied to the tree for an hour or an hour and a half as witnesses a quarter to a half mile away could clearly hear the blows and the screams for help and begging for mercy by the negro, Jeff Davis.

—State v. Wall, *189 Louisiana 653, 1938*

28

Abduction

SOUTHWEST MISSISSIPPI

Historians mark the demise of the Jim Crow era in the mid-1950s, with the Supreme Court's 1954 *Brown v. Board of Education* decision striking separate but equal from the Constitution, and demonstrations signaling the dawn of the "Montgomery to Memphis" civil rights movement. Yet despite the triumphal, if belated, official shift to equal protection, prominent features of the Jim Crow legal system continued to thrive. One particularly heinous phenomenon, a feature of both slavery and Jim Crow, was the decriminalization of kidnapping. A capital offense in some jurisdictions at the time, kidnapping was punished harshly throughout the country, but in the South, abducting a Black person was rarely the subject of law enforcement attention. Although crimes against Blacks were generally underenforced as compared with crimes against whites, the refusal to enforce the kidnapping laws speaks especially clearly to historical constructions of crime, mobility, and citizenship. White conceptions of Black capture and submission created an unambiguous racial gulf in criminal law that persisted for fully a century after slavery was officially over. Inasmuch as reading kidnapping as "lawful" was the legal bedrock of the African slave trade, it was perchance not so coincidental that it was still a racial marker in the second half of the twentieth century.

Conduct forbidden by criminal law can be categorized in three ways: crimes against property; crimes against a person; and crimes against public order. As North Carolina's legendary chief justice, Thomas Ruffin, explained in 1848, one who kidnapped an enslaved person from his owner committed the property crime of "stealing a man." But if the kidnapping of an enslaved person was a crime against property, Emancipation should have ushered in a new regime and changed the kidnapping of a Black person to the category of crimes against a person. Nothing of the sort occurred, at least as to the actual enforcement of the criminal law. Rather, kidnapping virtually disappeared as a crime when it came to the Black victim. Still vulnerable to the grasp of those seeking to maintain control over their lives and labor, Blacks were abducted from their homes, churches, fields, and other workplaces by whites—private citizens and police alike. The kidnappers suffered no legal consequences. They were, in effect, immune from punishment, or, to put it another way, their whiteness conferred upon them a legal right to do a legal wrong. The experiences of African Americans living in Southwest Mississippi illustrate how slavery's rules regarding Black mobility slithered into the post-slavery legal regime and lingered there well into the 1960s.

SOUTHWEST MISSISSIPPI, the site of important nationally sponsored civil rights activity in the 1960s, was long reputed to be a particularly violence-prone area in the most violent state of the Old South.* The region's eleven counties comprised 8.3 percent of the state's population in the 1960s. Anchored during that time by the growing industrial cities of Natchez in Adams County and McComb in Pike County, the area was largely rural and poor, with a population roughly divided by

---

* In 1964 the State Highway Patrol divided the state into regions for law enforcement purposes, one of which was Southwest Mississippi.

race in the two most populous counties and with Black majority or large minority populations in the remaining nine. Natchez, which had been at the center of the region's antebellum slave economy, hosted one of the largest Klan rallies in US history in 1965, with well over 3,000 people in attendance. The seeds of that 1965 rally would have been planted in the earliest years of Jim Crow, for in the 1890s, Southwest Mississippi was the center of the Whitecap movement, whose stated mission was to control Black labor by terror:

> We therefore pray the white farmers to combine forces and gain control of the negro labor, which is by right ours, that we may tend the soil under white supremacy. . . . Our first object is to control negro laborers by mild means, if possible; by coercion if necessary.

This style of junto justice prevailed without hindrance across the region for decades.

In 1964, the Student Nonviolent Coordinating Committee pried Mississippi open by bringing in hundreds of college students to pursue voting and education initiatives—the Freedom Summer Project. By one count, that year there were nine recorded kidnappings of Black men in Southwest Mississippi. Given the low reporting rate, the true number is likely to be far greater. Indeed, in a report to the Mississippi State Sovereignty Commission, one Adams County deputy sheriff put the number of kidnappings in the first few months of 1964 at sixteen Black men and one white man in that county alone.

LIKE THE SIX MILLION who fled the South in the decades before him, Burl Jones got off a train in Chicago in 1964, settled down, and lived a full life. Then, four decades later, as his senior years neared, Jones put his lifelong savings into a small but comfortable ranch house in Natchez, the nominal capital of Southwest Mississippi. In July 2004, about six months before Jones left Illinois, Natchez had sworn in its first Black mayor since Reconstruction, so Jones felt it was safe to go back home.

Natchez lies thirty-three miles northwest of Meadville, in neighboring Franklin County—the small town from which Jones had fled in 1964, leaving behind a family, a job at a local lumber company, and high school buddies in the area. He knew little about the civil rights movement in Southwest Mississippi—not about the famous SNCC voting rights campaigns led by Robert Moses in the towns of McComb and Liberty in 1961, and not about the Mississippi Freedom Summer that would, in the weeks following Jones's journey to Chicago, bring hundreds of students from across the country into the state. Southwest Mississippi was the headquarters of a recently revived and particularly virulent branch of the Ku Klux Klan, the White Knights, whose members, upon hearing the call "KiWi," would drop what they were doing and join an "action," most often a criminal enterprise targeting Blacks.

Though it was the seat of Franklin County, Meadville, with a population of about 400 in 1964, was really not much more than its Main Street and a few short offshoots. Justice was dispensed from the county courthouse next door to the sheriff's office and jail. On a Friday evening in June, Jones, then twenty-five years old, was arrested in his Ford on Main Street by a local police officer who claimed to have received a complaint that Jones ran a red light. Locked up for the violation, Jones got in contact with his father, who came down and paid the ten dollars to get his son released. The sheriff, Wayne Hutto, refused to release the young man to his father, but instead kept him in jail. When Hutto finally released Burl Jones, it was just after daybreak three days later.

Jones did not make it out of the jailhouse door. In the hallway leading out of the jail, two men wearing white hoods grabbed him, pounded him to the ground with baseball bats, and then hauled him, blindfolded, into the trunk of a car. The kidnappers had covered Jones's eyes, but as he later pieced it together, the Homochitto National Forest was where his captors were headed. Homochitto is federal land, 189,000 acres of beautiful raw forest covering several of Mississippi's southwest counties, but in the 1960s, the Klan appeared to have as much claim to the territory as did the United States Forest Service. The Klan's whipping ground of choice, Homochitto was where, one month earlier, Klansmen had taken two other young Meadville men to flog, nineteen-year-olds Henry Hezekiah Dee and Charles Moore, before nonchalantly tossing them, still alive, into the Old Mississippi River. It was Homochitto where, in June 1966, the Klan killed the sixty-seven-year-old sharecropper Ben Chester White, whose murder they thought would lure Martin Luther King Jr. into the state so that they could assassinate him.

On the day in question, Burl Jones was tied face front to a tree deep in the forest and beaten with a bullwhip. A favored punishment of the KKK, whipping, turned into a fine art during slavery, continued to mark Blacks as virtual slaves long after Emancipation. Flogging and slavery were joined at the hip. Indeed, in the nineteenth century, the common belief that flogging should be reserved for slaves influenced the debate over the legitimacy of corporal punishment. In slavery the whip "impress[ed] upon the slaves that they were slaves," and in Jim Crow, it made plain how close to slavery they still were. Jones's tormenters, five or six in number, demanded to know something about whether workers were seeking to unionize at a local lumber company that was owned by a onetime president of the White Citizens' Council. It was a subject on which Jones, motivated to help though he might have been, could not enlighten them. In the end, the kidnappers let Jones hold on to his life. Cutting the ropes that bound him to the tree, they threw him back in the car and deposited him on Highway 98 in Meadville, where eventually his family found him huddled on the ground, with the clothes stripped from his body and nearly unconscious, blood oozing from his face and back.

Although he was half dead, Jones's ordeal was not yet over. "Get out of town," his captors warned him. And so he did. A few days after the abduction, Jones was aboard the Rock Island line, headed to Chicago.

There he lived and worked—ironically, for the Cook County Sheriff's Department—for forty years until, in 2005, he decided the time was right to head back home to Mississippi.

In 1964, the news of Jones's disappearance was greeted with barely a whisper, despite the fact that kidnapping was an offense punishable by death under Mississippi law. The Franklin County sheriff received a report of the attack from Jones's father and from a local Black minister, whose contemporaneous journal entry about the incident was discovered in 2007, forty-three years later. While the sheriff had custody over the jail from which Jones was kidnapped, no legal action was taken by local authorities. Though Jones was beaten on federal property, the FBI, it appears, did not investigate. Though capital crimes were not an everyday occurrence in the county, not a word about the kidnapping appeared in the Franklin *Advocate*, the local paper. And it seems that no one at the lumber company where Jones worked took any particular notice of his abrupt disappearance.

In 1965, the US Commission on Civil Rights held hearings in the state on racial violence in Mississippi, and there was a cursory mention of the Jones kidnapping. Indeed, setting aside the minister's diary entry, the single contemporaneous written reference to the Jones event was an FBI agent's notes of a wide-ranging interview with a Klan informant who claimed to have known about, but not participated in, the crime. The abduction of Jones had the familiar markings of a Klan operation. At once capricious and calculated, random and regular, the assault on the young man could not have but terrorized and silenced hundreds who did not know Burl Jones but heard about his fate. Everyone knew what happened, but none could speak of it. The distinct features of the crime—the law enforcement endorsement, the tethering to a tree, the flogging—each reprised, in 1964, customary disciplining rituals from slavery, Reconstruction, and the early decades of Jim Crow.

In short, what happened to Burl Jones was rendered invisible. There were no media reports, no police report, no personal testimony. Jones did not go public with his story until 2007. In essence, Jones bore the mark of the criminal while his tormentors, using the jailhouse as their stage, hoisted the flag of law. Jones was outside law and they were inside: his victimhood was erased for forty-three years until he "reappeared" himself. The man and the harm were obscured, living on only in the backdoor memory of those privy to the rumors. The criminal conduct, enacting as it did—on the very stage of law—the rights, privileges, and disabilities of the two racial castes, never surfaced as a crime.

And there were others.

In February 1964 in Natchez, Alfred "Juicy" Whitley, a fifty-four-year-old man, was abducted by about ten hooded men on his way home from his job at the Armstrong Tire and Rubber Company. The men drove Whitley around for some time short of an hour. He was blindfolded and taken to the Homochitto Forest, where his clothes were stripped from his back. For more than an hour he was beaten with bullwhips and a cat-o'-nine-tails. The men forced Whitley to drink a bottle of castor oil. Ordered to leave his clothes behind and run naked out of the forest, Whitley tried to follow the commands, but tripped and fell down. His captors, who had accused him of NAACP activity and membership in the Masons organization, shot off their guns within inches of his prone body. Escaping death, Whitley got up after his attackers drove off and walked naked until he reached the road. His body a mass of welts and gouges, Whitley spent three days in a hospital. The beating cost him an eye and a lung. His niece would later tell a Mississippi journalist that he never truly recovered. No arrests were made in the case.

Also in February 1964, Archie Curtis, fifty-six, a widely respected mortician in Natchez who was chairman of the Natchez Business and Civic League's voter registration drive, and his assistant, Willie Jackson, forty-five, were ambushed. For many years before the attack, Curtis had been known for his voter registration work, and he was named in state investigative files as a clandestine NAACP supporter. Lured away from the funeral home by a false ambulance call at midnight, Curtis and Jackson were kidnapped in vehicles driven by five armed men in white hoods. Taken to a forest, they were stripped of all their clothing, whipped, and quizzed about their alleged NAACP membership. One of the men threatened to kill Curtis and Jackson, but ultimately the group decided to leave them, without their clothes, in the forest. The two men made their way to a friend's home.

The Adams County sheriff would later claim that he had no leads in the Curtis kidnapping, although state investigators named a local constable as a suspect. In a cursory report that focused on the beating but not the abduction, the sheriff wrote that he "received a call to . . . investigate a report by two Colored Males that they had been beaten."

Ivey Gutter, fifty-four, fell victim to a similar kidnapping in McComb. Gutter did not have extensive civil rights connections, although he was an NAACP member who had for many years worked for the Illinois Central Railroad. In June 1964, three men, clad in black hoods and armed with pistols and shotguns, kidnapped Gutter from his home, forced him into their car, took him to the woods, threatened him with death, and whipped him. They rifled through Gutter's wallet for an NAACP card but couldn't find one. They then released him on the open road.

From his hospital bed, Gutter reported the event to the Pike County sheriff and gave him a description of the car. The sheriff's half-page investigative report, titled "Ivey Gutter—C.M.," describes the abduction in the following shorthand: "[A]fter [three hooded men put] Gutter in car a hood was placed over his head and he was carried into woods. One of the men said you and CC Bryant [a well-known civil rights campaigner] goes to lunch everyday together." There were no arrests. Perceiving caution to be the better part of valor, Gutter, a lifelong resident of Pike County, gathered his wife and five children and disappeared from the area.

The consistent failure to charge these cases as kidnappings—their legal essence and political meaning—reflected the gap between law on paper and law in practice. The prevailing social norm, that whites had absolute control over the bodies of Blacks, shaped the perceptions of all the actors—victims, perpetrators, and investigators. The law enforcement records of these seizures do not refer to the abductions; rather, they describe the incidents as "whippings" or "beatings" of Negro men. Like Burl Jones, most victims were too terrified to report these assaults, but when they did, it was the beatings, not the abductions, that they complained about. Nor, apparently, did the KKK perceive that it was engaged in kidnapping. A White Knights internal instructional guide ranked the "actions" they could take from category one, the least violent (threatening phone calls and visits) to category four, the most violent (extermination). A "category two" action was burning a cross "to instill community fear among Negroes and as an advertisement for recruitment of radical whites," while "category three" consisted of "beating or flogging; burning of property; wild shooting into property; and bombings."

29

"Negro Leaders Cry for Justice in Kidnap Outrage"

Mississippi was hardly the only former slave state that, from the inception of Jim Crow in the late nineteenth century until well past the mid-mark of the twentieth, allowed white people to abduct Black people with impunity. During the height of the Klan era, such abductions were sporting events for white gangs, meant to test members' appetites for violence and to control territory. Chosen at random, or because they were suspected activists, or had transgressed racial rules, the victims were, as with Burl Jones, often left for dead on the open road. From time to time, dead men were discovered on the roads, their prostrate bodies testifying to abduction and other macabre crimes. NAACP leader Medgar Evers investigated the slaying of a man named Sylvester Maxwell, found dead and castrated on a highway in Mississippi. The case was never solved.

An unusual case in 1938 suggested that where a local prosecutor was so inclined, he could in fact win a kidnapping conviction, even where the abduction was all within the same county and incident to a beating. In Tangipahoa Parish—a stone's throw across the Louisiana border from Pike County, Mississippi, where Ivey Gutter was beaten in 1964—a case proceeded against several white men for kidnapping forty-six-year-old Jeff Davis, seized because one of the defendants, for whom he worked, claimed Davis owed him three or four dollars and had walked off the job. The Louisiana Supreme Court described what happened next:

> They took this negro some two and one half or three miles out of town of Kentwood, in the woods, where they administered a most brutal beating. The negro, Jeff Davis, was tied with his hands around a tree and all of them beat him. Pistols were used in the beating as well as some instrument that left a broad scar all over the negro's back and legs. The negro was also stamped in the stomach and kicked.

After the whipping the defendants strapped the unconscious man to a railroad track an hour before the Illinois Central's next train, the northbound Merry Widow, was due to pass through. Passersby saw Davis and, in the nick of time, cut him loose. On those facts a jury returned a conviction for kidnapping and a trial judge sentenced four of the five defendants to fifteen years of "hard labor" at the penitentiary, a result that was sustained on appeal.

There was also one rare Mississippi prosecution of whites for falsely imprisoning a Black man. In the 1946 matter, a local sheriff brought kidnapping charges against three white men who seized two young Black men and took them to a neighboring county. This was self-help: the wife of one of the abductors claimed that one of the young men had entered her room. The sheriff, however, described the white men's crime as "an out and out piece of hijacking, blackjacking and kidnapping." The sheriff's effort to protect his turf from private, self-appointed law enforcers was thwarted when a circuit court judge threw out the charges, vindicating the cross-county kidnappers with his ruling that the "right of private arrest is just as sacred and just as important to the public interest as that of arrest by an officer armed with a warrant."

A 1956 Florida case presented another exception to the pattern of non-prosecution. Sumter County officials charged seven men with false imprisonment in connection with the abduction of Jesse Woods from a jail cell, where he was being held on drunk and disorderly charges. It was said that Woods had yelled "hello there, baby," to a white teacher. A group of men seized Woods from the jail, took him to a secluded area, and beat him up. Woods fled to Alabama, but he was returned to Florida to testify against the perpetrators, who had been charged with false imprisonment as well as assault. Terrified of being targeted again, Woods claimed he could not identify his assailants because his head was down during the flogging. The men were all acquitted.

These were exceptions. In the vast majority of cases, kidnapping was not pursued even when other charges were. In Georgia in 1950, two white farmers were arrested in connection with the flogging of a Black tenant farmer, Jessie Lee Goodman, by a mob. Night riders had seized the man from his home, where he was sleeping with his wife and children, and carried him into the woods. The sheriff refused to follow the mob into the woods, but later, responding to federal and state pressure, charged two of the group with assault and battery. The abduction did not figure in the prosecution.

In a gruesome Alabama case, arrests were made, but not for abduction. On Labor Day 1957, several Klansmen came up with a hazing ritual for their new leader. That evening the six men, choosing their target at random, spotted Judge Aaron, a thirty-three-year-old handyman who was taking a stroll with a female friend in Birmingham. Forced into a car, blindfolded, and pistol-whipped, Aaron was transported to a Klan lair on the outskirts of town, made to crawl into a hut, and castrated by the new leader. One of his abductors told Aaron, "I want you to [tell] Shuttlesworth [the civil rights leader] to stop sending nigger children and white children to school together or we're gonna do him like we're fixing to do you." Surviving the ordeal, Aaron testified against the Klansmen at their trial for mayhem, a charge on which they were convicted. The crime of kidnapping never featured in the criminal proceedings, although arguably it would have been easier to prove a kidnapping than a conspiracy to commit mayhem (at least against some of the participants), for the castration was performed by one man wielding a razor while the gang acted jointly in kidnapping their victim.*

Women and children, as well as men, were seized against their will. In February 1949, three high school students were abducted, taken out of state, and whipped by Klansmen in Georgia. Their crime: participating in a Brotherhood Week event at their school. In 1960, forty-three-year-old Allene Redwine was stripped naked, flogged with a leather strap, and left with no clothes in the woods in Whitesburg, Georgia, a town she had lived in her whole life.

In abductions aimed at deterring political activism or racial "mixing," usually no charges of any kind were brought. Typical was what happened to one Willie Dudley, a Black man snatched and flogged in 1946 because he refused to resign from an American Federation of Labor local in Georgia. The mob told Dudley that he would be killed if he did not leave the union, which they were determined to prevent Blacks from joining. In 1949, Shelton Lorick, seventy-six years old, was dragged from his bed in the middle of the night and taken into the woods in Columbia, South Carolina, where he was stripped of his nightclothes, beaten to unconsciousness, and left for dead. The night riders claimed whites had been visiting the Lorick home; the old man later explained that he had been selling his eggs and farm products to all comers. More likely this was a "one-drop rule" enforcement action: a light-complexioned man, one census classified Lorick as "mulatto." In the summer of 1957, five men in the town of Maplesville, Alabama, chosen randomly, were snatched by Klansmen from a private home where they were watching television. Beaten first, they were then made to "run and dance to pistol shots." And in 1960, a twenty-six-year-old

---

* When the defendants were charged in 1957, under Alabama law kidnapping carried a two-year-minimum, ten-year-maximum sentence (Code 1940, Tit. 14, sec. 6). The defendants were all charged with conspiracy to commit mayhem and claimed on appeal that the prosecutor failed to prove the conspiracy. It is clear from the facts that all the defendants participated in the kidnapping but not evident why the prosecutor did not charge it as a backup to the charge of mayhem.

man in Houston was targeted in the wake of sit-in activities by students at Texas Southern University. The victim, Felton Turner, was taken into the woods, strapped by his feet to a tree, and beaten with chains. The perpetrators carved six Ks on his torso and left him tied to the tree.

BY CONTRAST, Klansmen who abducted and then flogged whites were readily brought within the scope of the kidnapping charge. That precedent was set in a 1929 Alabama case; its rationale could have been applied across the board. The victim, a white man, had been seized by a group of robed Klansmen for drunkenness and bootlegging, taken into the woods, and flogged. While an intermediate appellate court had trouble finding a kidnapping on these facts, the Alabama Supreme Court reversed, ruling that, if proved, such facts would constitute kidnapping under Alabama law. From 1951 to 1952, the federal government, alongside state and local officials, used federal kidnapping laws to combat a wave of floggings, largely of whites, in the southeast coastal areas of the Carolinas. The yield was significant: close to a hundred Klansmen were arrested in North Carolina, and four separate trials were held. In the first prosecution, the FBI pursued kidnapping and related charges that resulted in convictions and prison terms for ten men for abducting and flogging a white couple who had been taken across state lines. Not to be outdone, North Carolina state authorities followed with indictments for kidnapping and related offenses against sixty-four men. Of the thirteen victims, ten were white and two were Black women. Seven of the defendants went to jail, including the Imperial Wizard.

30

Black Captive,
White Capture

Although we will never know the real numbers, between the time of the Klan's post–World War II renaissance and its gradual demise after 1965, a reasonable conclusion is that thousands of Black people across the South were dragged away from their homes or jobs, carried into some remote woods, flogged with straps, pistols, rubber hoses, or cat-o'-nine-tails, threatened with death, and then let go. These narratives of captivity underscore that even at the end of the Jim Crow era, personal liberty was, as a matter of law, shaped by slavery. In the Burl Jones case, the sheriff's brazen participation in the Klan action explicitly immunized the perpetrators. When local authorities were not directly complicit, the seizure of Black people was still not treated as criminal behavior. Some kidnapping victims, bravely ignoring the warning to get out of town, complained to the police that they had been abducted, but these cases were almost never treated as kidnappings. When the coin was flipped, however, Black-on-white seizures were charged up as kidnappings—if the Black suspect made it to court before the mob got to him or her. And all sides contributed to this legal erasure of the crime of white-on-Black abduction. This rule of non-enforcement, rooted in well-known historical, visceral social norms, reinforced the profound alienation of Blacks from law and revealed the symbiotic relationship between formal and mob law in the Jim Crow South.

The kidnapping laws in these states were themselves a relic of slave law, which was meant to benefit owners whose kidnapped slaves would be either liberated or resold. Consider the stated intent of an 1816 slavery-era Louisiana kidnapping statute: "to 'take the most effective measures in order to prevent the transportation, or carrying away of slaves out of this State, against the will of their owners.'" And the hangman's noose was the penalty prescribed by the 1779 North Carolina code for "seducing and conveying away" a slave—or "carrying off" free Negroes. In one case, dating back to 1848, that state's renowned chief justice, Thomas Ruffin, puzzled over whether a conviction for larceny could be sustained on evidence that the accused transported and sold a runaway slave. Famously adroit at conceptualizing the slave legal personality as part-chattel, part-human, Ruffin observed that the central mission of the law—control over slave mobility—justified bending the common law meaning of larceny to cover "lost" slave property:

> This is a remarkable feature in the condition of a runaway slave, which distinguishes it from that of lost goods or stray beasts; for in these last the finder gets the property until the owner appears, and therefore the idea of larceny by using the property in any manner is repelled. But that wholly fails in the case of a runaway slave, as the person who takes him, must know that he has no interest in the slave. . . . Hence . . . the understanding is almost universal . . . that slaves cannot be reckoned among lost things, and that a runaway is . . . as much a subject of larceny, as any other slave.

Codified in 1848 as a capital offense in Mississippi, the crime of kidnapping outlived one of its central purposes after Emancipation and provided no protection to former slaves robbed of their precarious freedom and returned, by ruse or force, to post-slavery peonage and debt servitude. Formal law collaborated in this push back into a new form of slavery. The Mississippi Black Codes, enacted in 1865, included a provision subjecting to arrest any freedman who left his labor before the expiration of his contract and permitting the apprenticeship of any freedman under eighteen years of age, even against his will, with preference given to the former owner. Upon their repeal, these Black Codes were replaced by other legal mechanisms to immobilize Black labor, especially as the Great Migration gained momentum and Blacks attempted to flee to more promising venues. Mississippi was one of six states in which, as of 1915, it was lawful to force a man to work for another against his will. In the early twentieth century, Blacks were chased down by former white employers, often working hand in hand with law enforcement; kidnapped; and returned to their old plantations. These were crimes against which state prohibitions on kidnapping proved to be no safe harbor, and federal prosecutors were almost as ineffectual. Law paved the way for the peonage system, mirroring, echoing, and embodying custom and politics, and blurring lines of authority and control over the legitimate use of force. Judges and police collaborated with plantation owners to re-seize laborers as did the federal judge in Georgia who, in 1941, refused to extradite for trial in Illinois defendants in a peonage prosecution there. And sometimes private employers in the South would make their own "arrests" and hold their own "courts." Yet another thinly disguised form of kidnapping was the convict-lease system that turned men arrested on charges of vagrancy and petty crime into prison laborers.

Erasing the boundary between lawfully constituted authority and raw racial violence, all of these methods of controlling Black movement and labor reprised the structures, legal rationales, and material effects of chattel slavery. They presaged the ongoing carceral racial punishment practices that have, in the wake of the Jim Crow era, constituted the criminal justice system in the United States, and which we have just begun to take stock of.

To build a social order that does not depend on carceral punishment to address social challenges, it is necessary to confront these root causes, revive the tenets of antislavery abolition, probe the myriad facets of slavery's afterlife in law, and embrace the global movement for reparation and redress.

PART VII
"A MINT OF BLOOD AND SORROW"

The past has been a mint
Of blood and sorrow
That must not be
True of Tomorrow

—Langston Hughes, "History"

31

Redress

THE PROBLEM OF THE TWENTY-FIRST CENTURY

In February 2019, the descendants of African Americans murdered one hundred years earlier by white vigilantes in Elaine, Arkansas, gathered in that small Delta town, located about an hour and a half southwest of Memphis. They were there to commemorate the lives lost and measure out the debt owed. Triggered by the organizing efforts of Black sharecroppers and tenant farmers who sought to form a union, the 1919 massacre had claimed somewhere around two hundred lives. When the pogrom was over, entire Black families lay strewn across the countryside. The US Army, said to have killed some of the victims, took its leave. Eventually, the sharecroppers' and farmers' lands, cattle, and equipment passed into the hands of local whites. The sheriff told "the Negroes of Phillips County [to] stop talking" about the killing fields. He also told them, "Go to work."

At the centennial Elaine Truth-Telling Hearing in 2019, one of the descendants, William Quiney III, was asked what he thought justice required today. He replied with a hashtag: #GiveItBack.

But why? To whom? From whom? How? And what?

Pronouncement of Sheriff F. F. Kitchens, Phillips County, Arkansas, in the wake of a massacre of Black residents of the county on October 2, 1919.

TO THE NEGROES
OF PHILLIPS COUNTY
Helena, Ark., Oct. 7, 1919

The trouble at Hoop Spur and Elaine has been settled.

Soldiers now here to preserve order will return to Little Rock within a short time.

No innocent negro has been arrested, and those of you who are at home and at work have no occasion to worry.

All you have to do is to remain at work just as if nothing had happened.

Phillips County has always been a peaceful, lawabiding community, and normal conditions must be restored right away.

STOP TALKING!

Stay at home---Go to work---Don't worry!

F. F. KITCHENS, Sheriff   COMMITTEE
Edward Bevens   J. C. Meyers   S. Straub   E. M. Allen
T. W. Keesee   D. A. Keeshan   Amos Jarman
H. D. Moore   J. G. Knight   Jno. L. Moore   E. C. Hornor

Nicholls Print, Helena, Ark.

ADDRESSING THE HISTORICAL INJUSTICES of the twentieth century is the project of the twenty-first century. It is not just an American project. All over the world, generations who live under the shadow of past wrongs are having to acknowledge their forebears' behavior. Permeating the lives of Germans today are the butcheries of the Third Reich: *Vergangenheitspolitik* describes the never-ending integration of the past into the daily rituals of schooling, praying, and paving sidewalks.*

---

* That Germany's recognition of its genocidal past is limited to the Holocaust of the Third Reich suggests that even when states repent and remember, their practices are partial. The first genocide of the twentieth century was that of German forces against the Herero people and their lands in the German colony of South West Africa (now Namibia) in 1904. A full accounting and reparation have yet to be made, and while

Spain kicked off the century in October 2000 by unearthing the mass graves where lay the remains of victims of the Franco regime. Four years later, it adopted a reparation law. In 2013, the British government conceded that it brutalized the Kikuyu during the midcentury Mau Mau Uprising in Kenya; the former colonial regime settled the victims' claim for about 20 million pounds. In 1992, the Chilean government awarded lifelong compensation to victims and their descendants of the Pinochet dictatorship. Italy signed a treaty with Libya in 2008 to apologize for the injustices of colonialism, repatriate ancient art, and pledge $5 billion in damages in the form of investment. And Prime Minister Stephen Harper of Canada, also in 2008, made material amends for his country's cultural war against the Aboriginal peoples, pronouncing that the burden of this history is "properly ours as a government and as a country."

Projects of reparation, commemoration, and reconciliation abound, some targeting histories of racial domination, others meant to reconcile age-old political enemies, and still others to rectify colonial atrocities and injustices. Activists emphasize the origins of current oppression as they seek to imagine strategies of contemporary redress. Reparation claims, long part of the racial justice vocabulary in the United States, have taken on fresh urgency as projects reexamining the very nature of justice and equality intersect with those aimed at upending postcolonial hierarchies. The United States must catch up.

Certainly the law requires it—the imperative to redress historical injustices is embedded in international human rights principles. But more to the point, democratic practice requires it. Human communities are constituted in part by the intergenerational claims and obligations transmitted across history. It falls upon each successive community to recognize and interrupt the regenerative tendencies of ancestral harms until the inequities they spawned have disappeared. Every generation must take up the duty to repair the damage of slavery if we are to prevent its

---

schooling on the World War II Holocaust is required, little, if any, attention is given to Germany's colonial atrocities.

habits, beliefs, systems, wounds, and identities from endlessly rejuvenating. Because to err is to live, the business of repair is the business of life.

The duty of repair extends beyond the primary violators whose actions caused the wrong. Of course they bear responsibility, but so, too, do those who should have but did not protect the victims, or who failed to mete out justice after the harms occurred. Although human rights law does not address this, people at a temporal and geographic remove from the wrongs who nevertheless benefited—"implicated subjects," as the literary scholar Michael Rothberg teaches us—have a moral duty to participate in the project of repair.

Even when the perpetrators are beyond the reach of criminal and civil law, human rights norms impose upon states a duty to remember histories of oppression, to honor the victims' right to truth, and to make reparations. Societies coming to terms with a legacy of atrocities must seek accountability, justice for the victims, nonrecurrence, and reconciliation—obligations that can persist for centuries after the actual events. Because their identities and debts are ongoing, political entities, such as law enforcement departments, have a unique obligation to engage with redress.

It is still within the United States' power to provide reparation for the violence that made Jim Crow possible; that is the ultimate teaching of the stories recounted in this book. This discrete and finite project—recognizing these victims and restoring justice for their families today—is both possible and necessary. The descendants of the victims, those specific descendants of racial murders recounted here as well as those who suffered in other ways, demand that undertaking.

Three questions shape a reparations inquiry. What is the injury? What is the redress? What contemporaries bear responsibility for rectification? The case for reparation for the victims of racially motivated, state-sanctioned murder is particularly compelling. It is a natural starting point. If not sufficient, it is nevertheless necessary. The cases that follow explore the steps that might be taken in the early twenty-first century to address racial homicides that took place during the Jim Crow years, and, as William Quiney, the descendant of the Elaine massacre demanded, to #GiveItBack.

32

"Found Floating
in River . . .
Cause of Death Unknown"

The death certificate reads: "Found floating in river; inquest held; cause of death unknown; neither an accident nor a homicide." So stands the official record of the death of Elbert Williams, although it is indisputable that in 1940 he was lynched and then cast into the waters of the Hatchie River by a mob led by a local police officer, who would later become the county sheriff. In August 2018, the Haywood County prosecutor reopened an investigation into Williams's murder.

Williams, who had no children, enjoyed a quiet life with his wife, Annie, in Brownsville, Tennessee. In June 1939, then thirty-one years old, he became a founding member of the newly formed Brownsville branch of the NAACP, whose charter members included fifty-two men and women. Williams held no office in the branch, but he was a good friend and relative of Elisha Davis, one of the chapter's lead organizers. The branch was launched with the 1940 presidential election in mind: many Haywood County Blacks, who then comprised about 61 percent of the county's population, wanted to vote for Wendell Willkie, the presidential candidate of the Party of Lincoln. They carefully selected as leaders of the branch men and women of some means; people who could get a hearing from the county registrar, mayor, and police officials in town; and who were, it was thought, financially insulated from white retribution.

Buster Walker and Elisha Davis were such men. Walker was a minister whom the branch elected as its president. Davis, an executive committee member, owned property in the county, operated a service station, and had resided outside the South for many years. He had lived a remarkable life, following in the footsteps of his father, Isaac Davis, known all over the county for his industry, thrift, and moral fiber. Isaac, the son of a white man, had been allowed to do what few others could in the county: in 1900, he purchased forty acres of lush, rich farmland. Eventually he would pass the farm on to Elisha and his other children, having admonished them: "I got the land; you just need to hold on to it." Born in Haywood County in 1900, Elisha and his wife, Nan, left the area and joined the Great Migration, landing in Chicago. However, when his father Isaac died in 1930, Elisha moved his family back to the homestead and, in short order, opened a filling station in downtown Brownsville and bought a house in town for his growing family.

Together with a few others, Buster Walker and Elisha Davis went to the courthouse on May 6, 1940, to pay a visit to the county registrar, ostensibly to ascertain the voter registration dates. They actually came to test if there would be safety in numbers and reputations and how much resistance they would face from whites to Black voter participation. It would be the first time Blacks sought to vote in significant numbers in Haywood since 1888, when Samuel McElwee, Haywood County's three-term Black state legislator, was forced from office by voter suppression.

On that day in May 1940, the delegation was sent on a wild goose chase from one office to another. The honest answer came not from the registrar but rather from Deputy Sheriff T. Bolden, who, the following day, warned Walker to stop the registration campaign, or there would be trouble. Davis received a call at his service station from a man who told him that "people down at the courthouse say they will run you and Walker out of town if you try to vote."

The threats quickly proved not to be idle. Several weeks after he had made the trip to the registrar, Davis was visited at his home, where he lived with his wife and their seven children, after 1 a.m. The visitor, accompanied by about fifty men, was Tip Hunter, who at the time was a night watchman; he had also intermittently served the white electorate as their sheriff. Surrounded by these armed men, Davis knew he had come to the end of his days. A quiet man, he was fiercely proud of his personal accomplishments, his family's history and standing, and his children. He would be forced to cast this pride aside as he pulled on his clothes and told his wife not to fire the handgun they kept near the bedside, and as he narrowed his shoulders, lowered his eyes, and transformed himself into the mob's "nigra." Officer Hunter shoved Davis, so attired in the accoutrements of the Black man's destiny, into the back of his car and drove him to the Forked Deer River bottom. There Davis suffered through an inquisition. Some among the crowd demanded he be killed on the spot, but before anyone could act, one man declared that if Davis gave up the names of the NAACP members, his own life would be spared. Finding his voice at the bottom of his fear, Davis identified some of the branch members, at which point the men who made up the mob—grocers, public officials, WPA workers, and farmers—got back into their cars. To be certain that the averted lynching was erased from public memory, the men told Davis that he would be killed if he did not leave the county, immediately and permanently.

It was not a threat he could ignore. Davis walked several miles to the highway and caught a ride to the town of Alamo in Crockett County (named after Davy Crockett, whose stand is honored in Alamo), eventually sheltering with Milmon Mitchell, the NAACP branch president in Jackson. When the heat died down, he crossed the state line out of Tennessee. He would never again see his home, his father's farm he so loved, or the service station of which he was so proud. Nan and the children, hustled away from Brownsville and hidden until they could travel north, would join him in Niles, Michigan, many months later. There they started afresh. Davis and Nan raised twelve children in Niles. Also banished were Davis's two brothers: Casher Davis hid immediately after his brother's kidnapping, then fled; Thomas Davis also fled.

Elbert Williams was not an elected leader of the new Brownsville

NAACP, but he was a good friend of the Davis family. There had been talk of his taking over the gas station after Davis's forced disappearance. Born in 1908, Williams worked as a boiler fireman in a local laundry. On June 20, 1940, a few days after Davis had been pitched out of town by a mob, Tip Hunter, the night watchman, and two other men, one of them the manager of the Coca-Cola plant, came to Williams's home, again well after dark. They were chasing down the information they had squeezed out of Davis and acting on the tip that Williams was planning to reconvene the NAACP. Elbert and Annie Williams had just gone to bed, having stayed up beyond their accustomed bedtime to listen to Joe Louis's championship fight with Chilean boxer Arturo Godoy. No doubt thrilled at Louis's knockout victory, particularly as the last Louis-Godoy matchup had gone the full sixteen rounds, Williams went to the door in good spirits. When he looked out he saw trouble. Carried off in Hunter's patrol car shoeless and in his pajamas, Elbert Williams did not return home that night.

Searching frantically for her beloved husband over the next few days, Annie Williams reported his disappearance to Sheriff Richard Hawkins. "They aren't going to hurt him. They may just ask him a few questions but they'll let him loose," the sheriff assured her. "If he doesn't come back home in a day or so, come back and let me know." Annie next beseeched answers from her employer, Spence DuPree, whose frankness stood in sharp contrast to the sheriff's insulting prevarication. "Annie," he said, "these laws are just wrong. . . . There's just a bunch here we can't do anything about." On June 23, three days after the Joe Louis fight, a fisherman found Elbert Williams's body in the Hatchie River.* The corpse was roped at the neck and ankles to a log. Although his head was twice its normal size and his body showed signs of having been beaten and stabbed before being shot, Anne recognized her husband.

---

* The name "Hatchie" echoes what the Chickasaw, whose land it was until 1818, called the river: Bokoshi. The Hatchie should not be confused with the Tallahatchie, the waters that would sixteen years later saturate the body of fourteen-year-old Emmett Till.

At the coroner's inquest, six white men convened on the bank of the murky Hatchie and hovered over the prone body as a crowd collected. This coroner's jury concluded that the death was "caused by foul means by persons unknown." Williams's body—swollen, waterlogged, pierced, and mutilated—was loaded onto a pickup truck and buried later that day in an unmarked grave. His family and friends would never know where his bones finally came to rest. No memorial commemorated his life, his sacrifice, and his courage, because his friends were too terrified to mourn him in public.

Annie Williams followed in the footsteps of the Davis family and Buster Walker, the branch president, and his family. She fled her home. She fled West Tennessee's undulating, fertile farmland, the only landscape she had ever known. She moved to New York, where she lived the remainder of her life, forever haunted by the lynching of her husband.

After Annie's husband's body was recovered, Sheriff Hawkins told her that Judge William West Bond, a circuit court judge, was committed to bringing the perpetrators to justice. Bond, whose antecedents settled in Haywood County in the early nineteenth century, could not keep his word. The Haywood County grand jury over which he presided declined to return any indictments, reporting that after a "careful and earnest investigation examining people from all walks of life, including relatives of the dead negro, . . . no evidence was brought out that might place the suspicion on anyone as having part in the case."

The Black press closely followed events in Brownsville. Writing about the lynching, the *Pittsburgh Courier* proclaimed: "[I]f Elbert Williams is not avenged, if Elisha Davis, Rev. Buster Walker and the other refugees dare not return to their homes, just because they sought to exercise their right to vote, then democracy has no meaning, is a grim and empty fiction, is a terrible jest." The NAACP sprang into action in the wake of the slaying, alerting its national membership and the Justice Department to the terror in Brownsville. Walter White, the national NAACP leader, was in Memphis to speak at a national Methodist Youth Conference, and while there he conferred with Milmon Mitchell, Elisha Davis, and possibly others about what happened in

Brownsville. Rev. Walker delivered a dramatic report to the 1940 General Convention of the NAACP, which met later in June of that year in Philadelphia. He went to the convention with only the coat on his back, for he and five other members of the Brownsville branch had fled their homes as soon as Williams went missing.

Thurgood Marshall, who in 1940 was special counsel to the NAACP, was deeply committed to solving Williams's murder. He undertook a full investigation and turned over his findings, which included detailed affidavits from Elisha Davis and Annie Williams, to Assistant Attorney General John Rogge in Washington, DC. FBI officers from the Memphis office, in accordance with directives from Washington, began interviewing witnesses in Brownsville. The G-men were accompanied by none other than Tip Hunter, the night watchman who had led the mob to Davis's home in the early hours of the morning and days later ordered Williams, in his pajamas, to get into his police vehicle.

About ten days after Williams's murder, William McClanahan, the US Attorney for the Western District of Tennessee, wrote to Thomas J. Dodd Jr., special assistant to the attorney general, Criminal Division, warning against federal intervention in the case, noting that the "racial situation in counties like Haywood [one of two majority-Black counties in the state] is such as to require extremely careful handling." He suggested that whites were more likely to be attacked by Blacks than the reverse, and, in a message that was clear even when trying to sound cryptic, declared that "Williams is the only negro that has been killed, if he was killed."

Not only was the FBI investigation compromised by the presence of Tip Hunter at the in-person interviews, but according to Milmon Mitchell, who sheltered Davis after his abduction, the agents were more interested in finding a communist connection to the Brownsville NAACP than with identifying Williams's killers. McClanahan and the local FBI agents stalled for the next five months while the evidence went cold, and, in November, the local Memphis office informed the FBI in Washington that there were no more fruitful leads.

Wendell Berge, head of the Criminal Division of the Justice Department, leaned heavily on McClanahan to keep the case open, and told him the department thought the matter warranted consideration by a federal grand jury. Ultimately, however, the department's lawyers in Washington, over the vehement objection of Thurgood Marshall, permitted the case to be dropped. Victor Rotnem, chief of the Civil Rights Section of the department, memorialized the decision almost a year and a half after the lynching. In December 1941, he wrote that the men accused of the crime were "prominent citizens of the community" and that the victims' account of the events, as pieced together from the affidavits of NAACP leader Milmon Mitchell, Annie Williams, and Elisha and Nan Davis, did not match that of the accused. Five years later, L. B. Nichols, assistant director of the FBI, reflected on the agency's handling of the Brownsville case and concluded that the matter had not received proper supervision in the field or in Washington. The agency had moved too slowly and cavalierly, and had not followed up on leads. It had, in other words, sabotaged the case.

Elisha Davis never abandoned his hope that those responsible would be brought to justice. He recounted:

> I gambled everything—my home, my business, my life, my family (wife and children)—in order to prove to those people in Brownsville that the NAACP was alright. I felt that whatever happened I would be safe under the wings of the National Association for the Advancement of Colored People. At present I am separated from my family. I am not making any money. I do not feel secure in the least. After having told all in this case, my life . . . is constantly threatened.

More than a decade after his harrowing escape from Brownsville, he wrote to the NAACP Legal Defense Fund in New York seeking relief for the death of his friend Elbert Williams. Constance Baker Motley, who at that time was an assistant special counsel for the NAACP and later would become a federal judge, responded with cryptic legalese— as she would also answer Robert Spicely's queries about the murder of his brother, Booker—but indubitably she did not know what terror

lay behind Davis's letter. It was too late to pursue a civil action against
Hunter, the future jurist wrote, because the three-year statute of limitations had expired.

The events of 1940 cast such a fearsome shadow over the Black community that it would be two decades before African Americans would
register to vote in any significant numbers in Haywood County. When
they attempted again in the late 1950s, Hunter, who served as sheriff
from 1959 to 1966, was still guarding the registrar's office. He had
this to say to a reporter from *Jet* magazine in reaction to Black voter
activism in October 1959: "You got to understand we got two types of
nigras in this town: niggers and colored people. Now the niggers make
trouble and ain't no count. The colored people go to church and get
something out of it. They don't cause trouble. They're decent."

FEW PLACES IN TENNESSEE can surpass the physical beauty of Haywood County, where gently rolling hills press fertile dark soil up to
meet a bright sky, or the rich cultural legacy of its Black community, whence hailed Tina Turner and dozens of nationally renowned
musicians, artists, and educators. I joined a group of law students
who visited the area in 2011 and 2012 to investigate the Williams
and Davis case. Those visits left us with a distinct sense that Haywood County had yet to come to terms with the events of June
1940. Although still a majority-Black district, Brownsville had not
yet elected a Black mayor. When the students inquired about the
events of 1940, Jo Matherne, mayor in 2011, explained that opinion
in town was still deeply divided over whether the role played by city
and county officials was proper. The Davis family had not returned
to Brownsville, and the properties they left behind had ended up in
the hands of strangers.

As for the forty acres so carefully protected from tax collectors and
covetous neighbors by Elisha's father, Isaac, since he bought it in 1900,

it had been sold for what seemed like a song to a man named Guy Harrell, the overseer of the Haywood County Work Farm, a penal institution adjacent to the Davis property. The students found what appeared to be the old Davis property on Harrell Road.

Sometime after our visits to Brownsville, Davis family members and local citizens came together to rediscover their history and articulate a path to reparation. Three factors would be key to the success of this endeavor. First, the victims' descendants held strong memories of their parents' suffering and loss. Second, due regard for their appeals for justice animated the initiatives launched by public officials and private citizens in Haywood County. Third, in 2014, William (Bill) Rawls Jr. became the first African American elected as mayor of Brownsville. Embracing this story and appreciating its centrality to the city's future, his approach was different from that of his predecessor.

In 2015, the seventy-fifth anniversary of the murder of Elbert Williams was marked by a commemorative gathering, and the wheels of justice finally began to turn. In 2017, Tennessee adopted a civil rights cold case law modeled after the federal Emmett Till Unsolved Civil

Members of the Brownsville, Tennessee, branch of the NAACP at their second meeting in 1939. The branch sought to launch a voting campaign for the 1940 presidential election. The effort led to the lynching death of Elbert Williams, back row, far left in the photograph, and the banishment of his friend Elisha Davis, back row, third from left.

Elbert Williams was lynched in 1940 after members of the Brownsville, Tennessee, NAACP chapter announced its plans to encourage voter participation in the 1940 presidential election.

Rights Crimes Act. The Tennessee measure—the first in the country—called on its legislature to create a special joint legislative committee to examine unsolved civil rights crimes and cold cases. In 2018, responding directly to the new state law's requirement that viable cases be pursued, the district attorney for Haywood County reopened that county's 1940 investigation into the death of Williams. The prosecutor declared that "justice today may not look like justice could have looked in 1940. Today justice may consist of locating and examining Elbert Williams' remains and giving him a dignified burial with honor and a permanently marked grave. . . . If this can be accomplished, we believe the Williams family and this community will benefit from knowing as much of the truth as we can today determine and in that truth find a measure of justice."

It only took three-quarters of a century. The blame game was over. He drowned. He was under the influence of Communists. He was a Communist. He was a "no-count" nigger who "made trouble." He was a stand-in for the "no-count" nigger. He was an object—and a lesson.

He was a man lynched for thinking about voting. He is an unsung hero. Three-quarters of a century later, this, still, is true.

33

"A Fight with Some Sailors"

When she was not working as a nurse's aide or cleaning other women's homes, Lillian Williams, née Alveris, sold sno-balls to her neighbors in New Orleans. In 2012, at ninety-nine years of age, she passed away. At the Beautiful Zion Baptist Church in Algiers, a long line gathered in front of the pulpit to extol her virtues and accomplishments, among them, providing for her five sons, whose well-being depended, in some measure, on the accumulation of small coins from sno-balls.

At her funeral, her son James eulogized Lillian Williams, for he was the pastor at Beautiful Zion Baptist, the church where Lillian and her husband, Edwin Williams, had worshipped, and where, in 1943, Edwin's funeral was held. At Edwin's funeral as well, sixty-nine years before Lillian's, mourners filled the pews and spilled over into the aisles. They praised the deceased and then walked quietly to the front pew to comfort the young widow and her fatherless sons, of whom at the time there were four. Maybe Edwin Williams's brothers, two tenors in the New Orleans Gibbs Quartet, sang the group's most well known song, "Guide Me, O Thou Great Jehovah." A local newspaper reported that ministers from churches across the city were in attendance, as were the deceased's friends, "white and colored."

Somewhere within her body, Lillian Williams buried for those sixty-nine years and took to her grave the calamity of Edwin's murder. Only rarely did she talk to her sons about it. She never shared it with her congregation, although some of the older parishioners would have remembered the well-publicized event. What lay beneath the years of silence she placed in divine hands, and there, perhaps, she thought it should remain, unresolved, unexplained, and unexplored. A personal burden, she did not register her story in the archive of African American sorrow. She neither passed it down to her sons and their children as a cautionary tale about the perils of whiteness nor offered it up as an inscription on the Williams totem pole. All of that, Lillian Williams left for others to do. On her mantlepiece she placed a photograph of Edwin and moved on with a life that was at once pious and plenteous. She took in a brother's child, adding another son to the four she and Edwin had together. To her neighbors who loved her sno-balls, she would come to be known as the "Cold Cup Lady"; to her grandsons she was the best red beans cook in New Orleans and a ruthless Chinese checkers player. She sang in the church choir, as had her husband for ten years, and served as senior deaconess at Beautiful Zion Baptist. She stayed put in the home where she and Edwin had begun their family, only a short walk from church and from the place where he was slain. She was grateful for the support of her family, especially her brothers-in-law, who took a keen interest in their nephews, tutoring them in the gospel music that nourished the Williams clan and knit it together from one generation to the next.

Lillian Williams's life was upended by an encounter near her home in Algiers in 1943. Hosting thousands of soldiers by 1943, the Algiers Navy Yard sat on the rim of the old Black New Orleans community where Lillian, Edwin, and their four children lived, and, there at Beautiful Zion Baptist, worshipped. Located on the west bank of the Mississippi River, Algiers has historically hosted commercial activities that keep the New Orleans of tourist fame, over on the east bank, humming, while preserving its pristine façade: the old slaughterhouse, dry docks, lumber yards, the huge Southern Pacific Railroad yards, and, during the war, the naval station. In the 1940s, the quiet neighborhoods of Algiers were home to some of the famous musicians and entertainers who worked in the hotels and clubs in downtown New Orleans. A viaduct that lifted cars and pedestrians over the sprawling rails of the Southern Pacific also served as a passageway for sailors coming to and from their base.

It was there, on April 27, 1943, that a nineteen-year-old sailor from Texas, Walter Sherwood, slashed thirty-two-year-old Edwin Williams to death.

The day after the murder, Lillian Williams found her way to Daniel Byrd, one of the NAACP's most effective staffers. She told Byrd that late the previous night, she and Edwin had been walking home from church with their four children when they were accosted by three uniformed white sailors on the viaduct above them. One of the sailors, likely Walter Sherwood, stood over Lillian and poured beer on the baby boy she was carrying. Edwin remonstrated them, to which the sailor replied, "If you don't like that nigger I'll come down." Quickly descending the steps of the viaduct, the three men pounced on Edwin while Lillian watched in horror. With a broken beer bottle in hand, one of the soldiers "stabbed [Edwin] in the face and body. I was helpless having my baby in my arms. . . . I ran to my house to phone the police and when I returned I found my husband lying face down in the gutter dead." Police promptly arrived to investigate, finding broken glass strewn about the dead man and, in a stroke of luck (or providence), a sailor's hat, which would lead them to the naval station, Sherwood, and the two other men.

An Orleans Parish grand jury indicted Sherwood for manslaughter, but by the time the case went to trial several weeks later, Sherwood's story had significantly improved over the initial statement he gave to the New Orleans police. He was the victim, not the aggressor, he told the jury. Edwin Williams had "insulted his uniform," and when he came down from the viaduct to confront him about it, Williams, with his wife looking on, attacked him with a club and a knife, which Sherwood seized and, in self-defense, used to stab Williams. To put a cherry on top of the story, Sherwood testified that a group of angry Black men then came, it seemed to him, out of nowhere, and rushed in on him as Williams attacked, but he made his escape back up to the viaduct, where his two friends were standing, looking down at the fight. If the mayhem he inflicted on Williams with his beer bottle was supremely senseless, the story Sherwood peddled to the jury was insipid and caricaturish. In one fell swoop, the sailor had traumatized a community and animalized his victim. The forensic evidence solidly supported the prosecution, but the two women who served as the key prosecution witnesses—Lillian Williams, now a widow with four kids, and a neighbor, an African American single mother who did not work outside the home, who saw the murder and testified to its gratuitous brutality—were no match for the young Texan, uniformed, blond, blue-eyed, nearly six feet tall, and luminously white. The jury had no trouble with its verdict. Acquitted, Sherwood was promptly returned to duty.

The NAACP closed its file. And Lillian Williams went out to look for a job. After a decade she would marry again, but, as one of her sons would later recall, it did not "go well."

One could say that the trial of Sherwood marked some sort of progress in Louisiana, where, in 1943, whites were infrequently tried for crimes against Blacks. On the day he was indicted by the Orleans Parish grand jury, of the five men against whom the grand jury returned criminal indictments, he was the only white person charged. In a perverse sense, however, perhaps it was worse for Lillian Williams to have to play a part in a legal charade that dehumanized her husband and despoiled the respect to which her truth entitled her. The trial provided a semblance of transparency while obscuring and compounding the harms to Lillian and her boys. If Lillian Williams would bury this ordeal for most of her life, one might ask whether she was keeping her silence or whether the false verdict had silenced her.

In the summer of 2020, a law student, Erin McCrady, was tasked with researching the death of Edwin Williams. At the outset of her investigation, she was provided with the affidavit Lillian had written at the behest of Daniel Byrd on the day that followed the killing. McGrady collected press clippings and legal documents about the events, in preparation for an interview with members of the family. Her plan was to inform them of her discoveries and gather whatever information they might be willing to share with her. For weeks, she worked studiously but made no progress finding the right James Williams with a father named Edwin. When, after many hours of digital genealogy, she finally connected with a Reverend James Williams, the two talked for a long time, but not about what happened in 1943. He did not want to recall those events, and certainly not with a stranger; too far in the past and yet still too raw. To McGrady, the pastor posed the question of whether her family had ever experienced anything resembling what his had gone through, and that was as close as he got to the afterlife of unspeakable scars, to naming the chasm between her world and his, her America and his, her generation and his.

From the files she gathered from the local newspapers and the Louisiana NAACP, McGrady discovered how the story of Edwin Clifford Williams entwined, through no fault of Williams, with Walter Curry Sherwood. Born in Bexar County, Texas, Sherwood could well have been anxious to escape Texas for a bigger world, for he was one of eleven children. In 1942, he enlisted in the armed forces, and in April 1943 was sent to the Algiers Naval Station to be trained for the war overseas. So far as we know, Sherwood was never held to account by the navy. Eventually promoted to gunner's mate third class, he would serve the Allied forces on a Coast Guard tanker carrying artillery and supplies to armies in the Pacific theater. After the war he returned home. He died at age sixty-nine and is buried at Fort Sam Houston National Cemetery in San Antonio. It is a safe bet that few, if any, of Walter Sherwood's relatives and friends ever knew he committed what looked a lot like a murder when he was still a teenager, and then lied in a courtroom about it.

ALTHOUGH REVEREND JAMES WILLIAMS initially declined to discuss his father's death with Erin McCrady, Lillian Williams's middle-aged grandsons were eager to talk with her. When she reached them in July 2020, they knew little about how their grandfather had perished.

In New Orleans, Louisiana, in 1943, Edwin
Williams was beaten to death by sailors as
he was on his way to church with his wife
and children. His widow, Lillian Williams,
is pictured here with her four sons after her
husband's death.

Completely new to them were the affidavits so presciently collected by
Daniel Byrd that related the events witnessed by Lillian Williams and
her neighbor. "Our grandfather got into a fight with some sailors,"
and he got the short end of the stick, was the story they had picked up
over the years. That on the night he died he was headed to church—
the Beautiful Zion Baptist Church, where their fathers were pastors
and deacons, where each of them had been baptized—this was new
information. That he was slashed to death, prosaically, with a beer

bottle; that no other weapon was retrieved at the scene; that Thurgood Marshall unsuccessfully petitioned to get the Department of Justice to take up the case; that a doctor reported that their grandfather's injuries were consistent with what Lillian Williams saw; that there was a jury trial at which their grandmother testified; that it took the jury—likely all white—just under an hour to acquit the slayer; that the navy hastily shipped Sherwood off—all of this was new to them. They took it on board, thanked Erin McCrady, and wondered why they had never known what kind of man their grandfather was.

34

Owed? What?
And By Whom?

Is something owed to the descendants of Elbert Williams, Elisha Davis, and Edwin Williams? And to William Quiney III, whose forebears' land in Elaine, Arkansas, was stolen in 1919? What about the others whose stories are related here, and the thousands like them? By what scale is the responsibility of those who benefited from the injustices to be calibrated? Has the passage of time dulled or strengthened the descendants' claims? In sum, what form of redress does justice require today?

Legal concepts alone are inadequate to work through these dichotomies, for law's rights, wrongs, and remedies are based on intractable dualisms and encrusted in Western ways of thinking about individual responsibility and "just deserts." To unpack intergenerational burdens and benefits, reparations theory must look to political morality, the semiotics of gestures like apology, and restorative justice. Like restorative justice, reparation sits outside the traditional legal regime; it picks up where law has failed. Legal analysis is necessary but insufficient to explain when reparation must be made.

Reparation is an interdependent bundle of gestures and practices that involve recognition, truth-telling, apology, and payment—owed to all the victims of Jim Crow injustice. Indeed, the enduring presence of slavery in American structures and institutions militates in favor of reparations, both to address the wounds of enslavement and to dismantle systemic racism. But we need not determine the full reach of a reparations project to agree that the families of victims of lynching and racial murder, whose cases are the subject of *By Hands Now Known*, constitute a distinct and distinctly deserving subset of victims. Their claims for reparation should be promptly addressed, particularly because the generation most affected by these crimes is aging.

Any theory of redress, including one for the specific descendants of twentieth-century racial murder, must establish why certain historically distant harms matter more than others, how redress can ameliorate the harm, why redressing wrongs decades after the deaths of the directly affected victims and perpetrators is nevertheless imperative, why the historical suffering of African Americans is relevant to rectification of these specific harms, and why contemporary institutions must answer this claim.

The lexicon of reparation raises fresh questions about the relationship of the Jim Crow violence documented in *By Hands Now Known* to semifeudal slavery, on the one hand, and wage exploitation, on the other; and it retrieves traditions of resistance once lost to history. Indeed, history provides the rationale, the empirical basis, and the imperative of reparation. Acknowledging the hold of the past on the present elucidates the profound obduracy of social death, underscoring that the contemporary subordination of Black people cannot be divorced from the history of subjugation and resistance. It is also true that reparation, at least any remedy that might be forthcoming in the current climate, cannot by itself dismantle the structures upon which the violence depended, or eliminate the everyday tracks of enduring subordination. Reparation is meant to be corrective and restorative in nature, not distributive. It ought neither to be conceived as a standalone remedy nor as a substitute for meeting other requirements of justice, like equal access to the necessities and goods of life.

However, reparation is more than simply palliative. Activists committed to solutions that unravel the warp and weft of racism, capitalism, and unjust history have identified culpability sites at major universities,

health care institutions, and the insurance and banking industries. They
are articulating ambitious initiatives that harmonize claims centered
around historical harms with proposals addressing present injustices.
For example, payments made in 2015 by the City of Chicago to Black
victims of police torture were based on reparation's four components—
recognition, truth-telling, apology, and payment—as were payments
made in 2014 by North Carolina to the white and Black victims of
that state's mid-twentieth-century forced sterilization program. The
Algebra Project, founded by Robert P. Moses, while not couched in
reparation discourse, tackles what he termed "sharecropper education"
by positing a demand for intensive math education for the lower quar-
tile of public school students whose forebears were victims of forced
illiteracy and who have been hurt by ongoing miseducation. Similarly,
the prison abolition movement draws on the structures of slavery to
reveal the origins of mass incarceration, and the battle to end slavery
to imagine a world without prisons. In these initiatives it is the victims
of historical dispossession who are the protagonists for change. Present
assaults on their rights, they assert, need to be historicized if they are to
be corrected.

The problem of time renders reparative justice theory a messy affair.
The concept of repair requires a line drawn between the past and present, but such lines are inherently artificial. For enduring injustices, the
past is by definition the embodied present. Those who survived histories of injustice are always in dialogue with those who did not. Some
things are not "over," as proofs on the afterlife of slavery teach. It is
only the beneficiaries of past injustices who are served by holding on
to the illusion of a finite and "done" past. Reparation practice rejects
the teleological "arc of justice" version of American history that offers
freedom as a destination within reach. Claims for reparation illuminate
the infrastructures of history that reproduce power relations over time
despite changes in the legal environment, in contrast with liberal concepts of equality that are stripped of historical context. Indeed, piece-
meal reparation such as payments to the victims of lynching is not a
coda so much as another stage in a reckoning with racialized capture,

extraction, and death. If slavery generates an afterlife, so certainly does its descendant, Jim Crow violence.

It is, in short, impossible to free ourselves from the past as long as it coexists with the present. To borrow a metaphor from the Rwandan holocaust scholar Richard Benda, to make sense of life's journey one must simultaneously check the rearview mirror, the windshield, and the side mirrors. It is the rearview mirror that insists on defining the road ahead.

TWO PRECEPTS ADDRESS the discrimination problem in reparation theory: Why this past wrong (that is, Jim Crow violence), and not that one? First: redress is called for when an historical injustice has been reproduced over time and continues to shape contemporary group inter-actions. In such a case the historical injustice fundamentally damaged the political relationship necessary to sustain community in the present. Some theorists, most prominently Jeremy Waldron, have argued that the passage of time weakens historical claims. On this reading, rather than divisive obsession with original sin, attention should be paid to current inequalities. But without reparation, the material and social results of the original harm will continue to impair current relationships. In our case, the specter of lynching is ingrained in the contemporary images of Black bodies destroyed by police violence. By contrast, Bostonians of Irish descent once faced "need not apply" signs, a discrimination now entirely superseded, as evidenced by their political and economic standing in the city today. Access to "whiteness" largely erased the history of exclusion.

Psychoanalytic theory offers a slightly different approach to broken political relationships. In interpersonal relationships, repair interrupts the duplicating cycle of trauma that turns victims into perpetrators. As the psychoanalyst Jessica Benjamin argues, repair enacts the "moral third" to which the toxic dyad, trapped in the memory of a traumatic injustice, must surrender to create an alternative relationship. Repair is liberating because it empowers victims to confront the self-abnegation and self-hate

that flow from violent subordination and to take responsibility for ending replication. Care must be taken, however, to retain the collective call
for a reparation practice that engages broad social transformation rather
than—or perhaps in addition to—individual healing. If the problem lies
in subordinating social, political, and economic apparatuses, then solutions focused on individual psychological relations will not unmask the
underlying generative frameworks of historical racial violence.

The second precept aligns with debtor-creditor scales. In Aristote-
lian terms, and the language of tort law, corrective justice calibrates
what is owed to the victims of historical injustice by placing the burden
of loss on the shoulders of the perpetrators' successors. Reparation rests
on the same ethics that require a person to pay up on a debt. The problem of debt as grounds for reparation is that successful reparation must
include a political injunction: Never Again. Without the commitment
to change the relationship, payment of the debt cannot count as true
reparation. Whereas a debt based on a legal tort can be met without any
interrogation of the intent of the debtor, successful reparation turns on
political intent. Indeed, the concept of debt can be seen as a variation of
the first precept to make reparation. Redress helps repair political relationships damaged by longstanding injustices and reduces the residual
damage caused by an ancient debt—one that may no longer be legally
binding but is nevertheless alive as a moral matter.

In the cases described in *By Hands Now Known*, legal institutions
expedited and endorsed the injustices even when formal law afforded
remedies. Had the courts been open to the victims when these atrocities took place, their suffering would have been ameliorated. At the
very least, their losses would have been public. Genuine criminal trials
would have resulted in severe punishment for both official and private
perpetrators. Civil trials would have translated the families' injuries
into remunerable "pain and suffering," lost wages, and burial expenses.
These are the American tools to set things right after a murder.

But the courts were not there. Courts cast eyes on our private trans-
gressions when they cross into the crime zone, rendering them hyper-
visible. However, the residue of ruined lives ripped apart by Jim Crow

violence was hidden from view. Edicts from officials and others ordered victims and their families to "stop talking" and "go to work." In effect a "closed for business" sign hung on the door of the courthouse when Negroes knocked. Once the lynching was done, or the police bullets spent, the dead man's kinfolk had two no-win choices: stay shuttered in their homes in shame, or flee. Elisha Davis fled. Others fled. What they could not do is mourn in public, and certainly not take their grief to a courthouse. Charles Dickens famously observed: "It is a capital crime to mourn for, or sympathize with a victim of the guillotine." And so it was here. To mourn was to dissent. To mourn was to defy what law wrought.

What then, should be done decades after the events to bring a measure of justice to these families?

At a minimum, an official record must be created. The natural impulse, which is to expose the injustice for what it actually was, was chilled by the weight of manufactured uncertainty. Perhaps the deceased did pull a knife on the officer or commit the heinous rape. Perhaps, by his actions, the victim brought about his own death. The fabrications surrounding these killings stole from Black people their sorrow, their righteous rage, and their mourning. Bodies considered too dangerous to bury were left untouched by their survivors; and spurned and banished families were treated as if they, too, were dead. These actions have never been formally repudiated, leaving the lies in place and the survivors suspended in a liminal space between knowing and not knowing, the burden of the events still haunting their lives. Trauma, psychoanalysts teach, comprises the repetition of the original psychic wound long after the event, and sometimes it is only the repetition that reveals the full force and meaning of the event itself. The heavy, blurry shadow of the traumatic event cannot be addressed unless the fundamental facts of the event are made clear. Establishing the forensic truth; undoing the fear, the fraudulence, the fantastical, and the fabricated; and acknowledging the trauma that casts a pall over a life and its progeny can mark the road to meaningful repair. Recognition, the negation of invisibility, is the essential work of repair.

The reopening of the Elbert Williams case marks an important start on the road to reparation. When Williams was lynched in 1940, the local US Attorney for the Western District of Tennessee told Department of Justice officials in Washington that there was no need for federal intervention because "Williams is the only Negro to have been killed, if he was killed." As the official record stood until 2018, when the investigation was reopened, Williams drowned in a Brownsville swamp. Alternatively, his death was at the "hands of persons unknown." The county prosecutor's announcement in 2018—that "justice and historic truth demand that questions about the cause of . . . the death, and the identity of [Williams's] killer, be answered now if possible"—pronounces an official commitment to get it right. No, Williams did not drown. Those who lynched him are not "unknown." His bones, once washed over by the waters of the Hatchie, are now dry, but they are not at rest. The truth can still be retrieved seven decades later.

Nor is it enough to uncover the true story. An apology must be made. As in most cases in which prosecutions are no longer possible, an apology from an official representative of the state entity that bears responsibility for the harm can hold significance for families. An apology may, with good reason, be seen as too little too late, but most families want to hear the words "We're sorry." Samuel Bacon, sixty-one years old, was killed in 1948 in a jail in Fayette, Mississippi, because he refused to give up his seat to a white man on an interstate bus. In March 2018, Bacon's descendants gathered in Natchez, his hometown, to honor him and receive an official apology from Fayette's chief of police. James Darrell Broach, Bacon's grandson, fled the South after Bacon's murder, and he eventually became a New York City police officer. He deeply embraced the sentiments of the Fayette official: "Justice may be delayed, but sometimes it is not denied," Broach declared.

Royal Cyril Brooks died from a police bullet in February 1948 in his hometown of Gretna, Louisiana. Brooks wanted to exchange the nickel bus ride with another passenger, who had paid but was on the wrong bus. Brooks gave her a nickel to ride the correct bus. He expected, as was the custom, that he would then ride on the nickel already paid. Instead, the driver had him thrown off the bus by a police officer. Moments later, the officer shot the unarmed Brooks in plain sight, and as his son looked on, Brooks took his last breath on the sidewalk. In April 2018, Gretna mayor Belinda Constant apologized to her constituent, Roy Leo Brooks Jr., the victim's nephew, and other descendants. Brooks declared Gretna to still be a danger zone for Black people. Indeed, in 2016, Gretna was dubbed "the arrest capital of the United States." Nevertheless, Brooks accepted the apology as a step in the right direction.

For the families, apologies are an opening gesture on the path to reparative justice, and they offer a teaching moment for the institutions that extend them. An apology amounts to an official determination that the victim died at the hands of the state or that the state was in some way culpable. It also constitutes a forward-facing promise, much like the declaration when two people marry: "I do" hereby declare my intent from this point forward to infuse our relationship with justice and equality. For the state, the apology creates an official record. It is also performative in that it constitutes, or is an invitation to constitute, a fresh justice–respecting relationship. Finally, it is imperative in that it compels a new relationship. An apology fosters a practice of redress. It makes clear that, like individuals, institutions will inevitably err and must therefore customarily apologize and make amends for their wrongdoing. Apology must be the norm, not the exception. Not least of the reasons to apologize is to honor those who did not survive the virulence of Jim Crow terror. Their skeletal vestiges, often never properly interred, remain unattended, unmarked, and scattered across history's terrain. Apologies render them visible, urgent, and—despite the passage of time—still morally deserving.

Apologies and truth-telling alone are not enough, however; some kind of material remedy must also be forthcoming. As discussed earlier, historical wrongs litter the geography of the twentieth century, such that a reparation practice must distinguish between those injustices that call for material redress and those that fall outside that frame. Reparation theorists generally agree that claims associated with ongoing political disequilibrium require redress, as do claims that are akin to legal debts. On the first grounds, for example, reparation payments to Japanese Americans in response to World War II internment were owed not because the Supreme Court decision justifying internment, *Korematsu v. United States*, was wrongly decided, but because the failure to acknowledge the moral wrong of internment reflected disinterest in the harms suffered by Japanese Americans and Japanese nationals at the hands of the white majority. Denying or trivializing the injustice demeaned the political standing of the group, reiterated the dogma of second-class citizenship that was the basis for the injustice in the first place, and impugned the ideal of e pluribus unum. By definition, all injustices require some form of recognition, remediation, and restoration; and grave historical injustices require reparation. In the Japanese internment case, payment alone would not have been sufficiently reparative. The payment enacted a symbolic remembrance of the "pain and suffering" and recognition of the internment's material injustice. The apology corrected the historical record.

Norms in place at the time of the injustice may on some accounts also affect the validity of a claim for redress. Some theorists argue that reparation is justifiable only when legal standards extant at the time of the wrong were violated. In other words, if law supported the claims of the victim, then and only then should reparation be made. Claims for reparation for enslavement would on this ground fail because slavery did not violate positive law. This limiting criterion favors the claims of the families in *By Hands Now Known*, for murder was then, as it is now, unlawful. But the limitation also obscures the reality that racial violence was not confined to the spectacular murder or even lesser criminal assaults. Rather, it saturated Black life in the Jim Crow era. Moreover, the limitation ignores the distinction between corrective justice based on legal theories of fault, on the one hand, and political claims for reparation on the other hand. While a claim for reparation might be strengthened by demonstrating that the conduct giving rise to the harm violated existing legal norms, claims should not be limited because the laws upholding white hegemony provided no relief.

The cases of lynching, mob violence, and police killings in the Jim Crow South reflect the failure of the law as well as the failure of justice.

After the overthrow of slavery, Jim Crow reset the terms of racial subordination and reinscribed political domination, economic subordination, and social subservience. The injuries of slavery, both stigmatic and economic, were visited upon the children of the enslaved, and the privileges of slave owners were transferred to their progeny. Catalyzing most effectively the racialized roles of law were police and penal authorities. And corrective measures, which were not instituted as a legal matter until the 1950s, have never been adequate to repair the damage.

Scholars have established that the hallmarks of slavery and Jim Crow are most evident today in slavery's densest zip codes. The sociologist Geoff Ward has identified "microclimates of racial meaning" as places where current racial legal systems still reflect slavery's legacy. His research distinguishes these "microclimates" as places with higher death penalty rates, greater resort to corporal punishment in public schools, and sustained cycles of racialized violence. If the argument for broad reparation for the injustices of the Jim Crow period is sound, then it follows that the subset of claims by families who lost loved ones to murderous violence during Jim Crow are also sound. In fact, the argument for the subset is a good deal stronger than the argument for general reparation, because it is supported both by law on the books and by generally accepted principles of justice.

Federal law provided a civil remedy for those whose civil rights were violated, but it was not available to the families of men like Elbert Williams. His life was beaten out of him on the banks of the Hatchie by the Klan, or a stand-in for it, having been dragged to the waters by officers of the law. It was murders of this very type that federal law was meant to redress, but the law was then so weighted down with the detritus of sixty years of Jim Crow that even if Williams's wife, Annie, had been able to find a lawyer to take her case and a federal court willing to hear it, the federal statutes would likely have been unavailing.

Regardless of whether the murders could have entitled the victims' families to redress when they occurred, reparation to the descendants of these individuals is in order because their loved ones' unresolved deaths at the hands of the state enacted the penultimate norm that Black lives do not count. The practice of immunizing the perpetrators of racial murder changes the fundamental structure of law. It assigns an explicit racializing function to law and law enforcers. Rather than working as public guardians of community safety, law enforcement officials operate as protectors of privilege. Recall here Trayvon Martin's killer, George Zimmerman, who was the self-appointed overseer of the unspoken Jim Crow–like rules at a gated community in Sanford, Florida. Reparation has the potential to reduce the normative impact of injustices done under the flag of white supremacist law.

To de-racialize formal law and imbue it with the values of other traditions—for example, *ubuntu,** social equilibrium, and relationship—past wrongs must be purged. Here, again, redress requires more than the financial benefits that would have been due litigants' survivors had they sued under the applicable federal law at the time of the murders. Reparation requires the intentional recognition of the scope and impact of the injustice by those officials who caused or facilitated the abuse. Corporate law suggests that the officials' successors inherit this duty of repair. This brings us back to the four components: recognition, truth, apology, and payment.

In sum, reparation is particularly appropriate for the descendants of victims of lynching, police killings, and other racial murders. Such a program is both practicable and politically feasible because the beneficiaries constitute a finite group. Their claims are judicially cognizable and easily verifiable. They were denied relief to which the law entitled them at the time of the crimes. Those directly associated with the events—victims and perpetrators—are declining in number. Material reparation should be a part of a larger program of redress, including public educational initiatives and memory projects like memorial markers. Practically speaking, such a program cannot carry the full weight of redressing centuries of racial oppression, but it should be possible to design one that retrospectively addresses the specific losses suffered by the families of lynching victims, and prospectively speaks to improving the lives of their descendants.

---

* Nguni Bantu term translated as "I am because we are."

Epilogue

After the murder of George Floyd by police in Minneapolis, Minnesota, in 2020, a search of our archive of Jim Crow racial homicides revealed a striking (but not shocking) coincidence: a man of the same name was killed by a police officer in 1945. In October of that year, Thurgood Marshall received a letter from the secretary of the NAACP branch in St. Augustine, Florida, seeking an investigation into the "untimely death of our brother George Floyd whom we believe to have met his death unjustifiably so." Forty-six at the time of his death, the "other" George Floyd, a turpentine worker, was accused of being drunk on a Saturday evening and thrown into a cell in the St. Augustine jail. Floyd's protest against a second invasive search at the jail so incensed the arresting officer that he beat Floyd to death, in the presence of other detainees and the jailer. Just two documents have survived from which to render an account of this killing: the investigation of the branch NAACP, and the Florida death certificate.

Yet unmet, at the time of this writing, is the task of establishing true facts from these skimpy and contradictory papers. The official one, the death certificate, labels as an "accident" a death "caused" by "resisting officers of the law" and describes a killing "due to" "being hit with [a] black jack." The unofficial record, that of the NAACP, describes the execution of a prone man as he lay on the floor of a jail cell. Aside from a cursory coroner's inquest, no evidence of a state, local, or federal investigation could be located when we opened this case in 2015. The national NAACP was unable to lend support to its local branch when it was notified of Floyd's death in 1945. Floyd's wife of over twenty years followed him to the grave two years later, and a younger brother died a year after that. George Floyd's death destroyed his family.

It was not entirely unforeseeable that we would find this name-fellow in our archive, pleading to be exhumed and put in conversation with the iconic inspiration for what would come to be known as the 2020 "reckoning" with Black death at the hands of the state. After all, the Equal Justice Initiative identified more than 4,000 lynchings in the United States between 1877 and 1950. George Floyd's fate would not register in the EJI's report: it was not a lynching.

One might ask whether counting is even worth the candle, if "X" is not ascertainable. In this case, we count for Floyd Number 1 and Floyd Number 2. We count because George Floyd's younger brother, Charlie Floyd, beseeched the local branch of the NAACP to count. We count because the secretary of the branch, K. W. Calhoun Sr., wrote Thurgood Marshall in New York City, and asked him to count. And because Marshall's assistant, Robert Carter, who would later become a federal judge in New York, did his best to help. We count because George Floyd's paternal grandfather, Robert Floyd, was born into slavery in 1852, and with his paternal grandmother, also born a slave, had eight children. We count because across four generations of Floyds, the men worked in the woods chopping down the towering longleaf pines that would build our country and tapping out the turpentine to seal the boards on the ships that would transport our nation's merchandise, and the women cleaned houses, raised children, ran make-do infirmaries, and took in laundry. We count because the Floyds' payday wages were their only asset, indebtedness their constant companion, and the perpetually incomplete project of slavery their grinding geography. We count because for the Floyds, the bonds of slavery were replaced by unyielding indigence and debt, monetary debt, yes, but also debt living within the "calculus of blame and responsibility that mandated that the former enslaved both repay this investment of faith and prove their worthiness." We count because day after day and year after year, George Floyd worked in a forest alongside convicts whom he was only nominally freer than, from "can't see in the morning to can't see at night," dipping turpentine. We count because George and Rosa lived in the back of a camp that looked more like a prison, forbidden to keep a car on the premises because they might flee, and labored under the constant scrutiny of white bossmen even when the work was done. We count the years of sweat and blood, never calculated, never compensated. We count the suffering of the living and the savagery of the dying.

We count because we do not know who preached George Floyd's funeral or where he is buried. Or what happened to the man who killed him.

We count, and contest, because George Floyd counted. Number 1. And Number 2.

ACKNOWLEDGMENTS

This project started in 2007. That year I met Thomas Moore at a conference at Northeastern University. He told me about his brother, Charles Eddie Moore, who, together with Henry Hezekiah Dee, was lynched by the Ku Klux Klan in 1964 in Mississippi. I got to know the families of these two young men well. And I had the honor of representing Thomas, Charles's brother, and Thelma Dee Collins, Henry Hezekiah's sister, in a federal lawsuit. Though there was an opportunity to take legal action on behalf of these two families forty-three years after the lynching, I quickly learned that there were hundreds of others like them, at that point yet unnamed, for whom the courtroom doors were closed. To research their stories, I engaged students at Northeastern University. I've been at it since then, guided by the wisdom, grace, and fury that Thomas Moore and Thelma Collins imparted in 2007.

Around the same time, my good friend Melissa Nobles, a political scientist, began research along similar lines. We joined forces to create the Civil Rights and Restorative Justice Project at Northeastern University. From the beginning, Melissa forced me to discipline this project: to give it a geography, a time span, and a rationale. But for her insights and keen knowledge of US politics this book would not have been publishable. At my law school, my colleague Rose Zoltek-Jick helped to design the CRRJ project and to shape the research contained in this book. Emily Spieler, CRRJ's senior advisor, has provided invaluable advice and a steady hand as our project has grown. Over the past decade many other colleagues and students at Northeastern (where a fertile intellectual community is committed to research that furthers social justice) have helped me transform a set of random, fragmentary ideas into a book. It has been my good fortune to have generous colleagues and friends whose critiques of versions of the manuscript have, I hope, sharpened my thinking and tamed my writing. For their careful reading and discerning comments I am especially grateful to Libby Adler, Michael Meltsner, Jonathan Kahn, and Patricia J. Williams at Northeastern, and I thank my many colleagues at the school who have commented on my project at workshops, in the halls, and over a beverage.

Many friends and associates beyond Northeastern have offered their thoughts on the work. Nan Woodruff reminded me that I am not a historian, but that I am a writer with a duty to get the history right. She read and reread many versions of this book, with a red pencil in hand, and counseled me that good ideas deserve good writing. I thank my dear friend Nan. Ongoing conversations about these issues with Diane Harriford, Monica Martinez, Geoff Ward, Fania Davis, Hank Klibanoff, and Jennifer Llewellyn have helped me pose more incisive questions and put to proper use the research to which we are all committed. They have reminded me that behind each case is a family, and that family history is US history. Cheryl I. Harris pushed back, thankfully, on some of my legal analysis. Jim Emison generously reviewed my work on events in Brownsville, Tennessee, about which he has written a book. Robin Reshard was a wonderful source for Viola Edwards's story, and she has composed an opera about the case. Without Jay Driskell's several years of research at the National Archives and the Library of Congress, the book would not have been possible. Jay is more than an astute historian; to the task of uncovering every government document to be found on cases of Jim Crow racial violence he brought an enviable memory and eye for detail, not to mention patience, wit, and a generous spirit.

I thank those who commented on my work, and allowed me to learn about theirs, at many workshops and conferences. Of particular value was the convening "Rethinking Violence in African American History: History, Memory, Trauma" in 2017 at Pennsylvania State University, and the international conference "Recognition, Reparation and Reconciliation" in 2018 at Stellenbosch University in South Africa. I am grateful to the many knowledgeable librarians and archivists who have made the hunt productive. At Northeastern's Snell Library, the archivist Giordana Mecagni and her staff created the digital database housing the documents that underlie this project. CRRJ's archivists, Gina Nortonsmith and Rhonda Jones, and Northeastern's librarians Amanda Rust and Patrick Murray-John designed the database and website, and collected, catalogued, and digitized our materials, making my job infinitely easier. The librarians at Northeastern University School of Law met my every request. I thank the librarians and archivists who helped me at the Moorland-Spingarn Research Center at Howard University, the Birmingham Public Library, the Birmingham Civil Rights Institute, the Tuskegee University Library, the Mobile Municipal Archives, the National Archives, the Library of Congress, the Mississippi Department of Archives and History, the Amistad Research Center, the Schomburg Center for Research, the Tamiment Library at New York University, the Robert W. Woodruff Library at Emory University, the Valdosta State University Archives and Special Collections, the Abell Library at Austin College, the Hill Memorial Library at Louisiana State University, Howard-Tilton Memorial Library at Tulane University, and the Law Library at Southern University.

Without generous support from various institutions, I could not have undertaken this journey. I was awarded an Andrew Carnegie Fellowship in 2016. In 2008 and again in 2015, I spent sabbaticals at the Newhouse Center for the Humanities at Wellesley College, where I enjoyed a lovely office and benefited from rich exchanges with scholars and practitioners in the humanities. The Ford Foundation and the Andrew W. Mellon Foundation have provided generous support for this project. I thank Elizabeth Zitrin for her confidence in me, her friendship, and her support. Northeastern University has given me the space, time, and resources I needed, including many research stipends and grants.

Scores of my students worked on the cases described in these pages. It was for them an academic assignment, of course, but many students set out to learn more than how to measure a story or advise a client. The work changed them: it gave them that peculiar discernment that comes from seeing the past in the present, through another person's eyes. I cannot name them all, but I would be remiss if I did not mention some of those whose research figures prominently in this book—Kaylie Simon, Fraser Grier, Bayliss Fiddiman, Ada Goodly, Erin McCrady, and Lauren Hawkes—and some of the CRRJ lawyers upon whose work I have relied—Melvin Kelley, Raymond Wilkes, and Katie Sandson. Lydia Beal, my research assistant, spent a year working on every aspect of this project; I am deeply grateful.

I thank the families who shared with me their stories, and special thanks to those who allowed us to use their family photographs in the book. Conversations about Birmingham and Jim Crow with the esteemed Esther Cooper Jackson were always inspiring and informative.

After the cases were lined up, they had to be rendered readable. If they are, all the credit goes to my phenomenal editors, and if they are not, only I am responsible. John Glusman was an extraordinary editor who brought knowledge, enthusiasm, and a wickedly keen eye to this manuscript. I am deeply grateful to him and to all of his colleagues at Norton for supporting this project. Helen Thomaides, assistant editor and a consummate professional, persuaded me not to be too enamored of worthless prose. William Avery Hudson helped get me over the last hurdles. And before Norton took on this project, I leaned heavily on Lila Stromer to give to the work some form, and on Jill Kneerim to give it life. Without Jill Kneerim there would be no book. I am eternally grateful to Jill, and I cherish her memory.

Writing is lonely work, and revising even lonelier. Friends and family helped the medicine go down. My sisters Linda and Claudia and brother Charles tolerated countless progress reports at family Zoom meetings on Sunday afternoons, and my dear husband Max Stern and our children Hollis, Adjoa, and Dory encouraged and sustained me. My New Orleans family kept me and the writing going with superb nourishment for body, spirit, and mind.

There are bound to be some errors. They are mine. Incomplete references, awkward prose, no doubt. All mine. Blurred vision: mine. But here are the stories. Now they are yours as well as mine.

IN MEMORIAM

Ida Bessie Kelly, 1925–2022
Dora Belle McDonald, 1927–2020
Daughters of Washington and Josie Ellis
Bentonia, MS
Interviewed in 2017

Henry Gaskin Jr., 1948–2018
Nephew of Timothy Hood
Bessemer, AL
Interviewed in 2012

Rhetonia Perry Chisolm, 1920–2018
Friend of Walter Gunn
Tuskegee, AL
Interviewed in 2017

Marvin Roundtree Cox, 1934–2020
Acquainted with the Willie Davis family
Interviewed in 2013

Demetrius Newton, 1928–2013
Neighbor of the William Daniel family
Tuskegee, AL
Interviewed in 2013

Vida Rouse, 1932–2020
Daughter of Captain Butler
Edgewater, AL
Interviewed in 2019

Burl Louis Jones Jr., 1937–2019
Kidnapped in 1964
Meadville, MS
Interviewed in 2009

Elizabeth Bacon Sampson, 1912–2020
Daughter of Samuel Bacon
Natchez, MS
Interviewed in 2013

NOTES

INTRODUCTION

xi   **"Ride 'Jim Crow' in Georgia":** W. E. B. DuBois, *Dusk of Dawn: An Essay Toward an Autobiography of Race Concept* (New Brunswick, NJ: Transaction, 1940), 152.

xi   **"if there is any possible chance":** NAACP Records, Box II B47, Folder 12, Legal File-Crime.

xiii   **"public parks and playgrounds":** C. Vann Woodward, *The Strange Career of Jim Crow* (New York: Oxford University Press, 1966), 107–108.

xvii   **"house tops and cry aloud":** "Denied Chance to Preach Sermon, He Take His Protest to Lord in Prayer," *Norfolk Journal and Guide*, Sept. 30, 1933.

xvii   **a soldier on his bus:** "Mobile NAACP Wins Big Victory," *Pittsburgh Courier*, Sept. 12, 1942.

xviii   **"taught many lessons":** Eric Foner, *Reconstruction: America's Unfinished Revolution, 1863–1877* (New York: Harper & Row, 1988), 437.

xviii   **"blot on the page of history":** "Condition of the South," Report Number 261, in *Reports of Committees of the House of Representatives for the Second Session of the Forty-Third Congress* (Washington, DC: US Printing Office, 1875), 11–14; Committee of 70, "History of the Riot at Colfax, Grant Parish, Louisiana, April 13th, 1873: With a Brief Sketch of the Trial of the Grant Parish Prisoners in The Circuit Court of The United States" (New Orleans: Clark & Hofeline, 1874), 1, 4, 5, 6, 7, 8, 10–11, 12, 13.

xix   **the formerly enslaved:** *United States v. Cruikshank*, 25 F. Cas 707 (Bradley, Circuit Justice, C.C.D. La 1874) (No. 14, 897).

xix   **project of violent redemption:** James Gray Pope, "Snubbed Landmark: Why *United States v. Cruikshank* (1876) Belongs at the Heart of the American Constitutional Canon," *Harvard Civil Rights-Civil Liberties Law Review* 49, no. 2 (2014): 385.

xx **"bleeding colored men to the hospital":** Citizens' Protective League, *Story of the Riot* (New York: Citizens' Protective League, 1900), 2.

xxi **such state violence:** On the history of resistance to police violence, see, e.g., Elizabeth Hinton, *America on Fire: The Untold History of Police Violence and Black Rebellion Since the 1960s* (New York: Liveright, 2021); Bryan Wagner, *Disturbing the Peace: Black Culture and the Police Power After Slavery* (Cambridge, MA: Harvard University Press, 2009).

xxiii **a racial homicide case:** *Screws v. United States*, 325 U.S. 91 (1945).

1. "A NEW VERSION OF THE OLD, OLD STORY"

6 **recalled the Burns affair:** "A New Version of the Old, Old Story," *Cambridge Tribune,* Jan. 5, 1985.

7 **"his church and his family":** Ibid.

8 **warrant were determined:** *Ex parte Van Vleck*, 6 Ohio, Dec. Rep. 636, 7 Am. L. Rec. 275 (1878).

9 **"fair and impartial trial":** "New Version of the Old, Old Story," *Cambridge Tribune.*

9 **"given a fair trial":** "To Prevent Lynching, Ohio Judge Demands Assurance for Protection of Colored Persons," *Lewiston Daily,* Jan. 1, 1895.

9 **"humiliating guarantee":** "John Brown's Kick: The Governor of Kentucky Gives Judge Buchwalter Fits—Constitutional Question at Issue," *Cleveland Plain Dealer,* Jan. 3, 1895, quoted in Christopher Lasch, "Rendition Resistance," *North Carolina Law Review* 92, no. 1 (2013): 191–253.

9 **"from such unlawful death":** *In re Hampton*, 2 Ohio, Dec. 314 (1895).

2. "MR. FORD'S PLACE"

10 **between 1842 and 1862:** Roy Finkenbine, "A Community Militant and Organized: The Colored Vigilant Committee of Detroit," in *A Fluid Frontier: Slavery, Resistance, and the Underground Railroad in the Detroit River Borderland,* ed. Karolyn Smardz Frost and Veta Smith Tucker (Detroit: Wayne State University, 2016): 154–64.

11 **family kinship and church:** See *A Fluid Frontier: African Canadian and African American Transnationalism in the Detroit River Borderlands,* American Historical Association, Jan. 6, 2012.

11 **started a taxi business:** Karolyn Smardz Frost, *I've Got a Home in Glory Land: A Lost Tale of the Underground Railroad* (New York: Macmillan, 2007).

12 **to 60,000 in 1860:** Richard W. Thomas, *Life for Us Is What We Make It: Building Black Community in Detroit, 1915–1945 (Blacks in the Diaspora)* (Bloomington: Indiana University Press, 1992).

12 **provided aid to 1,045 fugitives:** Roy E. Finkenbine, "A Beacon of Liberty on the Great Lakes: Race, Slavery and the Law," in *The History of Michigan Law*, ed. Paul E. Finkelman and Martin J. Hershock (Athens: Ohio University Press, 2006), 83–107.

12 **jury trial with legal counsel:** Ibid.

12 **doubled between 1940 and 1950:** Joyce Shaw Peterson, "Black Automobile Workers in Detroit, 1910–1930," *Journal of Negro History* 64, no. 3 (1979): 177–90.

13 **20,000 members:** Parminder Kaur Mann, "A Comparative Study of the NAACP in Birmingham, Alabama, and Detroit, Michigan 1940–1965" (PhD diss., University of Surrey, 2000), 71.

13 **workers in the country were Black:** Peterson, *Black Automobile Workers in Detroit, 1910–1930*.

14 **"starin me in the face":** Paul Oliver, *Blues Fell This Morning: The Meaning of the Blues* (Cambridge: Cambridge University Press, 1990).

3. "THAT DUSKY HOSPITAL ON DEVILLIERS STREET": PENSACOLA TO BLACK BOTTOM

16 **their feet in Detroit.** Interview, Adrianne Sellers, Apr. 19, 2017 (interviewer: author) (on file with author).

17 **"send fugitive warrant":** "Lose No Time in Going After Negro Woman," *Pensacola Journal*, Oct. 8, 1928.

17 **demanding state's warrant:** Michigan Code of Criminal Procedure, 1927 PA 175, Chapter XVI: Miscellaneous Provisions § 776.7.

18 **across the entire city:** Donald H. Bragaw, "Status of Negroes in a Southern Port City in the Progressive Era: Pensacola, 1896–1920," *Florida Historical Quarterly* 51, no. 3 (Jan. 1973): 281–302.

18 **gaining valuable experience:** *Municipal Civil Service Commission of the City of New York: Minutes of the Commission for the Year 1920*, New York Public Library, 49.

18 **Black and white communities:** "Colored Hospital Will Be Open Soon," *Pensacola Journal*, June 4, 1922.

19 **"direct their own affairs":** See, generally, Booker T. Washington, "Chapter 2," in *The Negro in Business* (Boston: Hertel, Jenkins, 1907).

19 **"Pensacola, A Typical Negro Business Community":** Ibid.

20 **"the three Negroes and Tart":** Warren Carruth, "The Trials of Viola Edwards: A Window into the 1920s" (PhD diss., University of Southern Mississippi, 1983), 28.

20   **all of the defendants:** "Tart and Viola Edwards Freed," *Pensacola Journal*, Sept. 24, 1927.

20   **"hospital on DeVilliers Street":** Quoted in Carruth, "Trials of Viola Edwards," 37 (citing the *Pensacola Journal*, Sept. 24, 1927).

21   **"prejudice and bolshevism":** Ibid. (Sept. 26, 1927).

21   **"a group of Negroes":** Ibid, 50.

21   **ne'er-do-wells and criminals:** R. E. Lee, "The Negro National Business League," *Voice of the Negro*, Aug. 1, 1904, 327–31.

21   **based on the fetus:** See *Tart v. State*, 96 Fla. 77 (June 26, 1928), rejecting defendant Tart's appeal to the Supreme Court of Florida that the second indictment constituted double jeopardy.

21   **who was blameworthy and who was not:** Carruth, "Trials of Viola Edwards," 50.

22   **"do it if I die for it":** John Appleyard, *The Peacekeepers: The Story of Escambia County, Florida's 43 Sheriffs* (Pensacola, FL: publisher unknown, 2007), 7.

23   **"God Bless Our Home":** Quoted in Carruth, "Trials of Viola Edwards" (citing the *Pensacola Journal*, July 30, 31, and Aug. 5, 1908).

23   **beaten and murdered:** See *Lillie and Leander: A Legacy of Violence*, dir. Jeffrey Morgan, Sandy Hollow Productions, 2007.

23   **gusto and civic pride:** Linda Kim, "A Law of Unintended Consequences: United States Postal Censorship of Lynching Photographs," *Visual Resources* 28, no. 2 (2012): 171–193.

23   **"defense of white womanhood":** "Reaping the Whirlwind," *The Nation*, Nov. 5, 1908.

25   **"forty lynchings in that State":** *Twelfth Annual Report of the National Association for the Advancement of Colored People*, National Office, New York, Jan. 1922, 34.

25   **Progressive Women's Civic Association:** Cited in Carruth, *Trials of Viola Edwards* (quoting Fred Green Papers, Accession 49, Box 83, Folder 7 [c], State Archives of Michigan).

26   **the *Chicago Defender*:** "Michigan Governor Saves Woman from Florida Mob," *Chicago Defender*, National Edition, Dec. 8, 1928.

26   **"to barbaric mob murder":** NAACP Papers, Group I, Box G-96, Selected Branch Files, 1913–1939, Detroit, Michigan, Branch File.

26   **"arrest persons in other states":** "Michigan Governor Saves Woman from Florida Mob: Dixie State Loses Chance for Lynching," *Chicago Defender*, National Edition, Dec. 8, 1928; "Southerners May Kidnap Freed Woman," *Chicago Defender*, Dec. 22, 1928.

27   **relatives or the public:** Otis Bernard Jr., grandson of William H. Edwards, in discussion with author, Sept. 2017; Grace Hutcherson, granddaughter of William H. Edwards, in discussion with author, Sept. 22, 2017 (on file with author).

28 **"I won the case":** Telegram from J. Montrose Edrehi to Jack Ruby, Nov. 24, 1963, John F. Kennedy, Dallas Police Collection, Dallas Municipal Archives.

4. BENTONIA BLUES: YAZOO COUNTY TO BLACK BOTTOM

31 **hard work but never dull:** Interview, Daniel C. Moore and Timothy Moore, grandsons of Washington and Josie Ellis, Mar. 7, 2017, Detroit (interviewer: author) (on file with author).

32 **nearly froze to death:** Interview, Ida Bessie Ellis Moore-Kelley, daughter of Washington and Josie Ellis, Mar. 7, 2017, Detroit (interviewer: author) (on file with author).

33 **to locals as the "Yellow Dog":** "Brutal Death Bentonia Man Saturday Eve," *Yazoo City Herald*, June 4, 1935; Interview, Ida Bessie Ellis Moore-Kelley and Dora Belle McDonald, daughters of Washington and Josie Ellis, Mar. 7, 2017, Detroit (interviewer: author) (on file with author).

34 **places they were sharing:** Interview, Dora Belle McDonald, Mar. 7, 2017.

34 **had gotten into "some trouble":** Interview, Ida Bessie Ellis Moore-Kelley, Mar. 7, 2017.

35 **"nurturing of young radicals":** Beth Tompkins Bates, *The Making of Black Detroit in the Age of Henry Ford* (Chapel Hill: University of North Carolina Press, 2014), 172.

35 **murder of Boots Parker:** "Negro Long Wanted in Yazoo Picked Up in Detroit, Mich.," *Yazoo City Herald*, May 3, 1938, 1. *State of Mississippi v. Wash Ellis, Josie Ellis and James Allison*, Indictment returned on Oct. 22, 1935, Yazoo County Grand Jury.

36 **refused to honor the warrant:** "'Wipe Out Your Chain Gang!' Michigan Tells Georgia," *Chicago Defender*, Jan. 21, 1933

37 **until she could escape:** Interview, Dora Belle McDonald.

38 **"the chastity of his wife":** Letter, J. J. McClendon to Edward J. Kemp, July 28, 1938, NAACP Papers, Group I, Box D-41, Legal File: Extraditions, 1920–1939.

38 **"shown by that State":** William Pickens to Governor Frank Murphy, Aug. 2, 1938, ibid.

38 **"it was by Judge Frank Murphy":** Walter Francis White, *A Man Called White: The Autobiography of Walter White* (Athens: University of Georgia Press, 1948), 77.

39 **"cry of feared mob violence":** Governor Hugh White, telegram to Governor Frank Murphy, Aug. 5, 1938, RG 27, Series 915, Box 1636, Papers of Governor Hugh White (1936–1940).

39 **"where the indictment was found":** J. F. Barbour Jr., Esq., to Governor Hugh L. White, Sept. 9, 1938, ibid.

39   **bootlegging charge:** Ibid.

39   **"[for the murder of] Boots Parker":** General Laws of State of Mississippi, Chapter 191, July 26, 1938.

40   **befell the Ellises in Mississippi:** Governor Frank Murphy, letter to Governor Hugh L. White, Aug. 3, 1938, RG 27, Series 915, Box 1636, Papers of Governor Hugh White (1936–1940).

40   **"dangerous to your native citizens":** Governor Hugh L. White to Governor Frank Murphy, Sept. 19, 1938, ibid.

40   **Washington Ellis to Mississippi:** Governor Frank Murphy to Governor Hugh L. White, Dec. 7, 1938, ibid.

42   **"Yes, it was a mob":** S. Stuckey-Ellis 2002 Family Reunion Program Book (on file with author).

43   **"he is wanted in Mississippi":** Affidavit of Loyd Dewitt Talmadge Washington, Sept. 14, 1939, Papers of the Louisiana League for the Preservation of Constitutional Rights, Harold Newton Lee Papers, Manuscripts Collection 245, Louisiana Research Collection, Howard-Tilton Memorial Library, Tulane University.

43   **"nature was mending it":** Statement of Floyd [sic] D. T. Washington, Sept. 14, 1939, ibid.

5. THE ONE-WAY RIDE ON AIRLINE HIGHWAY: CRESCENT CITY TO BLACK BOTTOM

45   **banality on African Americans:** Jeffrey S. Adler, "The Greatest Thrill I Get Is When I Hear a Criminal Say, 'Yes, I Did It': Race and the Third Degree in New Orleans, 1920–1945," *Law & History Review* 34, no. 1 (2016): 1–44, 27.

46   **"warrant in a public building":** Official Report of the Proceedings Before the National Labor Relations Board in the Matter of Aluminum Line, et al. and International Longshoreman and Warehousemen's Union, vol. 12, the Elbert H. Gary Library of Law, Administrative Division Files and Dockets Section.

46   **"run them out of town":** "Without Form of Law," *Oakland Tribune*, July 1, 1938.

46   **"you're gonna leave town":** Burt Nelson to Harry Bridges, July 3, 1938, ILWU Papers.

46   **"we'll kill you":** Ibid.

46   **"agitate among the negroes":** Gorsch quoted in "Another Law, Another Straw," *Morning Post*, June 30, 1938.

46   **could be properly investigated:** "Workers Alliance Attempt to Stop Funeral Is Futile," *Louisiana Weekly*, Dec. 4, 1937.

46   **fatally shot two additional suspects:** Adler, "Greatest Thrill," 28.

47   **securing trial-proof "evidence":** "On Trial, Lad's Bodies Show Cuts, Bruises; Await Verdict," *Louisiana Weekly*, July 31, 1937, and Ethel Anderson, statement to

John E. Rousseau Jr., Apr. 22, 1945, Louisiana League Papers, quoted in Adler, "Greatest Thrill," 29 n138.

47 **at least nine months a year:** Janet K. Cavin, *Zachary Bicentennial Commission, Zachary Faces & Places: A History of the City of Zachary, Louisiana, 1975* (Baton Rouge: Land and Land Printers, 1976), 26, 56.

48 **ran along its Main Street:** The Back Street address is given in the 1910 US census for Wilbert Smith, East Baton Rouge, Police Jury Ward 4, District 0031.

49 **succumbed to his wounds:** "Policeman Shot by Negro, May Die," *Morning Tribune,* Jan. 18, 1930; "Police Hero Dies of Shot," *New Orleans Item,* Jan. 23, 1930.

49 **the city that year:** Jeffrey S. Adler, "'The Killer Behind the Badge': Race and Police Homicide in New Orleans," *Law & History Review* 30, no. 2 (2012): 495–531.

50 **and scores of others:** "Faces Extradition as La. Cop Slayer," *Chicago Defender,* Jan. 18, 1941.

50 **"tried by a New Orleans court":** "Habeas Corpus Writ Halts Ga. Extradition," *Chicago Defender,* Feb. 1, 1941.

51 **appeal to the Michigan Supreme Court:** "Faces Extradition as La. Cop Slayer," *Chicago Defender.*

51 **turned over to Grosch and Arnold:** "Fear Louisianan Murdered by Police," *Atlanta Daily World,* Jan. 22, 1941.

51 **its claim that Smith was murdered.** "Fear Louisianan Murdered by Police," *Atlanta Daily World.*

51 **the death as a "streamlined lynching":** "Say Extradition Victim Beaten to Death," *Chicago Defender,* Feb. 8, 1941, "Probe Streamlined Lynching," *Atlanta Daily World,* Jan. 30, 1941.

51 **against the officers:** "Suspension of 'Legal Lynchers' Demanded," *New Orleans Sentinel,* Feb. 1, 1941.

52 **open a file on the matter:** "Local Coroner to Hold Autopsy; Dr. N. R. Davidson, Representing Negro Organizations, to Witness Procedure," *New Orleans Sentinel,* Mar. 6, 1941

52 **right side of the head:** "New Probe Ordered in New Orleans Police Slaying," *Atlanta Daily World,* Mar. 13, 1941; "Grand Jury Frees Cops in La. Murder," *Chicago Defender,* May 31, 1941.

53 **"dragging Grosch with him":** "Fear Louisianan Murdered by Police," *Atlanta Daily World.*

53 **"safe delivery in the South":** Clinton Hamilton to NAACP, Jan. 17, 1941, NAACP Papers, Box IIA 407, Folder 4, General Office Files, Lynching.

53 **the story about the beating:** "Alleged Beating of Negro Woman Put Before Jury," *New Orleans Times-Picayune,* Mar. 13, 1941.

54 **to indict the officers:** "Grand Jury Frees Cops in La. Murder," *Chicago Defender.*

54   **was to no avail:** "Detectives Exonerated in Slaying of Wilmer Smith," *New Orleans Sentinel*, May 24, 1941.

6. RESISTING RENDITION: LEGAL STRATEGIES AND POLITICAL ADVOCACY

56   **the legality of slavery:** *Somerset v. Stewart*, 98 ER 400 (1772).

56   **"one another in this respect":** Quoted in Christopher Lasch, "Rendition Resistance," *North Caroline Law Review* 92, no. 1 (2013): 149–236, 170n116.

56   **non-slave fugitives from justice:** US Constitution Art. IV, § 2, Cl. 2: "A Person charged in any State with Treason, Felony, or other Crime, who shall flee from Justice, and be found in another State, shall on Demand of the executive Authority of the State from which he fled, be delivered up, to be removed to the State having Jurisdiction of the Crime."

58   **to leave her owner:** *Kentucky v. Dennison*, at 66, 67.

58   **"fair trial in the courts of Oklahoma":** In the Matter of the Application of the Governor of the State of Oklahoma for the Rendition of C. T. Smithie as a Fugitive from the Justice of that State, Nov. 23, 1921, NAACP Papers, Group I, Box D-43, Legal File: Extraditions 1920–1939, Smithie, Charles T.

58   **"service of legal counsel":** "California Refuses to Extradite Grocer," *Chicago Defender*, National Edition, Sept. 18, 1948, 5. See also Memorandum for Governor Earl Warren in re. Extradition of Wiley King to the State of Mississippi, July 26, 1948, NAACP Papers, Group II, Box B-68, Legal Files: Extraditions 1940–1955, King, Wiley.

59   **"Negro back to Mississippi":** Errol G. Gallagher to Thurgood Marshall, July 28, 1948, ibid.

59   **"bread winner back to prison":** "Warren Denies Extradition," *Salt Lake Tribune*, Sept. 3, 1948.

59   **to protect Black fugitives:** Eric W. Rise, "Crime, Comity and Civil Rights: The NAACP and the Extradition of Southern Black Fugitives," *American Journal of Legal History* 55, no. 1 (2015): 132.

59   **throughout the 1920s:** Ibid., 133.

59   **case in 1942 in Pennsylvania:** *Commonwealth ex re. Thomas Mattox v. Superintendent of County Prison*, 152. Pa. Super 167.

60   **thirty miles of Elberton:** Sara Kominers, *Interstate Extradition and Jim Crow Violence: The Case of Thomas Mattox*, Civil Rights and Restorative Justice, 2015 (on file with author).

60   **support to anti-lynching legislation:** "Clare Gerald Fenerty (1895–1952)," in *Biographical Directory of the United States Congress, 1774–Present*.

60   **"authorities for permitting murder":** "Judge Fenerty's Opinion," *Thomas*

Mattox v. Superintendent of County Prison, Court of Quarter Sessions for Philadelphia, no date.

60 **"such bias and prejudice":** Ibid.

60 **extradite young Thomas Mattox:** Fenerty's decision was subsequently upheld by Judge Keller of the Superior Court of Pennsylvania; see *Commonwealth ex re. Thomas Mattox v. Superintendent of County Prison*, 152.

60 **"story on the witness stand":** "Saves Chicagoan from Mob," *Chicago Defender*, National Edition, Mar. 25, 1944.

60 **for a physical examination:** "Catchings to Be Returning on Draft Violation Charge," *Jackson Clarion-Ledger*, Feb. 25, 1944, 2.

61 **"defendant back to Mississippi":** "Judge Refuses to Return Man to Face Dixie 'Law,'" *Chicago Defender*, National Edition, Aug. 26, 1944.

61 **straight extradition case:** "Huff Wins 77th Straight Anti-Extradition Victory," *Atlanta Daily World*, Oct. 21, 1949.

7. WHO STAYS UP NORTH, WHO GOES BACK DOWN SOUTH

63 **under duress but affirmatively:** "Court Blocks Woman's Extradition to Georgia: Mrs. Fleetwood Gets 20-Day Stay to Appeal Case," *Pittsburgh Courier*, Mar. 28, 1936.

63 **"in this case, please advise us":** Charles H. Houston to William T. Patrick Sr., May 22, 1936, NAACP Papers, Group I, Box D-41, Legal File: Extraditions 1920–1939, Fleetwood, Willie (Rejected Case).

63 **"one of my people is involved":** "Court Blocks Woman's Extradition to Georgia," *Pittsburgh Courier*.

64 **"my people to their jurisdiction":** William T. Patrick Sr. to Charles H. Houston, June 2, 1936, NAACP Papers, Group I, Box D-41, Legal File: Extraditions 1920–1939, Fleetwood, Willie (Rejected Case).

64 **one of the "Scottsboro Boys":** "Man Admits Being Escaped Convict—Fled Georgia Prison Camp in Cedartown," *Chicago Defender*, July 15, 1933.

65 **"severing all connections [with Crawford]":** Ibid.

65 **just three months earlier:** "Fugitive Must Return to Ga.," *Pittsburgh Courier*, Mar. 25, 1950.

65 **prospects for favorable legal precedent:** William T. Andrews to J. Montrose Edrehi, Nov. 1, 1929, NAACP Papers, Group I, Box D-41, Legal File: Extraditions 1920–1939, Edwards, Viola (Rejected Case).

65 **each year across the South:** Matthew J. Mancini, *One Dies, Get Another: Convict Leasing in the American South, 1866–1928* (Columbia: University of South Carolina Press, 1996), 68.

65   **based on Burns's memoir:** Rise, "Crime, Comity and Civil Rights," 120.

66   **"have been the chief victims":** Statement of Walter White, Secretary of the National Association for the Advancement of Colored People at the Hearing Before Governor A. Harry Moore of New Jersey of the Extradition Proceedings Brought by Georgia Officers of the Law Against Robert Elliot Burns, December 21, 1932, NAACP Papers, Group I, Box D-41, Legal File: Extraditions 1920–1939, Burns, Robert. E.

66   **held the men in peonage:** "Expose Peonage in Georgia: Fugitives Tell Tragic Story of Brutality," *Chicago Defender*, National Edition, Oct. 7, 1939.

66   **the Municipal Court of Chicago:** Ibid.

66   **"prosecuted for peonage and conspiracy":** "Governor Horner Saves 3 from Chain Gang: Extradition Denied," *Chicago Defender*, Oct. 21, 1939.

66   **conditions of slavery and peonage:** *United States v. Cunningham*, 40 F. Supp. 399, 400 (1941). See also "Two Indicted for Peonage: U.S. to Prosecute White GA. Planter and His Attorney," *Pittsburgh Courier*, June 7, 1941.

66   **support from peonage victims:** Erik S. Gellman, *Death Blow to Jim Crow: The National Negro Congress and the Rise of Militant Civil Rights* (Chapel Hill: University of North Carolina Press, 2012), 131.

67   **"substantial grounds for prosecution":** *United States v. Cunningham*, 40 F. Supp. 399, 401 (1941).

67   **"have violated the law":** "U.S. Judge Frees Peonage Boss: Won't Prosecute GA. Defendants for Trial," *Chicago Defender*, National Edition, Sept. 6, 1941.

67   **struck down Georgia's debt law:** *Taylor v. Georgia*, 315 U.S. 25.

67   **which had followed Emancipation:** "Gov't to Defend Civil Rights," *Indianapolis Recorder*, Apr. 4, 1942.

67   **"I would gladly go back to Oglethorpe County":** William Henry Huff to Thurgood Marshall, March 5, 1941, NAACP Papers, Group II, Box B-112, Peonage: Huff, William Henry, 1941–1942.

PART II: RACED TRANSPORTATION

71   **"you'd be in uniform yourself":** Corporal Fred Edwards to Jessie Flowers, Dec. 13, 1942; Office of Saline Waters, File-Camp Shelby, Mississippi, Entry 188, Box 186, Record Group 107; NARA II, quoted in John Daniel Hutchinson, "Sites of Contention: Military Bases and the Transformation of the American South During World War II" (PhD diss., Florida State University, 2011).

71   **"uniform of the United States Army":** Thurgood Marshall to Tom C. Clark, New York, NY, 1944.

8. THE COLOR BOARD

73 **The Color Board:** For description of the "color board" see, in Hood file, Greenberry B. Fant, Office Memorandum, May 14, 1946, DOJ Litigation Case File 144-1-30.

74 **in its immediate aftermath:** Blair L. M. Kelley, *Right to Ride: Streetcar Boycotts and African American Citizenship in the Era of Plessy v. Ferguson* (Chapel Hill: University of North Carolina Press, 2010); Robin D. G. Kelley, " 'We Are Not What We Seem': Rethinking Black Working-Class Opposition in the Jim Crow South," *Journal of American History* 80, no. 1 (June 1993): 75–112.

76 **"before this one is over!":** Wilkinson, Aug. 28, 1942, quoted in Robert J. Norell, "Labor at the Ballot Box: Alabama Politics from the New Deal to the Dixiecrat Movement," *Journal of Southern History* 57, no. 2 (1991): 227.

77 **to be mastered by newcomers:** On resistance to Jim Crow transportation, see Robin Kelley, " 'We Are Not What We Seem.' " See also Howard Griffin, *Black Like Me* (New York: Houghton Mifflin, 1960).

9. POB NOXUBEE, POD BACK OF THE BUS

79 **"handling, loading and related occupations":** Henry Williams, death certificate, Aug. 15, 1942, Deaths and Burials Index 1881–1974, Alabama, Alabama Public Health.

80 **the good, federally supported jobs:** See, generally, Scotty E. Kirkwell, "Mobile and the Boswell Amendment," *Alabama Review* 65, no. 3 (July 2012): 205–49; Melton McLaurin, *Mobile Blacks and World War II: The Development of a Political Consciousness* in *Gulf Coast Politics in the Twentieth Century,* ed. Ted Carageorge (Pensacola, FL: Historic Pensacola Preservation Board, 1973), v–89, 48–49. For population, see Pete Daniel, "Going Among Strangers: Southern Reaction to World War II," *Journal of American History* 77, no. 3 (Dec. 1990): 886–911; Department of Justice, RG 60, File 144-3-5.

81 **"asked to serve refreshments to the negroes":** Harry H. Smith to Gov. Chauncey Sparks, Sept. 30, 1943, Files of Dr. David Alsobrook, Mobile Municipal Archives.

81 **"more than a person can stand":** Quoted in J. Mills Thornton III, *Archipelagoes of My South: Episodes in the Shaping of a Region, 1830–1965* (Tuscaloosa: University of Alabama Press, 2016), 164.

82 **refusing to move from his seat:** William H. Craft to Gov. Chauncey Sparks, Sept. 6, 1944, Governor's Correspondence, SG 12491, Folder 8, Alabama Department of Archives; J. Mills Thornton III, "Segregation and the City: White Supremacy in Alabama in the Mid-Twentieth Century," in *Fog of*

War: The Second World War and the Civil Rights Movement, ed. Kevin M. Kruse and Stephen Tuck (Oxford: Oxford University Press, 2012), 51–69, 64; Charles A. Baumhauer to Major Thomas H. Vaden, Aug. 3, 1942, Mobile Municipal Archives, Race, Box 17027.

83 **the driver executed young Williams:** "Negro Private Killed Aboard City Lines Bus," *Mobile Register*, Aug. 16, 1942; "Negro Soldier Shot in Mobile in Bus Driver Row," *Birmingham News*, Aug. 16, 1942; "Alabama Soldier Killed: Investigation Ordered," *Birmingham World*, Aug. 18, 1942; "Negro Shot Six Times by White Bus Driver," *Birmingham World*, Aug. 21, 1942; "Ask Thorough Investigation," *Birmingham World*, Aug. 21, 1942.

83 **"as never manifested before":** John LeFlore to Roy Wilkins, Sept. 1, 1942, NAACP Papers, Part 26: Selected Branch Files, 1940–1955, Series A: The South.

83 **drivers remained all white:** On resistance to Jim Crow transportation as a subversive practice, see Robin Kelley, "'We Are Not What We Seem'"; Ella Baker to Lucille Black, Mar. 20, 1943, NAACP Papers, Part 26: Selected Branch Files, 1940–1955, Series A: The South; "Mobile Housing Survey," *Mobile Register*, Sept. 1, 1943; "Mobile's Colored People Call Off 'Walk' Campaign," Sept. 7, 1943; "Mobile NAACP Wins Big Victory," *Pittsburgh Courier*, Sept. 12, 1942; John LeFlore to Byron E. Pickering, Aug. 26, 1942, NAACP Papers, Part 26: Selected Branch Files, 1940–1955, Series A: The South.

84 **the murder of Henry Williams:** John LeFlore to Vincent B. Dixon, Oct. 27, 1942, Papers of John LeFlore, Box 1090, Mobile Municipal Archives; "Alabama Soldier Killed: Investigation Ordered," *Birmingham World*; "Negro Shot Six Times by White Bus Driver," *Birmingham World*; "Negro Private Killed Aboard City Lines Bus," *Mobile Register*; "Hearing Due Today in Negro's Death," *Mobile Register*, August 18, 1942; "Driver of Bus Allowed Bond on Slaying Charge," *Mobile Register*, Aug. 19, 1942; "Army Can Protect Soldiers from Civilian Violence—Why Doesn't It?" *Baltimore Afro-American*, Nov. 27, 1943; Record for Grover E. V. Chandler, enlistment date Nov. 9, 1943, World War II Army Enlistment Records, 1938–1946, NARA; Obituary, "Grover E. Van Chandler," *Smith County Reformer*, Aug. 26, 1981.

10. A BUS IN HAYTI

86 **"similar group in the nation":** Booker T. Washington, "Durham, North Carolina: A City of Negro Enterprise," *The Independent*, Mar. 30, 1911, 642–670, 646; W. E. B. DuBois, "The Upbuilding of Black Durham: The Success of the Negroes and Their Value to a Tolerant and Helpful Southern City," *World's Work* 23 (Jan. 1912): 334–338.

88   **"The room is crammed with people"**: Glenn Hinson, *The Bull City Blues* (Chapel Hill, NC: Creative Printers, 1976), 46.

89   **"equal rights with the white people"**: Hutchinson, *Sites of Contention*, quoting Long, letter to Cooley, Aug. 27, 1941, Harold Cooley Papers, Southern Historical Collection, University of North Carolina, Box 3, Folder 87, "Camp Sites."

90   **"not used to seeing things like this"**: Entry UD 15: Fourth Service Command, 1942–1946, War Department Decimal File No. 291.2; Records of US Army Service Forces, DOJ, RG 160 (hereinafter Army file, Spicely).

91   **in the heart and stomach**: Army file, Spicely.

91   **alcohol test was negative**: Army file, Spicely; "Bus Driver Is Bound Over on Murder Charges," *Durham Morning Herald*, July 11, 1944.

91   **more to conceal than to reveal**: Army file, Spicely.

92   **protest among communists or African Americans**: James J. Weingartner, *A Peculiar Crusade: Willis M. Everett & the Malmedy Massacre* (New York: New York University Press, 2000).

92   **his segregated unit at Camp Butner**: Army file, Spicely.

93   **as well as a misdemeanor record**: Army file, Spicely.

93   **the targets of that investigation**: Army file, Spicely.

93   **to mete out justice fairly**: Army file, Spicely.

94   **evoking wide-scale protests**: David S. Cecelski and Timothy B. Tyson, ed., *Democracy Betrayed: The Wilmington Race Riot of 1898 and Its Legacy* (Chapel Hill: University of North Carolina Press, 1998), 261; Timothy B. Tyson, *Radio Free Dixie: Robert F. Williams and the Roots of Black Power* (Chapel Hill: University of North Carolina Press, 2001), 15.

94   **"occurrence of overt racial disturbances"**: Daniel Kryder, "The American State & the Management of Race Conflict in the Workplace & in the Army, 1941–1945," *Polity* 26, no. 4 (Summer 1994): 601–634, 629 (Memorandum for the Commanding General, Army Service Forces, Subject: Racial Situation in the United States, Apr. 17, 1944, OF 4245, Office of Production Management, Committee on Fair Employment Practice, War Department Material Concerning Minority, Mar.–Apr, 1944; and Memorandum to Staff, W. D. Styer, Major General, Chief of Staff, June 8, 1944, OF 4245, Office of Production Management, Committee on Fair Employment Practice, War Department Material Concerning Minority, May–June 1944, Franklin D. Roosevelt Presidential Library and Museum).

94   **"regardless of local custom"**: Major General A. J. Ulio, Adjutant General, Letter to Commanding Generals, All Service Commands, July 8, 1944, quoted in Kryder, "American State."

95   **"whole trouble around the Spicely case"**: Thurgood Marshall to Carolyn

Dee Moore, Sept. 7, 1944, "Booker T. Spicely Killing by Bus Driver," Papers of the NAACP, Part 09: Discrimination in the US Armed Forces, Series B: Armed Forces' Legal Files, 1940–1950.

96   **prepared to respond to any unrest:** The NAACP was discouraged from becoming involved in the prosecution of Spicely by Durham's nationally prominent Black leaders, who thought widespread attention would scare off whites in the city who might otherwise speak up for fair legal proceedings. C. Jerry Gates to Thurgood Marshall, Aug. 11, 1944, Durham County Superior Court Minutes, Criminal Term 1944, July 19–Sept. 15, 1944, NAACP Papers, Part 09: Discrimination in the US Armed Forces, Series B: Armed Forces' Legal Files, 1940–1950; Army file, Spicely.

97   **not lost on the residents of Hayti:** "Scene at Durham's 250,000 Fire," *Charlotte Observer*, July 9, 1944.

98   **"Spaulding or anyone else":** Robert A. Spicely to Thurgood Marshall, Aug. 6, 1944, NAACP Papers, Part 09: Discrimination in the US Armed Forces, Series B: Armed Forces' Legal Files, 1940–1950, Spicely file.

98   **nothing further to be done:** Constance Baker Motley, letter to Robert A. Spicely, Jan. 18, 1949, NAACP Papers, Part 09: Discrimination in the US Armed Forces, Series B: Armed Forces' Legal Files, 1940–1950: Army file, Spicely.

11. "US COLORED . . . SAT WHERE WE WANTED TO"

99   **An official of the Southern Regional Council:** Robert J. Norrell, *Reaping the Whirlwind: The Civil Rights Movement in Tuskegee* (Chapel Hill: University of North Carolina Press, 1998), 60–61; Horace Bohannon to George Mitchell, Ft. Valley, Ga., Jan. 11, 1945, Southern Regional Council Archives document series VII:3 microfilm, reel 188, frame 257 (Special Collections, Robert W. Woodruff Library, Atlanta University Center).

101   **"demand for its products diminished":** Marilyn Davis Barefield, Compiler, *Bessemer, Yesterday and Today, 1887–1888* (Birmingham, AL: Southern University Press, 1986), 26.

102   **"to reside within the areas described":** For the Code of the City of Bessemer 1954, see S. Jonathan Bass, *He Calls Me by Lightning: The Life of Calif Washington and the Forgotten Saga of Jim Crow, Southern Justice, and the Death Penalty* (New York: Liveright, 2017), 365.

102   **watermelon and reduced prison time:** Chas. S. Johnson, "Southern Race Relations Conference," *Journal of Negro Education* 12, no. 1 (Winter 1943): 133–139.

103   **"former or present Klan members":** FBI File 44-95, Mar. 3, 1946; DOJ Litigation Case File, 144-1-30.

103   **commonplace in Bessemer:** Bass, *He Calls Me by Lightning*, 28, 56–57, 61.

105 **Weeks hollered:** DOJ Litigation Case File, 144-1-30.

105 **"All of you damn niggers, leave here":** Ibid.

106 **a Bessemer army investigator:** DOJ Litigation Case File, 144-1-30; "Birmingham Veterans Demand the Ballot," *Chicago Defender,* Feb. 2, 1946.

106 **response from federal authorities:** "1200 at NAACP Meeting Ask U.S. to Probe Killing of Marine," *Baltimore Afro-American,* Mar. 24, 1946.

106 **not the federal government:** DOJ Litigation Case File, 144-1-30.

107 **civic leader across the South:** On the Caliph Washington case, see Bass, *He Calls Me by Lightning.*

12. DOUBLE V ON THE BUS

108 **"as well as Hitlerism without":** "The Barometer of Negro Thought . . . ," *Crisis,* Dec. 8, 1947; "Industry's Failure to Use Negro Labor Held Glaring Obstacle to U.S. Defense Program," *Cleveland Call and Post,* June 21, 1941.

109 **"resulted in some minor racial conflicts":** Federal investigator, quoted in Pete Daniels, "Going Among Strangers: Southern Reactions to World War II," *Journal of American History* 77, no. 3 (Dec. 1990): 886–911, 905. Daniels also discusses bus problems in Mobile and Pascagoula (see "Some Problems of the Negro in Mobile," Oct. 8, 1942, Records of the Division of Program Surveys, Project Files, 1940–1946, Records of the Bureau of Agricultural Economics; "Pascagoula, Mississippi," Box 80, Pascagoula, Records of the Committee for Congested Production Areas).

110 **cost Spicely and Williams their lives:** Quoted in Leslie Hossfeld, Race Folder, Governor J. Melville Broughton Papers, Box 82, North Carolina State Archives.

110 **"That happened all over the South":** Johnnie Stevens, 761st Tank Battalion, quoted in Lou Potter, with William Miles and Nina Rosenblum, *Liberators: Fighting on Two Fronts in World War II* (New York: Houghton Mifflin Harcourt, 1992), 58.

111 **whereupon he whipped him:** Records of US Army Service Forces (World War II), Fourth Service Command, RG 160, Box 70, File 291.2 (Negro Transportation File: Occurrence of Racial Incidents on Local Transportation Facilities), NARA.

111 **"side of the white man also":** Ibid.

111 **"down with a Tommy gun":** Ibid.

111 **his revolver on them:** Ibid.

112 **terminated his military career:** "Jackie Robinson Insubordination Charges, and Segregation on Military Post Bus," NAACP Papers Part 9: Discrimination in the US Armed Forces, Series B: Armed Forces Legal Files, 1940–1950; Jules Tygiel, "The Court-Martial of Jackie Robinson," *American Heritage* 35, no. 5 (Aug.–Sept. 1984).

112   **to discipline the driver:** Fourth Service Command RG 160, Box 70, File 291.2.

112   **"making a test case of some sort":** Dudley Magruder Jr., Special Agent SIC, Fourth Service Command to Officer in Charge, Aug. 4, 1944, ibid.

113   **"keep from becoming bitter":** "Black Soldiers' Discrimination Complaints," 1943, NAACP Papers, Part 09: Discrimination in the US Armed Forces, Series C: The Veterans Affairs Committee, 1940–1950; Thomas Gibson Jr. with Steve Huntley, *Knocking Down Barriers: My Fight for Black America* (Evanston, IL: Northwestern University Press, 2005), 202–203; "Put 8 Soldiers on Chain Gang in South Carolina," *New York Amsterdam News*, Oct. 21, 1944; "NAACP Seeks GI Protection: Asks Stimson Support of Powell Travel Bill," *Pittsburgh Courier*, Feb. 17, 1945.

13. THE DEPARTMENTS: WAR AND JUSTICE

115   **federal government and its contractors:** Biddle to Stimson, Dec. 19, 1941, (citing *Chiles v. Chesapeake & Ohio Railway*, 218 US 71 (1910), and *Mitchell v. United States*, 313 US 80 (1941), Records of the Office of the Secretary of War, Transportation Discrimination File, RG107, Box 252.

115   **travel was nominally desegregated:** *Plessy v. Ferguson*, 163 US 537 (1896); *Morgan v. Virginia*, 28 US 373 (1946). See also *Bob-Lo-Excursion Company v. Michigan*, 333 US 28 (1948).

115   **custody of Beaumont police:** *Beaumont Enterprise*, July 28, Aug. 15, 1942; *Houston Informer*, Aug. 1, 1942.

116   **"result of his own misconduct":** DOJ RG 60, Box 579; Truman Gibson Jr. to Tom C. Clark, July 3, 1944, DOJ 144-3-9; Gibson with Huntley, *Knocking Down Barriers*.

116   **"without brutally killing him":** Irene Thomas to Attorney General Francis Biddle, Apr. 22, 1944, DOJ 144-3-9; Reverend S. R. Lee to Attorney General Francis Biddle, May 30, 1944, DOJ 144-3-9.

117   **Assistant Attorney General Tom Clark:** Tom C. Clark to Albert J. Truly, May 20, 1944, DOJ 144-3-9.

117   **a civil rights violation:** Quoted in Attorney General Francis Biddle to Eleanor Roosevelt, May 17, 1944, DOJ 144-33-14; DOJ Litigation Case Files 144-2-6; DOJ 144-33-14; DOJ 144-33-15.

14. THE "NEGRO TRANSPORTATION" FILE

118   **"to drop them again":** Jonathan Daniels to F.D.R., Nov. 24, 1942, OF 93 [Colored Matters], F.D.R. Library, quoted in Daniel Kryder, "American State."

119   **"unnoticed in a white offender":** "Fort Bragg's 'Night of Terror' Described,"

Pittsburgh Courier, Aug. 16, 1941; Stacy Knopf to War Department, Racial Difficulties in Fourth Service Command, Washington, DC, May 30, 1942, File 291.2; Records of Fourth Service Command, RG 160, Box 69, NARA; Racial Situation: Tabulation of Racial Incidents, Dec. 31, 1945, RG 160, Box 69, File 291.2, NARA.

119 **incidents of a racial nature:** War Department RG 107, Box 252, Transportation Discrimination File, 1941.

120 **"as he did, in the breast":** Fourth Service Command, RG 160, Box 70, File 291.2, NARA.

121 **for his impromptu protest:** Harvey J. Reid, Sept. 1, 1944, War Department RG 107, Box 252, Transportation Discrimination File, NARA.

15. RECONSTRUCTION STATUTES, JIM CROW RULES

126 **"the vengeance of the law":** Amos Akerman, quoted in Robert J. Kaczorowski, *The Politics of Judicial Interpretation* (New York: Fordham University Press, 2004), 66.

126 **their race or color:** Exclusion of jurors on account of race or color, 18 U.S.C. § 243 (1948).

126 **peonage or involuntary servitude:** Civil actions against the United States and agencies and officers thereof, 28 U.S.C. § 1581, 1583, 1584 (1930).

126 **federal criminal law enforcement:** Judicial treatment of Sections 51 and 52 is addressed in Part 4.

127 **"put in the constitution at all?":** Quoted in Eric Foner, *Reconstruction: America's Unfinished Revolution, 1863–1877* (New York: HarperCollins, 2002), 455.

128 **virtually every case it tried:** Lou Falkner Williams, *The Great South Carolina Ku Klux Klan Trials, 1871–1872* (Athens: University of Georgia Press, 1996), 49, 100. See also Foner, *Reconstruction*, 457–59.

128 **threat was significantly diminished:** Richard V. Valelly, *The Two Reconstructions: The Struggle for Black Enfranchisement* (Chicago: University of Chicago Press, 2004), 110.

128 **as well as Sections 51 and 52:** Charles Hamilton Houston Papers Manuscript Division, Moorland-Spingarn Research Center, Howard University, Box 163-25.

128 **taking on such a "local" matter:** On the 1933 Tuscaloosa lynching case, see Kimberly Sharpe, *Tuscaloosa 1933: A Summer of Violence*, 2015, Civil Rights & Restorative Justice Project paper (on file with author). See also J. Eugene Marans, *The Struggle for Federal Anti-Lynching Legislation, 1933–1945* (Harvard Honors Thesis, Department of History, Harvard College, Mar. 1962). The department's position would shift in 1940, when CRS issued its first set of guidelines to the attorneys responsible for enforcing federal civil rights law. The policy has been

interpreted as confirming that Section 52 protects a "federal right not to be lynched." *"Should the jailer . . . turn over the keys to the lynchers . . . the official's failure to protect amounts to discriminatory action in unleashing unlawful forces as a direct consequence of his unique position as an official, and both he and the private parties appear subject to Federal prosecution"* (1940 Policy Circular).

129 **Civil Rights Section in 1941:** The Civil Liberties Unit was renamed the Civil Rights Section in 1941, and in 1957 it became the Civil Rights Division of the Justice Department. I refer to the entity as the Civil Rights Section, or section, or CRS here.

16. "HER HIPS LOOKED LIKE BATTERED LIVER": TUSKEGEE IN THE MIDDLE DISTRICT

131 **with the fan belt from a car:** Investigative Report, Dec. 23, 1942, DOJ Litigation Case File 144-2-3. The case is described in Robert J. Norrell, *Reaping the Whirlwind: The Civil Rights Movement in Tuskegee* (Chapel Hill: University of North Carolina Press, 1998), 44–58; and Silvan Niedermeier, *Violence, Visibility, and the Investigation of Police Torture in the American South, 1940–1955, Violence and Visibility in Modern History*, eds. Jurgen Martschukat and Silvan Niedermeier (London: Palgrave Macmillan, 2013).

131 **and a fractured skull:** Interview with Rhetonia Chisolm, Tuskegee, AL, June 9, 2017 (interviewer: Margaret Russell) (on file with author).

132 **Readie Glenn Huguley:** *United States v. Edwin Eugene Evans and Henry Franklin Faucett*, Case Nos. 1297 and 1299, Eastern Division Middle District of Alabama, 1943, Grand Jury testimony.

132 **fatal assault on Gunn:** Norrell, supra., 53–54; "Witnesses to Slaying Won't Talk," *Chicago Defender*, Aug. 1, 1942.

133 **"future than they had ever given":** FBI interview with Chief of Police C. H. Thrasher, Dec. 23, 1942, DOJ Litigation Case File 144-2-3.

134 **back up in a sweltering cell:** Lillie Mae Hendon statement, Dec. 23, 1942, DOJ 144-2-3.

134 **"her hips looked like battered liver":** Ibid, *Reaping the Whirlwind: The Civil Rights Movement in Tuskegee*, 54.

134 **disparage her as sexually loose:** Ibid.; "Jury Frees 2 Ala. Police in Beatings," *Chicago Defender*, July 1, 1943.

134 **against the state's witnesses:** "Jury Acquits Macon Sheriff and His Deputy," *Atlanta Daily World*, June 26, 1943.

134 **Macon County's sheriff until 1950:** Ibid.; Norrell, *Reaping the Whirlwind: The Civil Rights Movement in Tuskegee*, 54, 75–76.

134 **the killers of a Black man:** *Mitchell v. Wright*, 69 F. 2d 924 (5th Cir. Ala. 1946).

135 **discriminated against Black voters:** *Sellers v. Wilson*, 123 F. Supp. 917 (D. Ala. 1954).

17 **"A LITTLE QUICK ON THE TRIGGER": UNION SPRINGS IN THE MIDDLE DISTRICT**

136 **so they banished him:** Interview, Whiley Thomas, Montgomery, AL, Oct. 25, 2012 (interviewer: Bayliss Fiddiman) (on file with author).

137 **and kept on shooting:** Statement of C. A. May, Feb. 12, 1946, FBI 44-HQ-1324-5.

138 **"son of a bitch on the street":** Ibid.

138 **never reside in Union Springs again:** Statement of Rev. J. L. Pinckney, Oct. 30, 1945, NAACP Papers, Box II B117, Folder 14, Legal File, Police Brutality; Report of Kenneth C. Kennedy, Southern Negro Youth Congress (undated).

138 **pronounced dead on the scene:** Statement of Ada Hightower, Donahoo Field Report, Oct. 13, 1945, FBI 44-HQ-1324, DOJ Litigation Case File 144-2-15.

138 **"too quick on the trigger":** Donahoo Field Report, Feb. 12, 1946, ibid.

139 **address Bradley's "reign of terror":** Louis Burnham to Mayor C. A. May, Dec. 31, 1945, Southern Negro Youth Congress Files, Moorland-Spingarn Research Center, Howard University Library; DOJ Litigation Case File 144-18-39; DOJ Litigation Case File 144-2-15,

139 **Washington followed his lead:** Theron L. Caudle to J. Edgar Hoover, June 20, 1946, DOJ Litigation Case File144-2-15.

18. "THE TESTIMONY . . . OF THE NEGROES SEEMS MORE PROBABLE":
TUSKEGEE IN THE MIDDLE DISTRICT

141 **and threw it at Elijah:** Kirby quoted in Donahoo Field Report, June 17–20, 1946, DOJ Litigation Case File 144-2-17.

142 **would see her two sons again:** Report of Henry A. Donahoo, June 21, 1946, DOJ Litigation Case File 144-2-17.

142 **requesting an aggressive investigation:** Thurgood Marshall to Turner L. Smith, May 8, 1946, DOJ Litigation Case File 144-2-17.

143 **Kirby told the FBI:** Interview, Eddie James Ray, Nov. 20, 2014 (interviewer: Quinn Rollins) (on file with author).

143 **"extremely shy and inarticulate":** Henry A. Donahoo, Donahoo Field Report, June 17–20, 1946, DOJ 144-2-17.

144 **without a grand jury:** Theron Caudle to Edward B. Parker, Jul. 30, 1946, DOJ 144-2-17. An offense under Section 52 was punishable by a sentence of only one

year's imprisonment, which meant the case could be prosecuted on an Information rather than an indictment.

144 **"this matter should be closed":** Edward B. Parker to Theron Caudle, Oct. 17, 1946, DOJ 144-2-17.

144 **closed in November 1946:** Parker's resistance—Undated memo to file, ibid.; file closed, Theron Caudle to E. Burns Parker, Nov. 15, 1946, ibid.

145 **sheriff who killed William Lockwood:** Theron Caudle to Robert L. Carter, June 24, 1947, ibid.

145 **"wanton killing by police officers":** Thurgood Marshall to Theron Caudle, July 3, 1947, ibid.

145 **the *Screws* case:** The *Screws* case, *Screws v. United States*, 325 US 91, 1945, is discussed in Chapter 4.

145 **what tipped the scales:** T. Vincent Quinn to Thurgood Marshall, July 25, 1947, DOJ 144-2-17.

146 **"X—will not go on anything":** Steven F. Lawson, *To Secure These Rights: Report of the President's Committee on Civil Rights* (Boston: Bedford/St. Martin's, 1947), 122.

146 **"violations will not be prosecuted":** DOJ 144-2-17, Nov. 30, 1948.

146 **talked about the tragedy:** Quinn Kareem Rallins, *The William Lockwood Case: A Legal History*, Civil Rights & Restorative Justice, Fall 2017, on file with author.

19. "HEAD . . . SOFT AS A PIECE OF COTTON":
LAFAYETTE IN THE MIDDLE DISTRICT

149 **"judge in New York or Michigan":** "Two LaFayette Officers Freed: Courtroom Greets Verdict with Cheers," *Alabama Journal*, Mar. 23, 1950.

149 **"permitted to remain on the force":** "LaFayette's Unfavorable Publicity," *LaFayette Sun*, Mar. 29, 1950.

150 **"vicious and dangerous men?":** "Police and Their Prisoners," *Birmingham News*, Mar. 24, 1950.

150 **right after the acquittal:** Memorandum, James M. McInerney to J. Edgar Hoover, Mar. 13, 1950, FBI File 44-3012.

151 **conduct a vigorous investigation:** Memorandum from J. Edgar Hoover to James M. McInerney, Apr. 6, 1950, ibid.

151 **"to punish a person":** US v. Clark, No. 1744-E, Middle District of Alabama, Trial Tr., 138–139, Oct. 31, 1950 (on file with author).

151 **sentence of ten months:** *Clark v. United States*, 193 F.2d 294 (5th Cir. 1951).

152 **from pursuing a civil case:** Interview, Leslie J. King, Jan. 14, 2013 (interviewer: Tasha Kates) (on file with author).

20. "NONE OF WASHINGTON'S BUSINESS"

153 **"Nation's history and its future":** *Younger v. Harris*, 401 US 37 (1971).

154 **control over Black communities:** For the relationship between small-town police departments and sheriffs, see Toby Moore, "Race and the County Sheriff in the American South," *International Social Science Review* 72, no. 1/2 (1997): 50–61.

156 **"in American legal history":** Frank Murphy to Franklin Roosevelt, July 7, 1939, Justice Department Files, Franklin D. Roosevelt Presidential Library.

156 **"organized to protect civil liberties":** Frances Biddle, *In Brief Authority* (Atlanta: Greenwood Publication Group, 1976), 154.

157 **"respect to a particular type of case":** *Federal Criminal Jurisdiction over Violations of Civil Liberties*, Memorandum with Circular No. 3356 (Supplement No. 1) from O. John Rogge, Assistant Attorney General, to All United States Attorneys, May 21, 1940.

157 **murky "constitutional issues":** Ibid.

157 **"state and local governments":** *Proceedings of the Federal-State Conference on Law Enforcement Problems of National Defense*, Great Hall, Department of Justice, Washington, DC, Aug. 5, 1940, RHJP Box 40.

157 **"to alter their conduct":** Robert Carr, *Federal Protection of Civil Rights* (Ithaca, NY: Cornell University Press, 1947), 163.

159 **"no better friend than our District Judge":** Lawrence S. Camp to Henry Schweinhaut, Mar. 26, 1940, DOJ Litigation Case File, 144-19-5.

159 **defendant's claim of good character:** R. W. Martin to John Rogge, Sept. 4, 1940, DOJ Litigation Case File, 144-19-5.

159 **Hoover wrote to the CRS:** John T. Elliff, "Aspects of Federal Civil Rights Enforcement: The Justice Department and the FBI, 1939–1964," in *Perspectives in American History: Volume V, 1971* (Cambridge: Cambridge University Press), 610 Silvan Niedermeier, "Selective Public Outrage: The Quintar South Case," in *The Color of the Third Degree* (Chapel Hill: University of North Carolina Press, 2019), 120–121.

159 **violated Section 52:** *United States v. Sutherland*, 37 F. Supp. 344 (1940). For a full account of the Sutherland case, see Elliff, "Aspects of Federal Civil Rights Enforcement."

159 **1876 case *United States v. Cruikshank*:** *United States v. Cruikshank*, 92 US 542 (1876).

159 **"It is secured by State laws":** Matthew F. McGuire to John Rogge, Sept. 30, 1940, DOJ Litigation Case File 144-19-5.

160 **Section 52 was "a little farfetched":** Alexander Holtzoff to James Rowe, Feb. 13, 1942, ibid.

160   **"to good race relations":** M. Neil Andrews to Francis Biddle, June 13, 1944, ibid.

161   **"for the prosecuting attorney":** J. Edgar Hoover, quoted in Lawson, *To Secure These Rights*, 124.

161   **and then go away:** Taylor Branch, *Pillar of Fire: America in the King Years, 1963– 65* (New York: Simon & Schuster, 1998), 368.

162   **unproductive "fishing expeditions":** J. Edgar Hoover to Tom Clarke, Sept. 12, 1946, DOJ 144-012; Hoover to Clark, Sept. 17, 1946, ibid.; Hoover to Clark, Oct. 2, 1946, ibid.

162   **walking the streets of Brownsville:** Patricia Sullivan, *Lift Every Voice: The NAACP and the Making of the Civil Rights Movement* (New York: The New Press, 2009).

162   **"the witness to tell the truth":** George Fisher, *Evidence 1*, 3rd. ed (New York: Foundation Press, 2009), 686.

162   **"cases of outright brutality":** Berge to Rowe, Mar. 3, 1942, DOJ Litigation Case File, 144-19-5.

163   **constitutional authority to act:** Lawson, *To Secure These Rights*, 123.

163   **in the South were segregated:** Michael Klarman, *From Jim Crow to Civil Rights: The Supreme Court and the Struggle for Racial Equality* (New York: Oxford University Press, 2004), 9.

163   **"none of Washington's business":** Francis Biddle to Oscar Henry Doyle, Dec. 11, 1943; *United States v. Erskine*, DOJ Litigation Case File 144-68-9; "County Citizens Pay Erskine Fine," *Anderson Independent*, n.d.

164   **"by a vindictive government":** "Jury Frees 2 Ala. Police in Beatings: Federal Court Case Lost by US Before Local Jurors," *Chicago Defender*, July 3, 1943.

PART IV: THE *SCREWS* EFFECT: RACIAL VIOLENCE IN THE SUPREME COURT

165   **"please take it up again":** Ethel Davis to Attorney General Tom Clark about the police killing of her son, Jul. 28, 1945, DOJ Litigation Case File, 144-20-9.

21. "LOOK TO THE STATES"

167   **impenetrable opinion in 1945:** *United States v. Screws*, 325 US 91 (1945).

168   **review in the Supreme Court:** Eric Foner, *Reconstruction: America's Unfinished Revolution, 1863–1877* (New York: Harper & Row, 1988), 530.

168   **reversed the convictions:** James Gray Pope, "Snubbed Landmark: Why United States v. Cruikshank (1876) Belongs at the Heart of the American Constitutional Canon," *Harvard Civil Rights-Civil Liberties Law Review* 49, no. 2 (2014): 385;

United States v. Cruikshank, 92 US 542 (1875). Section 51 was then Section 6 of the Enforcement Act of 1870.

170 **"but it is not so averred":** *Cruikshank*, 92 US 542, 556.

170 **"surrendered to the United States":** *United States v. Cruikshank*, 92 US at 552.

170 **utility for years to come:** See, e.g., *Slaughter-House Cases*, 83 US 36 (1873); *Ex Parte Siebold*, 100 US 214 (1879); *Minor v. Happersett*, 88 US 162 (1875); *United States v. Harris*, 106 US 629 (1883).

171 **the high court judgment:** Pope, *Snubbed Landmark*, 415.

171 **the beginning of *Hodges v. United States*:** *Hodges v. United States*, 203 US 1 (1906).

171 **"irrespective of party":** William G. Whipple, US Attorney for the Eastern District of Arkansas, to Philander C. Knox, Attorney General (May 8, 1903), quoted in Pamela S. Karlan, "Contracting the Thirteenth Amendment: Hodges v. United States," *Boston University Law Review* 85: 783, 785 n10 (2005).

172 **state actor's unconstitutional conduct:** *United States v. Classic*, 313 US 299 (1941).

172 **he never got to the bottom of the matter:** NAACP Papers Box I-D21, Folder H: Legal Files, General.

22. A "PATENTLY LOCAL CRIME"

175 **his head was smashed in:** These facts and quotes are drawn from *Screws v. United States*, Brief for the United States, Respondent, and a transcript submitted with the petition for *certiorari*.

175 **"struck him with a blackjack":** *Baker County News*, Feb. 12, 1943, quoted in in Christopher Waldrep, *Racial Violence on Trial: A Handbook with Cases, Laws, and Documents* (Santa Barbara, CA: ABC-CLIO, 2001), 75.

175 **"the attorney for the state":** *Screws*, 325 at 124.

175 **a person's constitutional rights:** NAACP Papers, Part 7, Series A, Reel 25, Notes for Spreadsheet.

175 **been used so infrequently:** *Screws*, 325 (Roberts dissent, joined by Frankfurter and Jackson), at 82.

175 **Justice Douglas put it, "trial by ordeal":** *Screws*, 325 at 106.

176 **"legislation were adopted to uproot":** *Screws*, 325 at 114–117.

177 **right to due process:** *Screws*, 325.

177 **"ugly abyss of racism":** *Korematsu v. United States*, 323 US 214, 233 (1944).

177 **"when he was hit":** Leo Meltzer, "Our Civil Rights," *An Address to the Chicago Civil Liberties Committee*, Feb. 18, 1950.

177 **"antagonism on States' rights grounds":** O. John Rogge, Assistant Attorney

General, to All United States Attorneys, May 21, 1940, Memorandum, "Federal Jurisdiction over Violations of Civil Liberties."

178 **"[explicitly deny racial equality]"**: *United States v. Cruikshank*, 25 F. Cas. 707, 714 (1874).

23. "VICTIM . . . OF A QUARRELSOME NATURE"

179 **"Uncle Sam's Man [now]"**: Eddie Lee Thomas Aff., Dec. 12, 1944, DOJ Litigation Case File 144-20-9.

180 **vindicating her son's death:** Interview, Marvin Roundtree Cox, July 16, 2013 (interviewer: Mia Teitelbaum) (on file with author).

181 **"of a quarrelsome nature":** Kimbrough FBI Report on James Bohannon, Apr. 3, 1944, DOJ 144-20-9.

181 **"received all relevant testimony":** Letter to FBI Director J. Edgar Hoover from Assistant Attorney General Tom C. Clark, USDJ, Apr. 13, 1944, DOJ 144-20-9.

182 **"we could prove . . . specific intent":** Memorandum from Assistant Attorney General Clark to Attorney General Francis Biddle, May 12, 1945, DOJ 144-22-9.

183 **"actions of the officers":** Judge Archibald B. Lovett to Ethel Davis, July 19, 1945, NAACP Papers, Legal Files: Soldier Killing, Davis, Willie, 1943–1945.

183 **"to please take it up again":** Ethel Davis to Attorney General Tom Clark, July 28, 1945, DOJ Litigation Case File 144-20-9.

183 **"justice that is this case":** *Crews v. United States*, 160 F.2d 746 (5th Cir. 1947).

183 **by fishermen sometime later:** Theron Caudle, "Sam Mcfadden, Victim," Memorandum, Nov. 30, 1945, DOJ 144-18-41.

184 **Justice Douglas affirmed the conviction:** *Williams v. United States*, 342 US 97 (1951).

24. "BAD BIRMINGHAM"

191 **per 100,000 people:** "11,000 Slain Yearly in U.S. A Sharp Rise," *New York Times*, Mar. 3, 1935.

192 **boasted 7,000 members:** Thomas R. Pegram, "The Ku Klux Klan, Labor, and the White Working Class During the 1920s," *Journal of the Gilded Age and Progressive Era* 17, no. 2 (2018): 373–396; Keith S. Herbert, "Ku Klux Klan in Alabama from 1915–1930," *Encyclopedia of Alabama*; Glenn Feldman, "Soft Opposition: Elite Acquiescence and Klan-Sponsored Terrorism in Alabama," *Historical Journal* 40, no. 3 (1997): 753–777.

25. NEGROES ARE RESTLESS

195 **the officers claimed:** "Negro Worker Is Shot to Death by Fairfield Police,"
Southern News-Almanac, May 1, 1941.

195 **a postman and two ministers:** "Extra! Officer Kills Negro," *Weekly Review*
(Birmingham, AL), Apr. 10, 1942.

196 **to shoot in self-defense:** "Officer Kills Negro in Downtown Area," *Birmingham News,* Apr. 9, 1942.

196 **drew 3,000 protesters:** "Policeman's Shooting of Negro to Be Aired Before
Grand Jury," *Weekly Review* (Birmingham, AL), Apr. 17, 1942.

196 **Black people were "restless":** "Ministers Petition City Commission," ibid.

197 **"segregation or lose their jobs":** *Alabama,* Sept. 18, 1942: 7; Bayard Rustin,
"The Negro and Nonviolence," *Fellowship of Reconciliation* 8, no. 10 (Oct. 1942):
166.

197 **"Shot Six Times by White Bus Driver":** "Negro Shot Six Times by White
Bus Driver," *Birmingham World,* Aug. 28, 1942.

198 **"a police power over slaves":** Ulrich B. Phillips, *American Negro Slavery: A
Survey of the Supply, Employment, and Control of Negro Labor as Determined by the
Plantation Regime* (New York: D. Appleton, 1940), 500.

198 **breaking the windows:** "Negro Shot Six Times by White Bus Driver," *Birmingham World*; "Negro Shot by Bus Driver," *Weekly Review* (Birmingham, AL),
Aug. 22, 1942.

26. "MR. VAN"

200 **put his hand into his pocket:** "T.C.I. Police Officer Shoots Negro Suspect,"
Birmingham News, Dec. 22, 1946.

200 **"he is going to steal":** Michel Foucault, "Security, Territory, Population,"
in *The Courage of Truth,* ed. Michel Senellart, trans. Graham Burchell (Lecture
Series at the Collège de France, 1977–1978).

201 **the man who shot him:** "Case of William Daniel's Death," SNYC Papers,
Box 1, Moorland-Spingarn Research Center.

201 **after her husband's murder:** Michelle Amelia Newman, "They Shot Me for
Nothing: A Legal and Historical Account of William Daniel's Murder," Apr. 5,
2014, Civil Rights & Restorative Justice Project (on file with author).

202 **"to the first rumor":** Interview, Demetrius Newton, July 2, 2013 (interviewer: Michelle Newman) (on file with author).

204 **"Big Mules into full scale panic":** Wayne Flynt, *Alabama in the Twentieth
Century* (Tuscaloosa: University of Alabama Press, 2004), 61.

204   **"the whole community, educated"**: Interview, Vida Rouse, July 26, 2019 (interviewer: Noah Lapidus) (on file with author).

204   **"it would be large crowds"**: Interview, Vida Rouse.

206   **"no contract dispute [was] involved"**: "Negro Miners' Death Halts Coal Production," *Dothan Eagle*, June 9, 1948.

206   **his way to the mine**: "Stoppage Hampers TCI Minework," *Alabama Journal*, June 9, 1948; "Miners Strike Over Shooting of Negro," *Shamokin News-Dispatch*, June 8, 1948.

206   **Butler's body from the back**: "Stoppage Hampers TCI Mine Work," *Alabama Journal*.

206   **"never in his life carried a pistol"**: "Bama Cops Slay Former Preacher," *New York Amsterdam News*, June 12, 1948.

206   **"10 days in Jefferson County"**: "B'ham Civic Groups Score Terror Reign," *Pittsburgh Courier*, June 26, 1948.

207   **covered in *Jet* magazine**: *Appeal to the Supreme Court of Alabama from the Circuit Court, Tenth Judicial Circuit of Alabama, Jefferson County, United States Steel Company vs. Allie Glass Butler, Appellee*, Transcript No. 20581-X, November 21, 1953; "Ala. Widow Awarded $10,000 Judgement," *Jet*, May 1, 1952.

208   **claim that Butler had a gun**: *Appeal to the Supreme Court of Alabama from the Circuit Court, Tenth Judicial Circuit of Alabama, Jefferson County, United States Steel Company vs. Allie Glass Butler, Appellee; United Steel Co. v. Butler*, 69 So.2d 685 (1953); "$10,000 Verdict OK'd in Alabama," *Pittsburgh Courier*, Jan. 30, 1954.

208   **"children received black lung money"**: Interview, Vida Rouse.

208   **screenings for black lung disease**: Robert Woodrum, *Everybody Was Black Down There: Race and Industrial Change in the Alabama Coalfields* (Athens: University of Georgia Press, 2003), 3.

27. "NEGRO YOUTH, SHOT NEAR WHITE RESIDENCE, DIES"

209   **"Negro youth, shot near white residence, dies . . .":** "Negro Youth, Shot Near White Residence Last January, Dies," *Birmingham News*, July 24, 1950.

209   **membership to 1,000 by 1940:** "Birmingham Gets Prize for Best NAACP Branch," June 20, 1941, Birmingham, Alabama, Branch Operations, 1940–1944, Papers of the NAACP, Part 26: Selected Branch Files, 1940–1955, Series A: The South. On Emory Jackson's life and career, see Kimberley Mangun, *Editor Emory O. Jackson, The Birmingham World, and the Fight for Civil Rights in Alabama, 1940–1975* (New York: Peter Lang, 2019) and Gene Roberts and Hank Klibanoff, *The Race Beat: The Press, the Civil Rights Struggle, and the Awakening of a Nation* (New York: Knopf, 2006).

210   **white supremacist organization in Georgia:** Letter, NAACP Birmingham

Branch Officials to Community Leader[s], Apr. 23, 1948, NAACP Papers, Box II C2 F2, AL Branch Files.

210 **because of the police killings:** "Ike Madden, 40, Killed by Policemen," *Birmingham World*, Mar. 30, 1948; "Negro Groups Ask Probe of Slayings in Jefferson Co.," *Opelika Daily News*, June 15, 1948. In addition to convening a presidential inquiry into civil rights matters in 1946, President Truman in 1948 issued an executive order desegregating the armed forces.

210 **to the committee's demands:** "B'ham Civic Groups Score Terror Reign," *Pittsburgh Courier*.

211 **targets for police vitriol:** "A Way to Stop Police Brutality," *Birmingham World*, Apr. 27, 1948.

211 **more alarming than the last:** "Birmingham Negroes Ask Killing Probe," *Alabama Journal*, June 15, 1948.

211 **"to grab the police driver":** "Ike Madden, 40, Killed by Policemen," *Birmingham World*.

211 **"pulled a knife" on him:** "Patrolman Kills Man; Coroner Investigating," *Birmingham News*, Apr. 27, 1948.

211 **"in his pocket for a knife":** "Police Kill Bessemer Man," *Birmingham World*, May 4, 1948.

211 **"his house with a knife":** "Officers Exonerated in Killing Near Flat Creek," *Anniston Star*, May 11, 1948.

211 **"cursed and drew an icepick" on police:** "Officer Kills Negro; Says He Drew Pick," *Birmingham News*, May 31, 1948.

211 **civil jury later rejected:** "Stoppage Hampers TCI Minework," *Alabama Journal*, June 9, 1948; "Miners Strike Over Shooting of Negro," *Shamokin News-Dispatch*, June 8, 1948.

212 **"attempted to pull a pistol":** "Negro Is Victim of Cop's Bullets; Becomes 7th of Race to Die," *Huntsville Times*, June 18, 1948.

212 **accused of breaking into:** "Police Shoot Negro," *Selma Times*, Aug. 12, 1948.

212 **"been drinking pretty heavy":** "Charles Wright Killed by Officer," *Atlanta Daily World*, Sept. 17, 1948.

212 **January 15, 1949:** "Negro Shot, Killed in Salvage Yard," *Alabama Journal*, Jan. 17, 1949.

212 **"knife after resisting arrest":** "Peace Officers Kill 5th Negro," *Birmingham World*, May 3, 1949.

212 **"and knocked him down":** "City Detective Shoots Negro in Shoulder," *Birmingham News*, May 31, 1949.

212 **selling illegal lottery tickets:** "Mother Wounded, Son Killed by Cops," *Pittsburgh Courier*, Aug. 6, 1949.

212 **"contact with Patterson's head":** James M. McInerney, Assistant Attor-

ney General to Thurgood Marshall, Dec. 18, 1951, DOJ Litigation Case File 144-1-121.

213 **"the commission of a crime"**: "Youth Shot Fleeing from Northside Home," *Birmingham News*, Jan. 4, 1950; "Negro Youth, Shot Near White Residence Last January, Dies," *Birmingham News*, July 24, 1950.

214 **as the extant records reveal:** Clarence Mitchell to Peyton Ford, Assistant to the Attorney General, July 17, 1951, DOJ 144-1-121.

215 **"white man's attack may be"**: Ida B. Wells-Barnett, "Mob Rule in New Orleans," in *Southern Horrors and Other Writings: The Antilynching Campaign of Ida B. Wells*, ed. Jacqueline Jones Royster (Boston: Bedford Books, 1997).

215 **"on the black charred ground"**: James Baldwin, *Going to Meet the Man* (New York: Dial Press, 1965), 251.

28. ABDUCTION: SOUTHWEST MISSISSIPPI

222 **"stealing a man"**: *State v. Williams*, 31 NC 140 (1848).

223 **"by coercion if necessary"**: From Whitecap organizational literature, in *Magnolia Gazette* (Aug. 19, 1893), quoted in William F. Holmes, "Whitecapping: Anti-Semitism in the Populist Era," *Jewish Historical Quarterly* 63, no. 244 (Mar. 1974).

223 **Black men in Southwest Mississippi:** Alfred Whitley (kidnapped 2/16/64, Natchez), James Winston (2/15/64, Natchez), Archie Curtis (2/16/64, Natchez), Willie Jackson (2/16/64, Natchez), Ivey Gutter (6/11/64, McComb), Wilbert Lewis (6/19/64, Natchez), Henry Dee (5/2/64, Meadville–killed), Charles Moore (5/2/64, Meadville–killed).

223 **white man in that county alone:** Report of Adams County Deputy Sheriff Hernandez to A. L. Hopkins, Feb. 18–20, 1964, MSSC 2-63-1-114.

224 **Jones had fled in 1964:** This account of the events involving Burl Jones is based on an interview with Jones on July 26, 2008 (interviewers: author and Janeen Blake) (on file with author). See also Donna Ladd, "Evolution of a Man: Lifting the Hood in South Mississippi," *Jackson Free Press*, Oct. 26, 2005.

224 **criminal enterprise targeting Blacks:** Charles Marcus Edwards, testimony in *United States v. James Ford Seale*.

225 **legitimacy of corporal punishment:** James Q. Whitman, *Harsh Justice: Criminal Punishment and the Widening Divide Between America and Europe* (Oxford: Oxford University Press, 2005), 173: "[p]eople who were flogged in America risked being thought of as slaves."

225 **how close to slavery they still were:** Orlando Patterson, *Slavery and Social Death* (Cambridge, MA: Harvard University Press, 1982), 3.

226 **by death under Mississippi law:** Under the state's criminal code, kidnap-

ping was a capital offense and remained so until the Supreme Court limited the death penalty to murder. Miss. Code Ann. § 97-3-53, derived from Code 1942, Section 2238; Laws 1974, Ch. 576 § 3, eff. from and after passage. Section 2238 (1956) applied at the time of the cases discussed herein. The statute defines the crime as follows: Any person who shall without lawful authority forcibly seize and confine any other person, or shall inveigle or kidnap any other person with intent to cause such person to be secretly confined or imprisoned against his or her will . . . (shall be guilty of kidnapping). In *Johnson v. Mississippi*, 288 So.2d 842 (1974), the Supreme Court of Mississippi upheld a kidnapping conviction where the defendant forced the victim into his car at gunpoint, drove several miles, robbed and threatened to kill the victim, then released him. The court held that "when one is forced at gun point to enter an automobile, and while confined therein is driven away against his will from a place where he has a right to be, along a route and to a destination unknown to his friends and acquaintances, he is, within the meaning of the statute, 'secretly confined and imprisoned.'" See also *McGuire v. Mississippi*, 231 Miss. 375, 95 So.2d 537 (1957).

227 **he never truly recovered:** Jerry Mitchell, "Spy Agency Files Detail '64 Beatings of Black Men," *Clarion Ledger,* June 10, 2007.

227 **No arrests were made in the case:** Gabriel J. Chin, ed., *United States Commission on Civil Rights: Reports on the Police* (Littleton, CO: Fred B Rothman, 2005) (hereinafter USCCR 1965 Report), 96–103, 463.

227 **clandestine NAACP supporter:** Investigation of Archie G. Curtis, July 17, 1961, Mississippi State Sovereignty Commission, 2-63-53A.

228 **their alleged NAACP membership:** USCCR 1965 Report, 96–103, 463.

228 **"two Colored Males that they had been beaten":** The sheriff wrote that he "received a call to come to the Adams County Jail to investigate a report by two Colored Males that they had been beaten by four or five masked men." USCCR, Investigative Reports Produced in Response to Subpoena, 496.

228 **released him on the open road:** The facts are drawn from hearings before the United States Commission on Civil Rights. *Hearings Before the United States Commission on Civil Rights, Vol. II: Administration of Justice, Hearings Held in Jackson, Miss., February 16–20, 1965*, at 451, in USCCR 1965 Report.

228 **"goes to lunch everyday together":** Ibid., at 493.

228 **disappeared from the area:** Ibid., at 451, 493.

229 **"beatings" of Negro men:** See, e.g., Report to the Mississippi State Sovereignty Commission, "Investigation of Whippings and Armed Robberies of Negro Men in Adams County by Hooded or Masked White Men," Feb. 20, 1964, MSSC 2-63-1-114.

229 **that they complained about:** Ibid.

229 **"wild shooting into property; and bombings":** *White Knights of the Ku Klux*

Klan of Mississippi (memorandum from Donald Appell to Francis McNamara, Apr. 22, 1964), HUAC 1965 KKK Investigation, Box 41, 3, Lib. Cong. One former Klansman described the murder of Vernon Dahmer in 1966 as a "project three and four—burning and annihilation." See also "Murder Conviction in Miss.," *Southern Courier,* Mar. 23, 1968, at MSSC 10-28-0-41.

29. "NEGRO LEADERS CRY FOR JUSTICE IN KIDNAP OUTRAGE"

230 **"Negro Leaders Cry for Justice in Kidnap Outrage":** "Negro Leaders Cry for Justice in Kidnap Outrage," *Pittsburgh Courier,* Nov. 10, 1956.

230 **The case was never solved:** Myrlie Evers and Manning Marable, *The Autobiography of Medgar Evers: A Hero's Life and Legacy Revealed Through His Writings, Letters, and Speeches* (New York: Civitas Books, 2006), 192.

231 **that was sustained on appeal:** *State v. Wall,* 189 La. 653, 180 So. 476 (1938).

231 **"officer armed with a warrant":** "Peace Officer, 2 Others Charged with Kidnapping," *Jackson Daily News,* Oct. 22, 1946; "Hearing Slated for Trio Held in Kidnapping Case," *Jackson Daily News,* Oct. 23, 1946; "Three Whites Freed in Kidnapping: Private Arrest of Negroes Given OK," *Chicago Defender,* Nov. 30, 1946; "Court Rules Citizen Can Make an Arrest: Trio Who Took Negroes Without Warrant Are Freed," *Hazlehurst Courier,* Nov. 21, 1946.

232 **The men were all acquitted:** "Negro Leaders Cry for Justice in Kidnap Outrage," *Pittsburgh Courier;* "Arrest 6 in Kidnapping of Farm Hand," *Chicago Defender,* Dec. 8, 1956.

232 **did not figure in the prosecution:** "Farmer Saves Negro Tenant from Lashing by Robed Mob," *St. Petersburg Times,* Mar. 5, 1950; "Shots at Klansmen Free Georgia Negro," *New York Times,* Mar. 5, 1950; "Held in Georgia Lashing," *New York Times,* Mar. 6, 1950.

232 **hazing ritual for their new leader:** *Mabry v. State,* 40 Ala. App. 129, 110 So.3d 250 (1959); *McCullough v. State,* 40 Ala. App. 309, 113 So.2d 905 (1959).

232 **"like we're fixing to do you":** This statement is drawn from an account in Diane McWhorter, *Carry Me Home: Birmingham, Alabama, the Climactic Battle of the Civil Rights Revolution* (New York: Simon & Schuster, 2001), 125.

233 **Brotherhood Week event at their school:** Donald L. Grant and Jonathan Grant, *Way It Was in the South: The Black Experience in Georgia* (Athens: University of Georgia Press, 2001), 368; "Negro Boys Charge Abduction, Beating," *New York Times,* Feb. 25, 1949.

233 **she had lived in her whole life:** "Two Negroes Flogged in Georgia Village," *New York Times,* Oct. 15, 1960; "Ga. Couple Flogged, Left Nude in Woods," *Chicago Defender,* Oct 17, 1960. See also "Mob Beats Negro Woman," *New York Times,* Jan 23, 1951, (describing flogging of Mrs. Evergreen Flowers in White-

ville, North Carolina, with sticks and a gun); "11 Former Klansmen Seized in Kidnaping," *Washington Post*, Feb. 28, 1952 (Esther Lee Floyd abducted, beaten in North Carolina); "Lest We Didn't Know," *Chicago Defender*, Oct. 2, 1951 (describing flogging of Mrs. Alberta Brinson of Dublin, Georgia, with an ax handle and strip).

233 **prevent Blacks from joining:** "Kidnap, Flog Dixie Worker," *Chicago Defender*, June 22, 1946.

233 **census classified Lorick as "mulatto":** "Mob Flogs Aged Man in Wild Midnight Raid," *Chicago Defender*, May 21, 1949.

233 **"and dance to pistol shots":** " 'Senseless' Klan Beating of 6 Negroes Disclosed," *Washington Post and Times Herald*, Aug. 16, 1957.

234 **left him tied to the tree:** "Negro Is Beaten by White Youths," *New York Times*, Mar. 7, 1960; "Police Probe Houston, Tex. KKK Branding," *Chicago Defender*, Mar. 9, 1960.

234 **kidnapping under Alabama law:** *Doss v. State*, 23 Ala. App. 168, 123 So.237 (1929); *Doss v. State*, 220 Ala.30, 123 So. 231,233 (1929).

234 **coastal areas of the Carolinas:** For an account of these events, see Horace Carter, *Virus of Fear: The Infamous Resurrection and Demise of the Carolinas' Ku Klux Klan* (Detroit: Mississippi River Publishing, 1992).

234 **taken across state lines:** "Say They Were Flogged by Klan," *New York Times*, Feb. 18, 1952; "Klan Chief's Trial in Flogging Starts," *New York Times*, July 22, 1952; "Klan Convictions Upheld," *New York Times*, Oct. 14, 1952; *Brooks v. United States*, 199 F.2d 336 (4th Cir. 1952); David Cunningham, *White Hoods and Tar Heels: The Rise and Fall of the Civil Rights–Era Ku Klux Klan* (unpublished manuscript on file with author).

234 **including the Imperial Wizard:** "Klan Chief Draws 4 Years in Beating," *New York Times*, July 31, 1952; "N.C. Klansmen Enter Prison," *Chicago Defender*, Sept. 13, 1952.

30. BLACK CAPTIVE, WHITE CAPTURE

235 **threatened with death, and then let go:** Reliable records of the number of kidnappings are impossible to come by, for, as illustrated by the Jones case, many who suffered never reported the crimes. Almost every lynching—in 1952 the Tuskegee Institute reported 4,730 nationwide (3,437 Black and 1,293 white)—was preceded by some form of unlawful seizure and detention. See Jessie P. Guzman., ed., *1952 Negro Yearbook—A Review of Events Affecting Negro Life (Economic, Social, Political, and Educational Progress)* (New York: Wm. H. Wise, 1952).

235 **mob got to him or her:** See, e.g., *Aikerson v. State of Mississippi*, 274 So.2d 124 (1973).

236   **"against the will of their owners":** *Buddy v. Steamer Vanleer et al.*, 6 La.Ann.
      34, 1851 WL 3748 (La). The code prescribed heavy penalties for kidnapping a
      slave and allowed the slave's owner to pursue private civil damages in the same
      legal action.

236   **"carrying off" free Negroes:** Act of 1779 (Rev. Code, c. 142). See *The State v.
      Hardin*, 2 Dev. & Bat. 407, 19 N.C. 407 (N.C.), 1837 WL 462 (N.C.). Kidnapping
      free Negroes with intent to make them slaves was also condemned by most of
      the slave states. See, e.g., Tennessee Code of 1858, Article 4, Section 4619-1625;
      South Carolina Act of 1837 (6 Stat. at Large, 674); Virginia Statute of 1787, 1
      Rev. Code of 1792, ch. 103, sec. 28; 1. Rev. Code of 1819, ch. 111, sec. 28.

236   **sold a runaway slave:** *The State v. Williams*, 9 Ired. 140, 31 N.C. 140 (N.C.),
      1848 WL 1278 (N.C.).

236   **"as any other slave":** *State v. Williams, supra* at § 6.

236   **The Mississippi Black Codes:** The principal provisions of the Black Code
      were set forth in five legislative acts. Act of Nov. 25, 1865, 1865 Miss. Laws,
      82; Act of Nov. 22, 1865, id., 86; Act of Nov. 24, 1865, ibid., 90; Act of Nov.
      29, 1865, id., 165; and Act of Nov. 24, 1865, id., 66. The first act was titled "An
      Act to confer Civil Rights on Freedmen, and for other purposes." See James T.
      Currie, "From Slavery to Freedom in Mississippi's Legal System," *Journal of Negro
      History* 65, no. 2 (Spring 1980): 112–125.

237   **given to the former owner:** 1865 Miss. Laws, Ch. IV, V, Vi, XXIII, and
      XLVII.

237   **legitimate use of force:** The Justice Department did prosecute one Mississippi
      peonage case in 1947 under the Lindbergh kidnapping law. "US Uses Lindbergh
      Law to Prosecute S.C. Peonage Case," *Chicago Defender*, Oct. 25, 1947. In a 1947
      case, the Justice Department charged four Alabama men with restraining a man
      and holding him in peonage. "Federal Court Peonage Trial Gets Underway,"
      Chicago Defender, Jan. 18, 1947. The department found it easier to hold on to
      convictions in peonage cases than in police brutality matters. Between 1940 and
      1946 it obtained convictions or guilty pleas in nine peonage prosecutions.

237   **peonage prosecution there:** *United States v. Cunningham*, 40 F. Supp. 399
      (1941).

237   **hold their own "courts":** Fred Cubberly Papers, Letter from Fred Cubberly to
      Richard Barry, Aug. 17, 1906, P. K. Yonge Library of Florida History, Univer-
      sity of Florida, cited in N. Gordon Carper, "Slavery Revisited: Peonage in the
      South," *Phylon* 37, no. 86 (1976): 85–99.

237   **petty crime into prison laborers:** Ibid.

31. REDRESS: THE PROBLEM OF THE TWENTY-FIRST CENTURY

243 **"as a government and as a country":** "Text of Harper's Residential Schools Apology," *Globe and Mail*, June 11, 2008

243 **inequities they spawned have disappeared:** See Janna Thompson, *Taking Responsibility for the Past: Reparation and Historical Injustice* (Cambridge: Polity Press, 2002) (arguing that intergenerational communities rely on their members "accepting transgenerational obligations and honoring historical entitlements," xviii).

244 **in the project of repair:** Michael Rothberg, *The Implicated Subject: Beyond Victims and Perpetrators* (Stanford, CA: Stanford University Press, 2019).

244 **after the actual events:** Farida Shaheed, *Report of the Special Rapporteur in the Field of Cultural Rights*, United Nations Human Rights Council, Jan. 23, 2014, A/HRC/25/49, at 4.

32. "FOUND FLOATING IN RIVER . . . CAUSE OF DEATH UNKNOWN"

246 **"out of town if you try to vote":** NAACP Papers, Box IIA406 F.3, General Office Files, Lynching. Excerpt from NAACP Annual Report for 1940, Chapter II, Anti-Lynching Bill.

247 **life would be spared:** Elisha Davis Affidavit 1, Dec. 12, 1940, DOJ Litigation Case File 144-72-2.

248 **"come back and let me know":** Anne Williams Affidavit 1, Sept. 11, 1940, DOJ 144-72-2.

248 **"can't do anything about":** Ibid.

249 **bringing the perpetrators to justice:** Anne Williams Affidavit 2, Sept. 11, 1940, DOJ 144-72-2.

249 **"having part in the case":** "No Blame Is Placed in Death of Negro," *Commercial Appeal*, Aug. 14, 1940.

249 **"is a terrible jest":** "Democracy in Brownsville, Tenn.," *Pittsburgh Courier*, Aug. 10, 1940.

250 **"require extremely careful handling":** William McClanahan, United States Attorney, to Thomas Dodd Jr., Special Assistant to the Attorney General, Criminal Division, July 2, 1940, DOJ 144-72-2.

250 **"if he was killed":** DOJ 144-72-2.

250 **no more fruitful leads:** Memorandum, Clyde Tolson, FBI Associate Director, to L. B. Nichols, FBI Assistant Director, Oct. 4, 1947), DOJ 144-72-2.

251 **that of the accused:** Memorandum, Victor Rotnem, Chief of the Civil Rights Section, Dec. 23, 1941, DOJ 144-72-2.

251   **followed up on leads:** Constance Baker Motley to Elisha Davis, Jan. 24, 1954 (on file with author).

251   **"is constantly threatened":** "NAACP Seeking Aid for Elisha Davis," *Atlanta Daily World*, July 16, 1940.

252   **statute of limitations had expired:** Letter, Motley to Davis, Jan. 24, 1954.

252   **"They're decent":** "Negroes Cannot Serve on Juries, Lack Representation," *Jet*, Oct. 1, 1959, 15.

252   **county officials was proper:** Interview, Mayor Jo Matherne, Aug. 2011 (interviewer: author).

253   **after our visits to Brownsville:** Heather Catherwood, *In the Absence of Governmental Protection: The Struggle of the Brownsville NAACP to Secure the Right to Vote*, 2012 Civil Rights and Restorative Justice (on file with author).

254   **"truth find a measure of justice":** Press release, Office of District Attorney General Garry Brown, Twenty-Eighth Judicial District, State of Tennessee, Aug. 8, 2018.

33. "A FIGHT WITH SOME SAILORS"

255   **deceased's friends, "white and colored":** "Police, Naval Authorities Silent in Taking Action in Algiers Man's Death," *Louisiana Weekly*, May 8, 1943.

257   **and the two other men:** Lillian Williams, Letter to Daniel Byrd, Apr. 28, 1943, NAACP Papers, Box II B53, Folder 6, Legal File-Crime.

258   **"go well":** Interview, Derek Williams, Nov. 7, 2020; Interview, Derrod Williams, Nov. 8, 2020 (Interviewer: Erin McCrady) (on file with author).

258   **the only white person charged:** "Service Man Indicted by Grand Jury," *New Orleans Item*, May 7, 1942.

34. OWED? WHAT? AND BY WHOM?

264   **a world without prisons:** Kim Gilmore, "Slavery and Prison: Understanding the Connections," *Social Justice* 27, no. 3 (2000): 195–205; Angela Davis, *Are Prisons Obsolete?* (New York: Seven Stories Press, 2011).

264   **stripped of historical context:** See John Rawls's theory of justice, for example. John Rawls, *A Theory of Justice* (Cambridge, MA: Harvard University Press, 2009).

265   **on defining the road ahead:** Richard Benda, "Time to Hear the Other Side," in *Time and Temporality in Post-Conflict Societies*, eds. Natascha Mueller-Hirth and Sandra Rios Oyola (Oxford: Routledge, 2018).

265   **be paid to current inequalities:** Jeremy Waldron, "Superseding Historic Injustice," *Ethics* 103, no. 1 (1992): 4–28.

265 **create an alternative relationship:** Jessica Benjamin, *Beyond Doer and Done To: Recognition Theory, Intersubjectivity and the Third* (London: Routledge, 2018).

267 **"victim of the guillotine":** Charles Dickens, *Tale of Two Cities* (New York: Dover Publications, 1999).

267 **meaning of the event itself:** Cathy Caruth, *Unclaimed Experience: Trauma, Narrative and History* (Baltimore: Johns Hopkins University Press, 2016).

268 **"if he was killed":** William McClanahan, United States Attorney-Memphis to Thomas Dodd Jr., Special Assistant to the Attorney General, Criminal Division, July 2, 1940, DOJ 144-72-2.

268 **commitment to get it right:** Wendell Berge, Assistant Attorney General, to William McClanahan, United States Attorney, Mar. 31, 1941, DOJ 144-72-2.

268 **on an interstate bus:** Mary Nguyen, *Law Enforcement Involvement in the Death of Samuel Mason Bacon*, 2013, Civil Rights and Restorative Justice (on file with author).

268 **hometown of Gretna, Louisiana:** Brittany Burk, *Royal Cyril Brooks: One Victim of a Corrupt Police Department*, 2016, Civil Rights and Restorative Justice (on file with author).

269 **arrest capital of the United States:** Mark Gimein, *Welcome to the Arrest Capital of the United States*, Fusion TV, June 22, 2016.

269 **step in the right direction:** Royal Cyril Brooks Memorial, Apr. 28, 2018 (on file with author).

269 **with justice and equality:** On the performative quality of apologies, Eve Sedgwick engages with the work of Jacques Derrida and Judith Butler. Sedgwick suggests that while certain utterances are distinctively performative—I apologize, I marry you, I christen you, I bequeath to you—all language constructs relationships. Eve Sedgwick, *Touching Feeling: Affect, Pedagogy, Performativity* (Durham, NC: Duke University Press, 2003), 4.

270 **hands of the white majority:** *Korematsu v. United States*, 323 US 214 (1944).

271 **cycles of racialized violence:** Geoff Ward, "Microclimates of Racial Meaning: Historical Racial Violence and Environmental Impacts," *Wisconsin Law Review*, no. 3 (2016): 575–627.

EPILOGUE

273 **"met his death unjustifiably so":** NAACP Legal Files II-Box 31-F23 (Crime).

274 **"prove their worthiness":** Saidiya V. Hartman, *Scenes of Subjection: Terror, Slavery and Self-Making in Nineteenth-Century America* (New York: Oxford University Press, 1997).

ILLUSTRATION CREDITS

INDEX